PRAISE FOR THE AUTHOR'S 'V2V' HISTORICAL SERIES

Mary Anne Yarde - author of the Du Lac Series

"These are not dry dusty books whose historical characters are one dimensional. Hughes has brought these men and women back to life with her quick wit and beautiful prose. The stories she tells are fabulously descriptive, as well as at times profoundly moving. She pulled it off beautifully."

D.K. Marley – Historical Fiction author of *Blood and Ink*

"What an incredibly fascinating walk through history with such in-depth historical research. I applaud Trisha Hughes for this immense undertaking, as well as the beautiful imagery and story-telling quality of her voice. I highly recommend taking this ambling journey into the pages of this historical series"

David Baird – David's Book Blurg

"Trisha Hughes did a great job of bringing each of these Kings and Queens to life. This is the kind of book that gives you the juicy, interesting facts and ignites the flames of passion for history"

Tony Riches – Historical Author of the *Tudor Trilogy*

"I wasn't disappointed as Trisha's lively and engaging style takes us on a grand tour of those who enjoyed wearing the crown. As Trisha Hughes says 'these stories span hundreds of years of lust, betrayal, heroism, murder, cruelties and mysteries.
What more could you ask for?"

Lyn Horner – Author

"Written in a lively, never boring style, I thoroughly enjoyed this historical epic. A definite 5 stars."

Paul Bennett – Author and Book Reviewer:

"Detailed research is evident throughout the book giving the reader a full picture of the events and the larger than life people who sought for the crown of a kingdom seemingly in constant turmoil and uncertainty. A fascinating tutorial of the
period of Canute to Elizabeth,
I'm looking forward to the next book.
5 stars"

PREVIOUSLY BY THE AUTHOR

Autobiography

Daughters of Nazareth

Historical Fiction

Book 1
Vikings to Virgin – England's story from
The Vikings to the Virgin Queen.
Book 2
Virgin to Victoria – England's story from
The Virgin Queen to Queen Victoria
Book 3
Victoria to Vikings – The Circle of Blood.

Crime/Mystery

Dragonfly
Chameleon
Scorpion

THE TARTAN KINGS
THE POWERFUL & RICH STORY OF SCOTLAND

TRISHA HUGHES

Copyright © 2025 Trisha Hughes

The right of Trisha Hughes to be identified as the author of this work has been asserted by her in accordance with the Copyright, Design and Patents Act 1988.

All rights reserved. No part of this publication may be reproduced, transmitted, or stored in a retrieval system, in any form or by any means, without permission in writing from the publisher, nor be otherwise circulated in any form of binding or
cover other than that in which it is published and without a similar condition being imposed on the subsequent purchaser.

This work is fiction based on real events in history.

Typeset in Garamond

ISBN 9798877914445

For David...

*My rock, my anchor, my best friend,
my life*

CONTENTS

Foreword	xi
1. The Early Picts	1
2. Early Kings of Scotland	8
3. The MacAlpin Dynasty	19
4. The Canmore Dynasty	59
5. Insurrection	101
6. The Stewart Dynasty	155
7. Robert II	156
8. Robert III	162
9. The Albany Years	169
10. James I	174
11. James II	180
12. James III	188
13. James IV	202
14. James V	211
15. Mary Queen of Scots	222
16. End of the Stuart Dynasty	257
17. The Tartan Kings Who Never Ruled	272

FOREWORD

At the heart of our present are the stories of our past. It's a story of all people, in all places, at all times and because we know of that history, we can decide what may happen in the future. It shows us models of good and responsible behaviour as well as teaching us how to learn from the mistakes of others. The more we know about the past the better prepared we are for the future because by remembering the past, we realise that we are responsible for building a legacy for the generations that follows us.

These stories are of ruthless kings, favoured queens, warriors, generals, battles and wars. But standing tall above them all are the strong, dependable ones who have persevered. The quiet ones. The resilient ones. The irrepressible ones.

And so, once again, as with my 'V2V' English trilogy, I share my interpretation of the world in which heroes and villains once lived in Scotland. The stories of Scotland and England mix and mingle throughout the ages in a broth that is never boring as they fought to survive and conquer.

This is the story of my ancestors, mostly through the women in history: the mothers, wives, sisters and daughters of powerful men. These women, some well-known some forgotten, were the glue that held the families together. The ones who kept the crops harvested, the household in good shape, who bore the children, who wept when their husbands and fathers failed to return from battles and raised their sons and daughters alone, hoping that their daughters would marry well to someone with a title and lands and funds to feed their own sons and daughters.

The blood of these brave women has flowed through my family tree for a thousand years and trickled down to me through the centuries.

And I couldn't be more proud.

THE EARLY PICTS

Geologists tell us that Scotland has been on a collision course with England for billions of years. They toss millions of years around like confetti when they tell us that Scotland's geological past involves a barely believable story of whole continents moving around like croutons half submerged in a bowl of soup. It's a story of great oceans forming and disappearing like seasonal puddles. It's a story of mountains being thrown up and worn down, of formidable glaciers and icecaps advancing and retreating behind mile-thick walls of ice as they melted and reformed again. Scotland has been a desert, a swamp, a tropical rainforest, and a desert again. It has drifted north over the planet with an ever changing cargo of dinosaurs, giant redwoods, sharks, bears, lynx, giant elk, wolves. And also, in the last twinkling of an eye in the geological time-scale, human beings. But always on this unavoidable collision course with England.

Some 800 million years ago Scotland was lying in the centre of another super-continent thirty degrees south of the equator. Over eons of time, it wandered the southern hemisphere before drifting north across the equator. By 600 million years ago, Scotland was attached to the North American continent, separated by an ocean called Iapetus from the southerly part of what was to become Britain and which was then attached to the European continent.

Then, some 60 million years ago, the Iapetus ocean began to close. North Britain and South Britain gradually came together, roughly along the line of Hadrian's Wall, and that collision produced the Britain we know today, although it was still connected to Europe. But the weld continued to be subject to stress after the land masses had locked together and over a 3 million year period, a chain of volcanoes erupting off the western seaboard of Scotland created many of the islands of the Hebrides, including Skye, Mull, Arran, Ailsa Craig, St Kilda and Rum. Edinburgh Castle itself would be built on the eroded roots of a volcano which had erupted some 340 million years ago when Scotland still lay south of the equator. Castle Rock was carved by the gouging passage of ice during the last glaciation.

The underlying rock of Scotland has shaped the landscape and has influenced through the soil, the kind of plants, animals, birds and insects in every part of the countryside. It has thereby shaped the lives and livelihoods of the human communities which have lived here.

Agriculture flourished on the productive farmland on the flatter east coast of Scotland but the more mountainous landscape of the west, with its thin, acid soils, was suitable only for subsistence agriculture. In the Central Belt, the abundance of coal and oil-shale entombed in the underlying rocks would fuel the Industrial Revolution and would foster the growth of the iron, steel, heavy engineering and shipbuilding industries.

The story of Scotland begins much like the story of England with a race of people struggling to survive. Look in the mirror and you'll see thousands of years of history looking straight back at you because written into our facial features are stories that go back countless generations. We look as we do through our genes, handed down through the centuries of conquest and bloody war.

The earliest evidence of people in Scotland comes from flint artefacts from around 12,000 BC with flint arrowheads at Howburn Farm indicating a hunter-gatherer population. Mostly nomadic, following seasonal rhythms of prey, they lived in groups of 10 to 20 with larger kinship networks.

Around 4,000 BC, evidence of new stone tools suggests an emerging farming economy, with the population producing enough food, such as wheat and barley, to stay in a particular location.

Copper and tin were discovered around 2,000 BC and the Bronze Age began when men with bronze could easily defeat men brandishing sticks and stones to protect themselves. But then the unimaginable happened. Bronze was dumped when iron was discovered and it could not be disputed that for smashing skulls, iron was certainly best.

This was a society of farmers and fishermen, speaking a Celtic language and living in scattered settlements strewn across the countryside, holding their main allegiance to local chiefs. These simple people owned sheep, pigs and cattle and grew oats and barley. But they still struggled to survive.

At this time in history, Egypt was also suffering its own crisis within the Ptolemian empire where a 14-year-old girl by the name of Cleopatra was growing up in an Egypt full of turmoil. Seven years later, the vivacious 21-year-old needed an ally to help her expel her brother, Ptolemy, from the Egyptian throne.

No one has ever called Cleopatra a wallflower. True to her legend, she rolled herself up in a carpet and had herself delivered as a present to Caesar, who at the time had troubles of his own after defeating his rival, Pompey, in a civil war. The rest, so they say, is history.

Imagine 52-year-old Caesar watching the carpet unroll and from within, a scantily-clothed, and let's admit it, precocious, guileful Cleopatra, unfolded herself. She would have stopped at nothing to excite the ageing Caesar and within a short time, he became her pawn, completely besotted with her, not necessarily by her beauty, which has been greatly exaggerated by Hollywood, but by her wit and intelligence. The fact that he was disastrously in debt after the civil war, and Cleopatra was possibly the richest woman in the world at the time, would certainly have been a dangling carrot to him.

The next three years hurtled ahead for Cleopatra. Within one year, she was pregnant with Caesar's twins and firmly seated on the Egyptian throne. One year later, she would deliver a son to Caesar and barely a year after that, Caesar would be assassinated.

This dynasty grew, as did Rome's influence and power, throughout Europe. Eighty years later, in 43 AD, Emperor Claudius in Rome had been watching and hearing interesting stories about a green island over a passage of water to the west of Gaul. It was an attractive target and he began planning a conquest with a massive invasion.

If things were hard for the Britons before, life was about to get even worse when they came up against the greatest empire the world had ever seen. Romans was on the march and things were about to turn ugly.

Emperor Claudius arrived in full Roman splendour with reinforcements, including elephants, and while some of the natives made reluctant deals with him, some fought savagely for their freedom and independence. It took the Romans thirty-four years of gradual advancement to become master of this new province they called Britannia and by 79 AD, all of England and Wales had been subdued. Only the far north remained – the Lowlands and Highlands of Scotland.

To the Romans, these were the Badlands inhabited by ferocious tribes with 'reddish hair and large limbs' and the newly appointed Governor of the Province of Britannia, Julius Agricola, turned his mind to an invasion of the untamed barbarians with a vigorous policy of subduing the native tribes north of Wales beyond current Roman control. In 83 AD he launched his blitzkrieg.

In those early days, to have a massive army of crack Roman infantrymen supported by cavalry and squadrons of battle-hardened auxiliaries amounting to 25,000 men meant serious business. To back him up there was a fleet of warships shadowing his army's progress. He began his march north and it took him a full year to advance up the coastal plains, taking out any native settlements on the way and building temporary marching camps. His plan was to bring the local tribesmen to their knees in a region called Caledonia.

Unlike their neighbours in the south, Caledonians were not content to stand by and let the Romans plunder their lands. More than 30,000 of the Caledonians gathered, both young and old, under the command of many local kings and chiefs in close-packed tiers on the slope of a hill at Mons Grampius, a name that later became the Grampian Mountains. They careened back and forth, taunting the Romans, daring them to advance. And advance they did. The squadrons moved forward and although the tribesmen fought recklessly and fiercely with the limited and primitive weapons they had, there was never going to be any other outcome except defeat. By the end of the day, 10,000 Caledonians had perished with only 360 Romans dead. The remaining survivors scattered and fled into the wilderness.

It was a crushing blow to the Caledonians and a significant victory to the Romans. Feeling buoyant by his success, and having already exceeded the normal 5-year period as Governor, Agricola sent a reconnaissance fleet further north to confirm that Britannia was indeed an island. Satisfied the terrain was too rugged and not worth his effort, he ordered the completion of a fortress seven miles east of Dunkeld before being recalled to Rome the next year.

Over the decades, uprisings by the highlanders became more and more violent and Roman emperors watched warily as governor after governor was sent to hold them back from Roman Britain. By the time Hadrian gained the imperial throne in 117 AD, the rebellions had reached a point where something major had to be done. A boundary had to be erected to keep the uncontrollable inhabitants of northern Britannia away from the more civilised southern people.

Hadrian was more than ready to make his mark in history. His dream was to build a stone wall, providing years of work for thousands of soldiers, to firstly build the wall and secondly, maintain the structure. The Wall's primary purpose would be as a physical barrier to slow up the raiders who were intent on getting into the empire for plundering purposes but it would also be a convenient observation point that could alert Romans of an incoming attack. It was to be the north-west frontier of the Roman empire and no one would be able to cross south of it without falling prey to Roman arrows. The way he saw it, it was a win-win solution.

Construction started in 122 AD and took six years to build. The entire 73 miles of Wall crossed northern Britain from Wallsend on the River Tyne in the east to Bowness-on-Solway in the west. It was built with an alternating series of fourteen forts, each housing as many as 600 men, with a guarded gate at every mile and two observation towers in between.

Hadrian's Wall appears to have continued successfully in its form until 180 AD when the tribes finally succeeded in crossing over, killing a general and the troops he had with him. Not many details are known but this probably led to the abandonment and deployment of the army.

By 214 AD, the Romans had finally withdrawn from the wall, leaving Scotland and its restless tribes to their own devices and their own domestic feuds.

Left to their own devices, the Scots slowly evolved over the next eighty years unbeknownst to the Romans, who perhaps secretly hoped they would just internally kill themselves off. Gradually, terrifying stories began to circulate of sightings of a more barbaric, warlike people popping up in a kingdom stretching from north of the Firth of Forth to the Moray Firth. These people were reported to have hair touching their shoulders and shaved beards with only the upper part of their hair left to trail down their chest from their lips. They had bird heads painted on their chests and the sun was shining around their nipples with the light reaching their thighs. Faces were painted on their abdomen and fish scales on their calves. On their shoulders the head of a griffin was painted and their arms are crawling with pythons.

To the Romans, coming across one of these barbarians was a terrifying thought to envisage. When the Romans actually did see them advancing towards them, it took a lot of courage to stand firm against them since their first instinct would have been to turn tail and run. Their whole presence screamed danger and the Romans gave these painted warriors an enduring name. The Picts. These 'Picts' were basically Celts who lived north of the Forth-Clyde line and were the tribal descendants of the Iron Age tribes. Their ancestors were the people who built great stone circles like Stonehenge during the 3rd millennium BC in the Neolithic times.

This new age was a ferocious time in the north. Tribal leaders tussled for power and in many parts they descended into bloody conflict where the need to fight and defend became the main focus of their lives. It was the age of ancient myths where warrior heroes rode on horseback armed with highly decorated glittering Celtic swords, creating romantic folklore.

While these legendary warriors attacked Roman Britannia simultaneously from all sides, Rome was having serious problems of its own back home. Germanic tribes had undergone massive technological, social and economic changes over the past couple of centuries and as they grew stronger, their main object was to challenge Rome. It was all rather good news for the Britons because it marked the end of the Roman Empire and the hold they had on Britannia as the Roman army finally left Britain's shores. Behind them they left towns, cities, bridges, roads and aqueducts and a written language. A vast improvement on what they had before the Romans arrived.

But if the Britons thought they would be left in peace, they had a shock coming. This peace was all coming to a terrifying end. There was a new enemy surfacing and life would change for everyone. The Saxons from

Germany had set their sights on Britain and of all the Germanic races, the Saxons were the most appalling. The Britons now lived under a worse menace coming from the sea that was more cruel and bloodier.

Saxons brought with them their own structure of Germanic life: fighting for life and control over men as hard-pressed as they were themselves and only winning because of their mastery, perhaps butchery, as war-leaders. With this new lifestyle came a long and intricate rivalry for leadership between the various Anglo-Saxon kings who all strived for mastery by force and savagery. To understand these days and their constantly changing rulers, we have to understand time frames. Five years was a lot in those days. Twenty years was the far horizon and fifty was antiquity.

These kings were the beginning of the House of Wessex south of Hadrian's Wall. It was the time of Cerdic and his son Cynric and with these two savage leaders, we see signs of fear spreading throughout the whole country. Where once there had been law and order and a respect for property during the Roman occupation, a dark time fell and dawn rose with a poor, barbaric, divided England. Not far away in Ireland, the light of Christianity was burning brightly with the efforts of Saint Patrick and followers of his doctrine were flowing into Wales and England. And as for Scotland, it was just waking up.

EARLY KINGS OF SCOTLAND

We can only view these days through dim telescopes in this vaguely recorded history. Romantic stories loom of a knight by the name of King Arthur and his Knights of the Round Table who won countless battles in those savage times. Around him and all his deeds, passion and bravery abound. Stories of 12 separate battles (all untraceable) against people (all unknown) are told. No one can say for sure where, or even *if*, Arthur actually existed, although it is assumed that if there was such a person, he would have been alive at this time of the Saxon invasion in 495 AD and quite possibly, he was Welsh.

The Picts heard these stories but they were basically protected in the north of Scotland by the uncompromising terrain. That was up until the seventh century when the Britons began reaching out with grasping hands for strongholds in Strathclyde. Between 631 and 653 AD, the Annals suggest the Picts had several kings descended from the British houses where Pict kings married daughters of Anglo-Saxon kings, as with King Bridei III whose mother was probably a daughter of King Edwin of Wessex and the first cousin of King Ecgfrith.

King Ecgfrith regarded Bridei as his sub-king but that's certainly not what Bridei thought. It was around 685 AD when Ecgfrith decided to put Bridei in his place and mount a massive cavalry attack on Pictland against the advice of St Cuthbert, Bishop of Lindisfarne, and all his counsellors.

Bridei felt he had righteousness on his side. He was fighting for his grandfather's inheritance of Fife and Circinn that were brutally taken away by the English and Ecgfrith was challenging that right. Enraged by the continued defiance, Ecgfrith marched an Anglian force north through the Lowlands to Edinburgh before crossing the Forth at Stirling and the River Tay at Perth. As he advanced up Strathmore from Perth, he was diverted from his planned route by the Picts using classic guerrilla tactics who fell back towards their own territory, luring the English into boggy, treacherous ground, instead of fighting a battle in open country.

It was somewhere in these narrow mountain passes that the Picts ambushed Ecgfrith's army on 20th May, 685 AD with devastating effect. They swarmed down from behind the top of Dunnichen Hill to attack the Northumbrian cavalry on its flank, cutting off any thoughts of retreat. As a result, the Northumbrians were virtually wiped out and Ecgfrith and his army was slaughtered.

It was a strong, decisive victory, and it had the momentous effect of temporarily settling the Picts who felt they had made their point. In a churchyard of Aberlemno, ten kilometres to the north of Dunnichen Hill is a magnificent Pictish cross-slab richly decorated with Pictish symbols depicting the battle-scene. The combatants are carefully distinguished: bareheaded Pictish warriors confronting opponents who are wearing Anglo-Saxon helmets with long nose-guards and distinctive neck collars. The Pictish cavalrymen are riding long-tailed ponies which they control with their knees and feet, leaving both hands free to wield their weapons.

This battle would just be the first of many.

Out of the carnage, Bridei continued attacking fortresses and strongholds such as Dunnottar and the hill fort of Dundurn in Perthshire. He was the king and his dream was nothing less than to bring together all the Picts in a single entity.

But as savage as these battles were, it was just a foretaste of what was to come. York had a terrible shock coming. Britain was waking to a new nightmare stirring beyond the seas. The Age of the Vikings was beginning and the force was moving slowly but surely towards Britain.

At this time in history, Scandinavia stood on the brink of the Viking

Age. Historically, it's important because we see the first powerful people begin to emerge; men who were not just chiefs and warlords, but a dynasty of kings on the make. These kings were not only interested in gold and silver, but they were in search of hostages as well. Captured men, women and children were shipped back to Scandinavia as slaves then on to Constantinople where they were traded for Middle Eastern gold and silver. This international slave trade not only swept thousands of natives halfway around the known world but also marked the emergence of a violent religion that included animal and human sacrifice.

All this combined to force the most adventurous, the most ambitious and the most ruthless to look across the vast expanse of water in the west in search of finding a new path to wealth and power. And so it was towards the end of the 5th century, war bands of Norwegian Vikings took to their lethally efficient longboats and headed west in search of plunder.

What we know about the Vikings is more myth than reality because they were basically warriors, not writers. What we *do* know is they didn't just spring out of nowhere, fully formed. They were the product of thousands of years of a cultural evolution with a dynamic and violent history.

These Vikings weren't just expert sailors and ship builders. They were warriors in every sense of the word who plundered and burned their way across the known world, heedless of their own lives or the lives of others, intent only on destruction, rape and pillage. Even to the Dark Age standards, Vikings were very adept in the messy business of killing. Their long boats were stunning craft, packed with two dozen men, that could sail up rivers and anchor in creeks and bays and their beautiful lines and construction could ride out the fiercest storms of the Atlantic Ocean. Every male Viking had a sword, an axe and a knife on him at all times but when going to war or on a raid, equipment like shields, spears, bows and arrows was added. On top of that, these heavily tattooed men held no semblance of moral code. They really were the 'bogeymen' of history.

While some Vikings were flexing their muscles in Europe, others had been invading parts of Ireland around County Munster for a couple of centuries and they had begun advancing further on to Northern Ireland where they established their own kingdom around Country Antrim. Within a few short years, they ventured further still, across to southern Scotland to Argyll, Kintyre and Bute and then further on to Alba. This dominating group of warriors, calling themselves Scots, had a king of their own who became known as the Dál Riata. As they expanded further and further into Scotland from their capital at Dunadd near Kilmartin Glen in Argyll, early Pict kings were coming and going at an alarming rate.

For a hundred years, Pictish kings reigned and fought to hold onto their throne from the Dál Riata. Some kings reigned for barely a couple of years, one for less than a couple of months, before a rival ousted him off the throne and took over. Then the pattern would repeat with another rival doing the same thing, resulting in rapid successions that became muddled by in-fighting. Eighteen times, rulers succeeded to the throne, then were removed brutally shortly afterwards due to the ugly problem of matrilineality (a line descended from a female ancestor instead of a male) which produced a large number of aspiring and eligible would-be aggressive kings.

It's difficult to know when to say the first 'king' rose so for the sake of my story, let's start at the House of Oengus with Oengus I who reigned the Pict throne for a massive period of time between 732 until 761.

Oengus (anglicised to Angus) was a true warrior king in every sense of the word, who seems to have been an extraordinarily brutal man in outstanding brutal times. Upon seizing the Pictish throne from his contenders, he turned his attention to the problem with the Scots. Together with his brother, he laid waste to the Scottish fortress of Dunadd, and many others during his entire thirty-year reign. After brutalising the Scots, he then turned his attention to Ireland, the source of the irritating problem, invading and annihilating them in their ancestral homeland in two great battles in the years 739 and 741.

Seemingly invincible, he captured and drowned the King of Atholl, then conquered the remaining Dál Riata Scots after beheading the current Scottish king. The Dál Riata Scots had been beaten on both Argyll land and in Ireland and a Pict finally ruled over them all as King of both Picts and Scots as their liege lord. Things couldn't have been worse for them.

The great military victories of Angus gave the Pictish nation the chance to rule unhindered without any hinderances. Drunk with victory and mad with power, Angus looked south for more territory to conquer in the lands of the Britons of Strathclyde, the kingdom that was formed south of the old Roman Wall.

Time and time again he marched his tattooed host south, at one time to the great Briton fortress at Dumbarton Rock where he was joined by a Northumbrian ally intent on destroying the Strathclyde kingdom.

Sometimes, all the preparation in the world is not enough to secure victory. This time the combined armies were nearly destroyed in battle and Angus retreated north where he died five years later.

With the mighty Angus dead, things unravelled a bit and there was a 7-year period of confusion in the list of Pict Kings. From his death onwards, four Pictish kings reigned and perished at the hands of the Dál Riata kings and their associated Irish clans. While the Pict kings hung on valiantly, with another four kings dying in the next seven years, this upheaval meant the beginning of a more powerful Dál Riata.

While both kingdoms blamed the other for the conflict, it was never quite one-sided. History seldom is. It was more a clash of personalities and an outright grasp for power and as always, the strongest man won.

Although there is an historical shadow engulfing both Pictish and Scottish history though the latter years of the eighth and ninth centuries, we should not be tempted to skip over these years. With a little effort, fine threads can be woven together and the result is not so much the workings of our imagination but an exciting and dynamic foundation to Scotland's future. We know that kings were succeeded by their brothers, probably because their young sons were too young to rule, and then these young men would leapfrog over their uncles later on to rule as cousins then leapfrogged them in turn.

We also know that in the thirty years after Angus I died, the Scots were busy rebuilding. By 768, a Dál Riata king, by the name of Aed Find, had grown up and had begun invading the Pictish territories. He managed to regain freedom for the Scots by the time of his own death in 778 when his brother Fergus took up the challenge. By then, Dál Riata was once again independent.

But this success was to be only temporary because of one major failing. Fergus had no male heir. When he died in 781, he left behind two daughters and the battle and confusion began all over again because the next two males in line for the throne were Caustantin aged seven and his younger brother Angus, roughly aged four.

Both boys were either grandsons or grandnephews of Angus I, so there was no question about bloodline, but they were still far too young to take over the throne. And of course, neither of the daughters were eligible.

Information is scarce for the years between 781 and 789, but you can believe would-be kings were coming and going regularly. So let's fast forward to Caustantin who suddenly emerges as a fourteen-year-old with ideas of his own. Even at this young age, he seems to have been amazingly ambitious and ruthless enough to look at the greener pastures of Pictland as well as the Dál Riata throne.

According to the Annals of Ulster, there was *'a battle between the Picts and Dál Riata in which Conall was defeated but escaped, and Caustantin was the victor'*.

Then eight years into Caustantin's reign, one cold miserable January morning in 795, Vikings suddenly arrived in their long boats 112 kilometres south-east of Edinburgh on the English holy island of Lindisfarne while the monks were enjoying their tranquillity.

Imagine an icy wind ripping through the trees after a savage night of arctic air cutting its way through cracks in walls, freezing everything. In the early morning light, no one heard the muffled sounds over the water. Everyone slept, still clinging to their dreams. Suddenly a hollow pounding was heard, at first in the distance, but gradually coming closer. The ominous sound broke the peaceful silence as monks were rubbing the sleep from their eyes.

The Vikings murdered viciously, only leaving when their boats were filled to overflowing with a rich booty of gold, jewels and sacred emblems. The unprecedented violence of this raid sealed itself into Britain's very being because now the English were confronted with a different type of enemy. They were the most treacherous and audacious type of pirate that had ever appeared.

Caustantin had blood ties to a Cashel dynasty in Munster, Ireland and it was from them he heard the frightening story of the Lindisfarne raid that was planned with care and knowledge and executed with complete surprise in the dead of winter. He had already heard vicious stories of the Viking raids in Ireland and I'm sure he had been wondering when his turn would come. The next year, when he heard of an attack that wreaked havoc on Iona, a part of the Gaelic Kingdom of the Dál Riata, the 18-year-old king was doing his best to hold on to his own Pict throne while the Vikings returned time and again, pillaging and slaughtering.

Dál Riata had once been an extensive sea kingdom, linking the coastline of Argyll with the fertile lands of Ulster through a network of islands and sea lanes and the Viking warlords saw the true potential of combining their nautical abilities with this natural crossroads. They had already established a strong bridgehead and base on the Orkney and Shetland Islands and they knew the Hebrides would provide them with a fertile platform to continue their raiding into the Irish Sea, and on to Ireland itself. The west coast landscape of islands and fjords was also very similar to their own homeland, which must have been a further attractive feature in securing this area.

Caustantin ruled for thirty-one years as the second King of Picts and Scots, (Angus I is regarded as the first king), at a particularly brutal time in history with the help of his son Domnal. When Caustantin died in 820 at the age of 45, he left the Pict throne to his brother Angus, with Domnal reigning nominally on the Dál Riata throne. In doing this, he effectively took the throne away from his cousin Alpin who had been waiting not-so-patiently for his turn.

You'll remember the leapfrogging that took place when new kings claimed a throne, and if all had gone according to that tradition, the throne perhaps should rightfully have gone to Alpin. What actually happened was Caustantin seems to have conveniently forgotten this tradition and bypassed that side of the family by giving the Pict throne to his brother Angus, as Angus II, and the Dál Riata to his eldest son Domnal.

You don't have to be clairvoyant to know that this was going to cause trouble.

At Caustantin's death, Alpin was the King of Dál Riata and he wasn't about to be sideswiped by Domnal, or from the more lucrative Pict throne. He was covered both ways with bloodline and he wasn't about to be pushed aside and forgotten.

It took almost fourteen years of stewing for Alpin to finally make his move and no one knows why he waited so long. Perhaps he was waiting for his sons to come of age, but no one knows. For some reason everything changed in 834 because the 56-year-old Alpin finally set his mind to removing Angus II from the Pictish throne and replacing him with, well, himself. After all, he had a direct blood link to both thrones covered through past ancestors.

The rebellion led by Alpin in the south forced Angus II to forego his total preoccupation with the Vikings in the north and split his army in two as he faced the Scottish rebel on Easter Sunday, 834. Angus suffered a disastrous defeat at the hands of Alpin and the Scots, and the *Irish Annals,* record that both Angus and Domnal died during the battle. Flush with victory, Alpin and his Scots army then marched north to attack the rear of the main Pictish army which was led by Caustantin's second son, Drest.

This time it was a very different outcome. Drest, who was both Angus' nephew and Alpin's cousin, met Alpin at Galloway. The battle was expectedly vicious and brutal but eventually Alpin and many of his nobles were annihilated. Alpin's head was then fastened to a pole and carried around by the Picts before displaying it in Abernethy, their capital. Later, the Scots would take their revenge on the town and raze it to the ground, calling it Bas Alpin, roughly meaning *'Remember the death of Alpin'*. Although there is no information on who the 'Scots' were, it would be a safe bet to assume that Alpin's two sons, Kenneth and Donald, aged 24 and 22 respectively, were in the foray somewhere.

Following the defeat of Alpin in Galloway, a joint rule began between Drest and Talorc. No one can agree why there would have been this joint rule between two brutal men in a time when most would have just lopped off the opposition's head, but that's exactly what happened. Perhaps it was because the combined armies of Drest and Talorc, (Drest's uncle who was married to Caustantin's second sister Bergoit) were stronger if Alpin's two sons took it into their heads to stir the melting pot and seek revenge.

However, it wasn't to be that simple. Seething in the shadows was Angus II's second son, Eogan, who also felt he had the right to be the king after his father's death instead of his cousin Drest. And he wasn't about to be left out either. Eogan decided that *he* was the rightful king and in 837, he stepped in and killed both Drest and Talorc before taking over.

To say it was brutal times is perhaps an understatement. No one felt safe and most kings chose their friends very carefully.

For forty guarded years, the English coast had been left unravaged by the Vikings. But in 835, while Scottish kings were dropping like flies, the Vikings returned to England in ferocity with three to four hundred vessels for the remainder of the booty they'd left behind and for another thirty years, Southern England was under constant attack from Denmark and Norway. Saxon England was at this time ripe for their savagery.

One Viking in Southern England stands out in particular during a twenty-year period of aggression and nobody was more ruthless than Ragnar Lodbrok. Before attacking England, he led his fleet up the Seine into Paris before a plague brought him to an abrupt halt, forcing him to turn his interests to Northumbria instead.

While Ragnar was busy ravaging the east coast of England, the escalating conflict between both Picts and Scots would all come to a screaming halt in a catastrophe for both kingdoms alike in a bloody battle known as the 'Great Disaster of 839'.

It all began to fester throughout the first half of the 9th century, Norse-Gaels from Ireland had been settling in the Hebrides, Orkney and Shetland, in some cases replacing the local population and removing all trace of native languages. These were no longer the wild warriors coming in on the morning tide, pillaging and heading home. These people craved peace and had come to settle. They wanted to watch their children grow, to plant seeds and live long enough to harvest their crops. But while they showed a semblance of peace, they were still Vikings at heart, hellbent on settling in this new region, whether the natives liked it or not. They were after all pure blood Vikings and they were still the brutal murderous kind ready to split skulls and spill blood if necessary to attain that peace.

As you can imagine, this created tensions with rulers in the rest of the country when they saw their homeland infiltrated by 'The Great Heathen Army' in their beaked prows, ready to raid, enslave, steal and kill. When dreams of peace are destroyed, when marauders destroy homes, ruin harvests, rape daughters and enslave sons, a type of madness emerges, the madness of hope, and you will stop at nothing to protect the little you have.

So while Anglo-Saxon England struggled to suppress the Swedish Vikings as well as the Danish Vikings who had established a huge empire centred in York, the Norse Vikings in Ireland were making their presence felt by pushing the Scots of Dál Riata in the western islands towards the east along Strathearn and on to the lands of Pictish Fortriu where the Picts were also under attack from Vikings in the east.

Despite the hostility between the Scots and Picts, there was a certain inevitability about the way in which the two kingdoms came together at this time against their common enemy.

The greatest hour of the Viking Age in Scotland was dawning. Orkney had become a prize for the Vikings, a befitting strategic location for them, and under the rule of powerful earls, they extended their authority all the way down the west coast of Scotland to the Isle of Man. The Hebrides were more of a loose confederation, nominally controlled by Norway, but the islands of Argyll, particularly Islay, played a significant role as a base by which the Norse could shore up their rule in Ireland and launch attacks on Alba.

The Picts were already weakened by assaults from the Vikings over the years, as well as the in-fighting between family members, but at a single stroke both peoples were about to be decimated.

The nearly invincible Vikings had already conquered and settled in the Shetlands, the Outer Hebrides and as far south as the mouth of the Clyde but now Caithness, Sutherland and even Dalraiada, the land where the Dál Riata resided, were being attacked and harassed by the 'heathens' in long boats.

No one can agree where the battle took place but given that the mention of warriors in the *Irish Annals* came from Moray, it seems likely that King Uuen led an army from Fortriu to a battlefield south of Perthshire. One thing is certain: the battle was a catastrophe for Picts and Scots alike.

The year 839 AD was a year when monsters walked the lands. There were the Saxons fighting the Danes while the savage Picts fought the ferocious Scots. There were Norse Vikings from Ireland marauding up and down the west coast of Scotland while Northumbria was a kingdom of rivalling lords squabbling and jostling for power. Then there was the obvious struggle between the Danish Pagans and Saxon Christians. In between, clans butchered each other in skirmishes as a means of survival. The Danes of East Anglia would raid the farmlands around London and they would retaliate by sending men deep into Danish territory to burn, kill and plunder. There was officially a peace treaty between King Alfred of Wessex and the King of East Anglia but a hungry Dane took no notice of words on parchment. A man who wanted slaves or livestock would simply take what he wanted. It was a dangerous time to live in.

But the brutalising defeat at the hands of the Vikings that year not only killed most of the Pictish nobility, but many others who were in line for the throne fell like dominoes as well. The kings and heirs of both Picts and Dál Riata, their sons, their brothers, many nobles and *'others almost innumerable'* according to the *Irish Annals*, were slaughtered by the marauding Norse-Gaels and almost immediately, the triumphant Vikings moved on to further plunder the lands of the Picts, sending raiding parties westward to let the Scots know who was the boss.

This culling of the Pictish royal houses and its warrior elite, delivered the decisive shift in the pattern of succession, and in the chaos, several ambitious figures claimed the vacant Pictish throne. In the ensuing chaos where both sets of royal families, the Picts and the Dál Riata, were crushed, one figure rose quickly to claim the vacant Pictish throne: Uurad mac Bergoit. But in the background, waiting and watching, was Cinaed MacAlpin (anglicised to Kenneth MacAlpin) and he wasn't about to sit back and be sideswiped like his father before him. Not by a long shot.

THE MACALPIN DYNASTY

The 9th century was a savage time in Scotland's history only proven by the fact that in the fourteen years between 834 and 848 we have nine Pict kings, as well as four Dál Riata kings, who reigned and fell. In the space of 8 chaotic years after 'The Great Disaster of 839", five kings ruled in quick succession, some for barely a year, one for barely a month. Their mutual desire to destroy each other was never diminished and almighty battles were always on the cards.

But the writing was on the wall for all of them because of one man: Kenneth MacAlpin, the son of the man who had made an attempt to secure the Pict and Dál Riata kingdoms for his family thirteen years before.

Kenneth's claim to the Dál Riata crown came through his father, a member of Clan Gabhran. which had produced more Scottish kings than any other clan. But it was the link that went back sixty years to his great-great uncle, Alpin mac Echdach, who died in 728 that sealed the deal. It's no wonder Kenneth MacAlpin saw himself as the most likely candidate.

What was clearly evident was Kenneth's aim to free Dál Riata from Pictish domination and establish Scottish rule over the Picts, as was his father's attempt many years before.

This warrior king is perhaps one of the most mysterious figures of ancient history. His life is surrounded by treacherous myths, dark stories and unproven allegations of shameful deeds and sinful accomplishments. That the first true Scottish king of the various peoples of Scotland is smeared with the stain of treason and backstabbing is as much a product from lack of knowledge as it is from the terrible bits and pieces from a story of treason which has survived for more than a thousand years. This story is called the 'MacAlpin Treason'.

Let me start by saying this is just a juicy legend passed down in history with a dribble or fact to back it up. The facts of how Kenneth MacAlpin, the avenging son of the slain Alpin, became King of Picts and Scots are shadowy and suspect to say the least. Indeed there is a lot of falsified or embellished documents from later Scottish Churchmen and Church historians, eager to create a 'Church approved' version of how the Gael line of kings (and its Church) came to conquer Alba and completely erase Pictish culture and destroy the Pictish Church.

However, two such sources, *The Prophecy of St. Berchan*, and *De Instructione Principus* both agree that in 841, MacAlpin invited the current Pictish king, Drest X, and the remaining Pictish nobles to Scone to discuss, perhaps even settle, the issue of Dál Riata's freedom and MacAlpin's claim to both the Scots and the Dál Riatic crown.

Faced with a recently victorious MacAlpin in the south, and a devastated army in the north, Drest X and all claimants to the Pictish throne from the other seven royal houses attended this meeting at Scone with what could only be assumed as nervous trepidation. And they were right to be suspicious. Legend has it that the MacAlpin Scots came secretly armed with murder on their minds. Very *Game of Thrones* you might be thinking.

Dr Alfred P. Smyth, author of *Warlords and Holy Men: Scotland AD 80 - 1000* is under no illusion that Kenneth MacAlpin was very well aware that Drest X knew his father, Uurad, was the son of a *daughter* of a past king by the name of Fergus mac Echdach. Unfortunately for Drest, this made him merely a great-nephew of a past Pictish King, Constantin mac Fergusa, via a *daughter*. It also meant that Uurad's three sons and successors, were based purely on the *matrilenial* transmission of the throne. Not good enough, it seems.

Not that Drest was too concerned about that minor little detail. He had the kingship in a strong grip and he meant to keep it.

What he wasn't aware was how far Kenneth MacAlpin was willing to go to change all that.

Giraldus Cambresis in *De Instructione Principus* recounts how a great banquet was held at Scone, where Drest and his nobles were plied with drinks and became quite drunk. Once the Picts were drunk, the Scots allegedly pulled bolts from the benches, trapping the Picts in concealed earthen hollows under the benches. Beforehand, the traps had been set with sharp blades and the falling Picts, stunned and foggy headed, were impaled. *The Prophecy of St. Berchan* tells that '*...[MacAlpin] plunged them in the pitted earth, sown with deadly blades...*'). Trapped and unable to defend themselves, the surviving Picts were then murdered from above and their bodies, clothes and ornaments "*plundered.*'

Although the royal houses had been murdered and their armies wiped out in the north by the Vikings and decimated in the south by the Scots, the Picts nonetheless wholeheartedly resisted Kenneth MacAlpin and his Scottish domination for the full ten years of his reign. *The Chronicle of Huntington* tells us that MacAlpin *'fought successfully against the Picts seven times in one day'*, perhaps wiping out the last remnants of an independent Pictish armed force and making himself King of Dál Riata, King of the Picts and King of Alba. The kingdom's Gaelic name was replaced with 'Alba' then later replaced with Scotia, then Scotland.

While Kenneth I's dominion was essentially limited to Fortriu, the Mearns and Dál Riata, in reality the rest of the Pictish lands were under the control of the Vikings. He reigned between 843 and 858 until he died of a tumour at his royal seat at Scone near Perth, having spent his 15-year reign invading the kingdom of Northumbria no fewer than six times and allying himself with the Vikings in England. Because of this, within a few generations the Pictish language would be forgotten, the Pictish Church would be taken over by the Scottish Columban Church and most vestiges of Pictish culture would be erased. This fateful sequence of events eventually led to the suffocating of Pictish culture forever.

His unification of Dalriada and Pictland as one entity was a landmark in Scottish history although his reign saw an increase in Norse settlement in the outlying areas of Shetland, Orkney, Caithness, Sutherland, the Isle of Man as well as parts of Ross.

His dynasty is the first recognisably Scottish one and as a result, Scotland's kings are numbered from him as Kenneth I. Although he had two sons, to strengthen his power even more, he then married his two daughters to the kings of Strathclyde and Ireland.

It was his 46-year-old brother Domnal, (anglicised to Donald I), who succeeded him in 858, only to die himself 4 years later in 862 of reasons unknown, although The Prophecy of Berchan states: *"the wanton son of a foreign wife .... dies of disease."* Although Donald is generally supposed to have died childless, it has been suggested that Giric, who we will see in the near future, was the illegitimate son of Donald.

The eldest of Kenneth's two sons, Constantine, was lucky his uncle died so soon after taking the throne. Many others in Scottish history had waited endlessly for their turn. So at 26 years of age, Constantine stepped up to the mark and for the next 15 years, the battle against the Irish Vikings continued in earnest.

Meanwhile, Britain was still having issues of their own with Vikings. King Ella of Northumbria had finally captured Ragnar Lodbrok and had thrown him into a pit of snakes where he died in a coiling mass of loathsome adders.

Ragnar's four sons were huddled together around a fire as snow floated over the barren icy wasteland waiting for news of their father's marauding trip to England. They were fully expecting every hull in the fleet to be laden with precious gold. What they weren't expecting was news of his death. When the news came, each son went silent.

Britain, more particularly King Ella, was to find that the Vikings believed that sons were expected to avenge the killers of their fathers. It was Ivar, nicknamed 'The Boneless' due to an early difficulty with fast growing limbs, together with his brother Hvitserk, sometimes called Halfdan Ragnarsson, who set out to attack York, East Anglia, Northumbria and Mercia to do exactly that. It was time to return while the wounds were still raw.

Ivar knew his way around the sea. But if you take your ships far from familiar land as the wind rises and the tides suck at the hulls with a venomous force, you have to hope you end up where you wanted to land. The long oars and full sails would help but you had to watch the darkening skies and listen to the wind howl and suffer the rain's sting while you prayed you would not end up on rocks.

It was 865 and three years into Constantine's reign that Ragnar's sons, Ivar and Hvitserk, arrived in York with between 300 to 400 vessels hellbent on revenge.

For six years, Constantine heard the stories of the Lodbroks plundering their way south attacking anyone who stood in their way. On both sides of the country there were abbeys and monasteries, churches and cathedrals all loaded with treasures of gold and silver, of jewels, wine, food and luxuries and they wanted it all.

If Ivar had wanted to stop in Northumbria and call himself king, no one would have stopped him. He could have put a pliable Saxon on the throne to collect taxes to keep them quiet while he did what his family did best: make war. But he was a war-besotted Lodbrok and no Lodbrok had ever died dribbling in his bed from old age. They died fighting with their swords in their hands rather than settle an argument with words.

During this uncertain and unstable time in Britain, local rival kings were reading the writing on the wall when it came to the Vikings. Rather wisely, they forgot their feuds with each other and united in one final effort to fight against Ivar and Hvitserk. And they were right to be worried. King Ella of Northumbria was the first to die as Ivar made him suffer the 'Blood Eagle' fate for his father's death. His flesh and ribs were cut and sawn off the spine and then Ivar's hands ripped out the palpitating lungs. Next in line was Edmund of East Anglia who put up a good fight but in the end, was used as target practice as the brothers shot spears at him. Then they cut off his head for good measure and threw his body in a thicket.

Rightfully alarmed, the King of Mercia called for help from Wessex and one of the greatest figures in English history appears. Alfred of Wessex.

It was a bleak winter's morning in January 871 when beautiful Wessex turned into a battlefield. The early morning fog had risen from the valley and drifted through the trees like cold grey smoke as Ivar and Hvitserk stood high on the hill overlooking the tents in the lowlands of Ashdown.

Despite Alfred's inexperience, he sounded the horn, raised his sword from the dirt and gave the command for his men to charge. With a roar, both lines of warriors broke into a lurching run through the mud, watching their men disappear into the grey rain and sullen mist like ghosts. The two sides collided violently and in the hissing rain, blood flowed and men screamed.

Alfred was the victor that day but while Hvitserk accepted a truce from Alfred and turned his attention to the Picts of Strathclyde in the north, Ivar joined up with two of his brothers in Ireland and started his own dynasty called the Uí Ímair dynasty (Dynasty of Ivar) in Dublin.

And that's when he began to notice Scotland.

It was probably from Orkney that his early raids on Iona were mounted. History tells us that Ivar's brothers had already been active in Ireland but now Viking armies penetrated deep into mainland Scotland in the north and the west, inflicting heavy defeats on the Scots and the Picts alike.

Three figures are identifiable as his sons, all reigning as Kings of Dublin, while five further individuals are termed as Ivar's grandsons, including Sitric Caech who settled himself in York. But while Ivar's descendants dominated the major seaports of Ireland and challenged the power of kings in Britain during the later ninth and tenth centuries, they did not have the strength they previously once had. A historian by the name of Alex Woolf has suggested that the Crovan dynasty who ruled as Kings of the Isles, including the Isle of Man and parts of the Hebrides, were descended from Ivar, as well as the Clan Donald and Clan MacDougall who were also descended from him through a female line.

Viking activity appears to have reached a peak during Constantine's reign. He managed to stay alive for fifteen years before being violently killed in a battle against Viking raiders at a time when Alfred was desperately trying to make peace with the Danish Vikings. Although there is a general agreement on time, the manner of Constantine's death is not clear. Most historians agree he was beheaded on a Fife beach following a battle at Fife Ness and the Chronicle of Melrose names the place as the *'Black Cave'*.

His 36-year-old brother Aed's reign lasted barely a year and by trying to put the messy stories together, it would seem the tanistry leap-frogging act was the reason.

You will remember that the Scottish monarchy of this period based its succession on a system called tanistry where all adult male descendants of previous monarchs were eligible for the throne. The kingship regularly switched from one bloodline of royal descendants to another and had the benefit of ensuring that there would always be an *adult* king on the throne, avoiding the usual problems of minority reigns, as in the case of the brothers Constantine I and Aed, both sons of Kenneth I.

But if things had gone correctly, Aed actually *did* jump in a little early for his turn at the crown. Donald I's son Giric, although illegitimate, certainly thought so.

While Giric appears scheming and manipulative, Eochaid, the son of Kenneth I's daughter, (Constantine and Aed's sister), who had married the King of Strathclyde, seems to have been a young man easily led and fooled. The main problem for Eochaid was that he descended through his *mother*, and as the *daughter* of Kenneth, she should have missed out. Not just that, but her son Eochaid should have missed out as well.

Both Constantine and Aed had young boys, so the future of the monarchy looked safe and secure because it was expected that both sons would marry and have more sons to carry on the dynasties. But both boys were very young and tanistry is based on '*adult male descendants of previous monarchs*'. If anything happened to Aed, both boys would be too young to take the throne. Which is perhaps why Aed jumped in early.

You can see how Giric's mind was working. What if Aed suddenly had an accident and died? If both boys were too young, surely the throne would go to the nearest adult male relative of Kenneth I even if it was through the female line? Oh. Wait a minute! Isn't that my friend Eochaid? He was after all the grandson of Kenneth I and the son of a Strathclyde king who in turn was descended from a long line of English kings. And of course, there was a cobweb of truth in there.

No one knows how Giric managed to lure Aed into a battle within a year of coming to the throne but lure him he did. Giric killed him in battle at Strathallan, just north of Stirling, and then promptly took over the throne in partnership with Eochaid.

We know where Eochaid's line of descent comes from, but Giric's familial origins are very uncertain. Some theories say he took his father's name *Mac Domnal*, making him the son of Donald I, perhaps an illegitimate son, but evidence of this is sketchy and uncertain. His role in the drama could have simply been as *kingmaker*, orchestrating the timely removal of Aed and installing Eochaid in Aed's place with himself firmly by his friend's side to help and guide. But if the parentage is correct, it would certainly mean that Giric thought he possessed a strong claim to the Pictish throne himself through Donald I, even though illegitimate. And if that fact is correct, then Aed succeeding Constantine I could indicate that Giric felt he had been leapfrogged and denied his rightful place on the throne. It could explain why he orchestrated the removal of Aed from the picture and it could also mean that he felt reliant upon the assistance from Eochaid, in this case his maternal cousin.

Whatever their relationship, the pair ruled jointly together for eleven years.

Although the apparent joint reign is obscure and uncertain, individually they have been remembered, although very differently. Giric came to be remembered as a legendary figure and the architect of military conquests in both Ireland and England. Eochaid on the other hand is portrayed as the weak link and is one of two kings not even noted in the *'King Lists.'*

While all this was going on, young cousins, Donald and Constantine, each one a son of Kenneth's two sons, were wisely swept out of Scotland for safe-keeping and sent to the Royal Court of the Irish King at Grianan of Aileach, anglicised to Greenan Ely. In this brutal world, everyone was aware that their lives were endangered since the two young cousins were the most direct threat to Giric's throne, especially knowing Giric had murdered Constantine's father.

The two cousins left as Pictish boys but over the next decade, they learnt a lot and as they grew to manhood, they fully intended to return home as Gaelic Princes. And they were out for revenge.

The two young men returned to carry out their revenge on Giric in 889 where a bloody battle took place at a hill fort at Dundurn in Perthshire. According to various king-lists, Giric was slain and Eochaid was exiled, possibly back to Strathclyde, but never heard of again. It's not until the first quarter of the next century that we hear of the death of Dyfnwal, King of Strathclyde, possibly a descendant of Eochaid through his daughter.

In any case, this is when Domnal mac Causantin, nicknamed 'The Madman' finally took the throne as Donald II.

During Donald's 11-year reign, he did a balancing act, embroiled in efforts to reduce the highland robber tribes on one hand while fighting off renewed invasions from the Danes on the other hand, even though these Danes had come more to occupy lands bordering Scotland and the Anglo-Saxon kingdoms than to plunder.

Donald's father, Constantine I, had told him stories of Ivar the Boneless and Hvitserk, aka Halfdan Ragnarsson, the two Norwegian sons of legendary Ragnar Lodbrok, and how their combined armies, called the Great Heathen Army, had murdered and plundered their way from East Anglia, Northumbria and Mercia through to Ashdown in Wessex where they finally suffered defeat. He told Donald how Ivar left Hvitserk and King Guthrum, the Danish king of East Anglia, bargained with Alfred the Great for a pact called the Danelaw then left to set up shop in Ireland.

These stories about rampaging Vikings would have turned Donald's bowels to water when he heard that Harald Fairhair was on his way to Dunnottar Castle in Stonehaven and was intending to take it for himself.

As far as castles go, it's difficult to imagine a more remote and dramatic location than Dunnottar Castle. It comes with a good dose of dastardly history with an intrepid mix of torching, smuggling and pillaging. Perhaps with the most impenetrable position of all Scottish castles, surrounded by steep cliffs that drop to the North Sea 50 metres below, this castle sits on top of its own cliff peninsula on the road to Aberdeen, defended on all sides by the forces of nature.

In common with all Scottish castles, Dunnottar is all about location, sitting on a red stone outcrop on the cliffs just outside Stonehaven. This fortress is the oldest discovered in Scotland, named after its very apt Gaelic name, Dun Fhoithear, literally meaning 'fort on the shelving slope'. It was built as the only route over land to Aberdeen and so of huge strategic importance in Scotland. Its high cliffs are pounded by the North Sea on three sides while the fourth is narrowly joined to the three acre parcel of land as the only access to the site. This section was once a peninsula, but its access was destroyed in favour of a cliff pathway. As a result, these days you can only reach Dunnottar via a narrow, twisting route that ends in a tunnel, making it one of the most difficult Scottish castles to enter.

In the future, during the Wars of Independence, the English would capture the castle, but would later be besieged by William Wallace and his Scottish troops in 1297. The 4,000 English soldiers, loyal to Edward II, would find themselves overwhelmed and would hide in the church. Wallace and his soldiers would then ransack the site and torch it in one of the bloodiest episodes – even by Medieval standards.

The heyday of Dunnottar arrived in the 14th century when the Keith family, one of the most powerful in the country, built the Tower House that dates from 1392. Almost 200 years later, the Keiths added the Palace, known as The Quadrangle, built to take in the magnificent views from the castle.

Making the most of the vistas and the luxury castle accommodation, many monarchs visited Dunnottar over the centuries. Mary Queen of Scots would stay for the first time in 1562 and her son, James VI, would make several visits with his longest stay in 1580. Charles II would also enjoy the Palace before Cromwell overthrew the monarchy.

Cromwell took centre stage for the next episode at Dunnottar in an era that rivals the best adventure novels. The castle was deemed the best place to hide the Scottish crown jewels during Cromwell's eradication of monarchists in Britain. The Honours, as they were called, including the crown, sceptre and sword of state, were taken to the castle to await the eventual restoration of the monarchy. However, Cromwell got wind of their whereabouts and his troops laid siege.

Those loyal to the Crown held out for a full eight months, but the continual bombardment was impossible to resist. Exactly how The Honours left Dunnottar isn't clear. Some sources say they were smuggled out under the skirts of a pregnant woman. Others claim they were lowered down the cliffs to a waiting fisherwomen. But when Cromwell's troops stormed the castle they found no trace of them. The Honours were buried at nearby Kinneff church and unearthed 10 years later when Charles II returned. These days, they lie in state at Edinburgh Castle.

But as intriguing as this story is, we're getting too far ahead of ourselves. Let's get back to the Picts who were the first to see the defensive possibilities of this impregnable spot. Seeing the endless possibilities this fortress was offering, King Bridei III had attempted to extend his power further from Fortriu to cover more of the northeast in 681. But the Vikings had already had their eyes on it for quite some time, long before Harald Fairhair set his sights on it.

Harald Fairhair's life and the unification of Norway is something of a love story. It begins with a marriage proposal that resulted in rejection and scorn from Gyda Eiriksdottir, the daughter of Eirik, King of Hordaland. She is said to have refused to marry Harald 'before he was king over all of Norway'.

Harald did not pine away for love of Gyda, although he did eventually sire five children with her. He managed to sire more than twenty other children as well with at least six other women, two of whom were Eric Bloodaxe and Haakon the Good, who eventually succeeded Harald to the throne.

In 866, during Constantine I's reign, while Ivar and Hvitserk were plundering Northumbria and Eric Bloodaxe was spending a lot of time raiding northern England, Harald made the first of a series of conquests over the many small kingdoms comprising of Norway, and including Varmland in Sweden, which had sworn allegiance to the Swedish king Erik Eymundsson. While Ivar the Boneless had joined two of his brothers in Ireland in 872 and was making his presence felt in Scotland, Harald was tidying up after a crushing victory at Hafrsfjord near Stavanger. Harald then proclaimed himself King over the whole country as Harald I of Norway and then began looking further afield.

His realm, however, was very small and threatened by large numbers of his opponents who had taken refuge, not only in Iceland, recently discovered, but also in the Orkney Islands, Shetland and Hebrides, as well as the northern European mainland. Many Norwegian chieftains who were wealthy and respected now posed a threat to Harald and were therefore subjected to persecution from him, prompting them to vacate the area. Harald felt he needed to spread his wings further still and embarked on a career of international piracy to the West to clear the islands and the Scottish mainland of the Vikings who were residing there.

Eric Bloodaxe was the favourite and probably the eldest of Harald's twenty children. The small kingdom did not provide much of an inheritance especially with so many children to provide for, so as any self-respecting Viking would do, Eric took matters into his own hands, methodically murdering most of his brothers one by one, except for Haakon who was safely ensconced in the English court as part of a hostage-taking exercise at the time.

But we'll get back to Eric later on. Right now, Donald II had managed to stay alive and hold onto his kingdom for eleven years until the raid by Harald Fairhair on Dunnottar in 900. Like his father, Constantine I, Donald died a violent death at 38 years of age and his 26-year-old cousin, Caustantin mac Aed, took over the kingdom as Constantine II since Donald's son Malcolm was only an infant.

Once again, the tanistry rule came into play, ensuring that there would always be an *adult* king on the throne, avoiding the usual problems of minority reigns. Despite his cousin and predecessor having a son of his own, Constantine was able to take the throne and hang on to it for 43 years while his cousin Malcolm was forced to wait for his turn.

There has never been a time in history when a Viking warrior sat back and enjoyed his spoils of war. And just because Harald had defeated Donald at Dunnottar didn't mean the Norsemen were happy to sit back and lead a quiet life. And it also goes to say that the Scots were not happy to let the Norsemen get away with killing their kin either.

Four years later, Constantine retaliated by attacking the Norsemen where Ímar, Ívar's grandson, and many others, were killed in a battle at Strathearn. This Ímar was the first of the Ui Íma, a grandson of Ívar, along with three other grandsons who would appear later on in Constantine's reign.

As Constantine fought the Irish Vikings, things in Northumbria were heating up dramatically as well.

In Wessex, Alfred the Great's daughter, Queen Aethelflaed, Lady of the Mercians, was busy herself exterminating the Vikings along with her brother King Edward. Here again, in front of an army, stood another imposing woman, almost a reincarnation of the legendary Boudica.

Everyone remembered well the legend of Boudica. Here was a woman with flaming hair and a piercing gaze. A woman out to extract revenge for her country and her people. Her wild beauty and courage had given them the strength to stand up and fight for what they believed in when for so long, they had only felt defeat.

And it was time to do it again.

After her husband's death, Aethelflaed went straight to work with anger rippling the muscles of her back and shoulders and her fiery hair streaming behind her. In those savage times, a woman ruler would have had to be extraordinary, and she and Edward, knit by blood, marched together at yet another onslaught from the Vikings. For ten years, brother and sister advanced mercilessly together, strengthening towns as they went as Vikings attacked from all directions.

From 914 onwards, there are reports of Viking fleets in the Irish Sea led by two grandsons of Ivar, Ragnall and Sihtric Caech, crossing the Irish Sea in separate fleets intent on establishing Ragnall as King of Northumbria. Later on, Sihtric would step up to the mark a well.

Then, in 918, Aethelflaed was dead, followed by Edward five years later, and the events that followed Edward's death became messy. With five aggressive sons from three different mothers, it was never going to be simple or easy.

Edward may have intended Elfweard, his eldest son by his second wife to be his successor in Wessex only, but that's not what Elfweard thought. He considered himself ranked above his older half-brother, Aethelstan, for succession to the *entire* English throne for two reasons. Firstly, the House of Wessex was the ruling house of Britain and if Elfweard was to be the King of Wessex, then surely he should also be the King of the English. Secondly, as Aethelstan was born in 893 *before* his father became king (and to a common-law wife, no less) and Elfweard was born *during* his reign, then Elfweard believed he should be ranked higher.

But not everyone saw his logic, especially not Aethelstan.

As fate would have it, Aethelstan was by his father's side in Mercia when he died, so the Mercians promptly elected him as their new king. Meanwhile Elfweard was in Wessex and he was elected the new king by the people of Wessex.

And no one dared to take sides.

Whether Edward intended a division of the kingdoms is uncertain and as it turned out, it didn't matter. Fifteen days later in Oxford, Elfweard rather suddenly, and conveniently, died under 'mysterious circumstances'. His death ended a civil war between the brothers and overnight, everything changed yet again.

Aethelstan took no time at all to mourn his brother. He pronounced himself King of the English, taking off the traditional helmet and replacing it with a shiny new gold crown.

But he wasn't finished yet. Not by a long shot. It was 934, plans were in motion and he had a very busy year ahead of him.

The arrangement of Sihtric being King of Northumbria rubbed Aethelstan up the wrong way. As soon as his coronation was over, he approached Sihtric with the suggestion that Sihtric marry his sister, Edith, to make peace. At her marriage, both kings would make a deal and agree not to invade each other's territories or to support each other's enemies. *Surely everyone could live in harmony?* Aethelstan asked.

All very friendly and civilised, you would think. A terrific outcome. And

Edith was certainly not a wallflower. She was a beauty anyone would be happy to wed and bed.

In Sihtric's rush to the altar, the question never popped up about what would happen when one of them died. After all, both were still in their prime so there seemed to need to dwell on that nasty little subject. Right?

Until a year later when Sihtric very suddenly and very mysteriously died as well.

Once again, Aethelstan took no time in the muddled business of mourning. He tucked Northumbria under his belt and gathered up his army to move on to Scotland. It would seem England was not enough for Aethelstan. He wanted the lot.

Sihtric's Irish cousin, Guthfrith, had heard of the unexpected death, and he had grand thoughts of his own to take the throne of Northumbria for himself. He even got as far as leading a fleet from Dublin. But Aethelstan had seen that one coming and was very well prepared. He led his army north so quickly that Guthfrith was forced to flee to Scotland since there was no time to return to Dublin. This set up a fresh wave of anger from the Northumbrians who were depending on his help while they gathered their own forces together to defend themselves against Aethelstan and his reign of terror.

This is where we return to Eric Bloodaxe who was still raiding northern England with a certain deal of relish. Aethelstan knew he had to do something to appease the Northumbrians. What he really wanted was to continue with his army north to Scotland, not settle petty squabbles in Northern England.

Which is when he had an idea. He could calm Eric Bloodaxe with the promise of power and glory which would free himself up to continue with his own agenda to Scotland. He suggested to Eric that he could rule as his proxy to protect his kingdom against the Danes and 'any other marauders', such as the Scots and the Norse in Ireland, but with the understanding that Aethelstan was his overlord. By then, Aethelstan had conquered York and was itching to march further north into Scotland to confront the Scots. With him were four Welsh kings, six Viking chiefs, eighteen bishops and thirteen earls, six of whom were Danes from eastern England. All were kicking their heels with adrenaline pumping through their veins waiting for Aethelstan to say the word.

The suggestion seemed to appeal to both Eric and the Northumbrians. Eric took the oath and settled in, leaving Aethelstan to continue his march north with his army.

Constantine II had never seen an army so vast and he panicked. The way he saw it, he had two choices: risk annihilation or surrender the kingdom of Scotland.

He chose to surrender.

The Scots had never given up *anything* in their entire history so when Constantine accepted Aethelstan's victory so easily, they were both dumbfounded and apoplectic. Not just that, he did it without so much as a squabble. The word 'coward' was never uttered but in dark corners, men spoke the word in furious whispers.

Constantine knew they were right. Neither option had been really acceptable to him but what were his choices?

It was only then he realised that there actually *could* be a third choice. He could still remain King of Scotland if it *looked* like he was accepting Aethelstan as overlord. By this one deception, he would save any more Scottish blood from being spilt and it would give him time to make plans of his own.

But submission was never the Scottish style and the nobles still thought he had cowardly sold them out. While the nobles fumed at him, he took a few deep breaths and thought long and hard about how and what he would do next. While he thought, Aethelstan's court bickered savagely amongst themselves.

Wessex was still not entirely happy with Aethelstan's leadership and his legitimacy was always in question. So while Constantine pondered and Wessex quarrelled, in other parts of the country a conspiracy was being hatched by impatient men who had no desire to wait. The plan was to have Aethelstan blinded at Winchester and have him replaced by the late Elfweard's full brother, Edwin. To do that, they had to have the full support of the Bishop of Winchester, and they had been smart enough to already have that.

Once again, Aethelstan was one step ahead of them with an army ready to subdue them. In the uproar, the nobles of Wessex wisely decided to send Edwin abroad to his cousin Adelolf, Count of Boulogne in France, for safe keeping until things quietened down.

But while on the boat to France, it seems Edwin inadvertently fell overboard and drowned.

It was yet another very opportune tragedy that Aethelstan took advantage of. A hat trick, one could say.

While events in England were coming to a head, Constantine had devised his plan and was waiting patiently for the right time to step in and reclaim some semblance of honour.

On reflection, the plan was a good one. But for a Scotsman, given the sheer brutality of that present time in history, it was almost unthinkable and the nobles must have been speechless when he presented them with his solution. His rabbit in the hat, he smiled, was an eligible daughter. Olaf Guthfrithson, the Norse King of Dublin, was itching to take back his father's kingdom of York from Aethelstan so why not kill two birds with one stone? Constantine would offer his daughter to Olaf in marriage and the marriage would seal an alliance between the Norse Vikings in Ireland and Scotland. Individually they were too weak to defeat Aethelstan but together, he knew they would be victorious.

If you'd been a fly on the wall, you'd have felt the atmosphere crackle with tension. Fuming amongst the nobles was Constantine's cousin, Malcolm, still waiting next in line to the throne, and not one to hold back his temper. After Constantine's first decision to surrender to the English, followed by this fresh proposition of siding with the very Norse Irishmen who had ravaged their coastlines and butchered their families for over a century, they would have been dangerously close to losing all semblance of restraint, almost tipping them over the edge.

Malcolm was born during his father, Donald II's reign, so by now, he was 43 years old and no longer a young man. He would have seen his life ending, either at the hands of the Norse Irish or the rampaging English, while still waiting for his chance at the throne. He would have envisaged his death without having had a chance to leave his mark.

At this time in history, the various Scottish kings had their lands and power bases in different parts of Scotland, preventing any single region from claiming full domination of the others, as well as helping the country to avoid significant secession movements. The downside was that it cut down the number of available kingdoms if you were the ambitious sort. For royal members who were out to better themselves, the only way to the top was to delete a family member. Kinsmen had their own aspirations and some were impatient to wait for a natural death from natural causes to achieve them. The succession was often decided through acts of warfare or murder, resulting in early deaths and high casualty rates in the extended royal family.

You can be sure all of this ran through Malcolm's mind and he would have had supporters from several kingdoms ready to back him up at the drop of a hat. He would have certainly spoken his mind. Nonetheless, he failed to change Constantine's mind.

History tells us that Olaf and Constantine *did* join forces with the Strathclyde Britons, but Aethelstan was already on his way north to meet them by then. Once again, one step ahead. The most ferocious battle yet to be fought on English soil was about to begin at Brunanburh.

This cruelly fought clash of 937 is remembered in poetry as 'The Great Battle'. The poem tells of 'hoary' Constantine, by now around 60 years of age, in this historic battle referred to as the *'greatest single battle in Anglo-Saxon history before the Battle of Hastings'*. Thousands of Scots were to lose their lives that day while Olaf would escape back to Dublin with the remnants of his army. Among the dead Scots was one of Constantine's sons, four Scottish kings and seven earls while Aethelstan lost two of his cousins, along with his younger half-brother Edmund. Despite, the terrible loss of life, the English seized an overwhelming victory.

It would be difficult to exaggerate the importance of this victory because it was not purely about blood and conquest. This was a showdown between two very different ethnic identities. The North Celtic alliance versus the Anglo-Saxons and it was meant to settle once and for all whether Britain would be controlled by one single power or remain several separate kingdoms. If Aethelstan had been defeated, the West Saxon domination over Britain would have disintegrated and Scotland would have taken over the whole realm.

But, for all the blood and suffering, nothing was solved at all.

Constantine never recovered from Brunanburh. The defeat of all his hopes for his kingdom and the death of his son seems to have drained the spirit out of him. A few years after the battle, he abdicated and withdrew to monastic life in St Andrews, leaving his successor, his cousin Malcolm, to stem the seemingly invincible Wessex domination.

The 11th century *Prophecy of Berchan*, states that it was not a voluntary decision that 65-year-old Constantine made when he abdicated to enter a monastery, leaving this kingdom to Malcolm. He had been under great pressure to leave, especially after the series of disastrous decisions he'd made.

It's probably a good time to mention that we are in the Dark Ages, a period of time where we find few facts handed down to us. It was a time of little or no law and order and the written word was at a low point, which means stories were passed down verbally through the generations. As stories were told, they changed so that many facts turned into myths.

Two years after Brunanburh, Aethelstan died and his 18-year-old half-brother Edmund Ironside from his father's third marriage took over the throne. And everything changed once again for England.

As soon as news of Aethelstan's death reached Dublin, Olaf Guthfrithson and his cousin Olaf Sihtricsson, both great-grandsons of Ivar the Boneless, took full advantage of the unstable situation and marched to York where they simply took over. Two years later again, Olaf Guthfrithson was dead and Sihtricsson was ruling alone.

Edmund came to the English throne in 939 and began the huge task of maintaining peace in England where most of his ancestors had failed. By 945, he had managed to expel Sihtricsson from Northumbria, more specifically York, devastate Cumbria and blind two sons of Domnal mac Eogain, the King of Strathclyde.

Edmund's quiet strength kept the north subdued but it wasn't to last. Six years into his reign, while Sihtricsson was still licking his wounds and Malcolm was enjoying the first two years of his reign in Scotland, Edmund was celebrating St Augustine's Mass Day in Gloucestershire and feasting with his nobles. While the air rang with laughter and clapping as delighted guests watched beautiful women dancing and revelling in the splendid waste of expensive wine and food, Edmund Ironside was stabbed in the stomach and died almost immediately. He left two young sons, Edwig aged 5 and Edgar aged 6 so it was his 23-year old brother, Edred, who took the throne.

In the power vacuum while Edred settled in, Archbishop Wulfstan and other Scandinavian magnates in York huddled together and made plans. Six years previously in 939, Archbishop Wulfstan had been reluctantly subdued in York by 17-year-old Prince Edred on the order from his brother King Edmund and the sting was still fresh in his mind. It seemed the perfect opportunity for Wulfstan to push the boundaries again and put Eric

Bloodaxe on the York throne. As for Eric, it was the perfect opportunity to improve his own personal lot.

In hindsight, it was unfortunate for Eric that he made his move at that particular time. Edred had only just stepped up to the throne and he was still just forming his court. He had Malcolm raiding Northumbria as far south as Tees taking cattle and hostages, along with five kings from the Hebrides and two earls of Orkney joining up with him to rampage the north. Then to top it off, Edred heard that Sihtricsson was restless again in Dublin and was itching to make his move back to York, ready to oust Eric from York and establish himself as king.

Edred must have taken a good hard look at what was happening in his kingdom and as you can expect, he exploded. He gathered his army together and stormed north to Ripon in Scotland and began burning the town and the monastery to the ground.

Eric's hold on York had been tenuous to start with but when he saw Edred practically outside York's gates, he fled. However, after his rather speedy exit, Edred's rear guard was taken by surprise by Eric Bloodaxe's troops, slaughtering many of Edred's men just outside Castleford. Edred threatened another full scale raid on York if Eric persisted and Eric finally, and reluctantly, retreated.

Once again, Edred reprimanded Archbishop Wulfstan and once again the Archbishop huffed and puffed and quietly seethed. This time, he waited one year before pushing the boundary again. This time he invited Sihtricsson over from Dublin and defiantly offered the throne of York to him.

Edred had finally had enough. He gathered his army together and marched north to have it out once and for all with the Vikings. This time, however, he decided to meet the Archbishop halfway. He agreed that Sihtricsson could remain King of Northumbria if he managed to keep Eric Bloodaxe well away. And of course, Sihtricsson wholeheartedly agreed.

The move may have been made to keep the peace but it actually did the opposite. When Malcolm heard that Sihtricsson was sitting on the throne of York in Northumbria, he instantly gathered up his army and headed south towards Northumbria to have it out with everyone.

By then, Edred had begun to suffer from a severe stomach illness, perhaps Crohn's disease like his ancestor Alfred the Great, and whether he had always suffered from it or the stress of his reign exacerbated it, no one knows. It stopped him from eating food properly and was so severe that he could only suck the juices from the food and spit the rest out. And Archbishop Wulfstan took full advantage of the situation by doing an about-face and deposing Sihtricsson from the throne and inviting Eric Bloodaxe back again.

The push and pull all came to an abrupt end in 954 in a lonely place called Stainmore where the Vikings, English and Malcolm finally came together to thrash it out.

Edred had already marched back to York and had captured the Archbishop but this time, he also came with a plan. Using the long-established tactic of setting one Viking leader against another, he bought another Viking into the picture by the name of Maccus, in conspiracy with Oswulf Ealdulfing of Bamburgh, both supporters of Edred.

Malcolm should have remembered that his father Donald II and his grandfather Constantine I had both died violently 54 years and 77 years earlier respectively in battles. He should also have remembered that his two sons, Dub and Kenneth, were still young children and if Malcolm died, his 30-year-old cousin Indulf the Aggressor would step in, following the rules of tanistry, and become the next king of Scotland. His own sons would then have to wait their turn like everyone else until Indulf died.

He would have been nervous, knowing that. He would have thought of ferocious battlefields and felt a surge of fear as he remembered the glint of helmets in the sunshine, the soaring spears, the pounding of hoofbeats and the screams of dying men. Fear would have crawled inside him like a beast, clawing his guts, weakening muscles and loosening bowels. Fear wants you to cringe and weep but you have to hope that savagery will see you through. He would have remembered his glorious past and he would have hoped to see remnants of that glory in the future. It would have been hard to bring thoughts into order knowing you can slide from glory to chaos so quickly.

He would have known that Edred and his Christianity-besotted family liked to believe they were bringing civilisation to a barbaric world. Alfred and his descendants spoke of an impending doom and chaos for pagans. His priests scurried like mice imposing rules as if obeying their rules would stop the doom. *Thou shalt not kill*, they preached, then screamed at warriors to slaughter all pagans. *Thou shalt not covet your neighbours goods*, they preached, as their eyes and spears pointed greedily towards the north. *Thou shalt not steal*, they preached, and yet warriors thundered into other men's kingdoms to do exactly that.

As he stared across the countryside, sodden with rain as a blanket of fog smothered the marshes, he would have seen the old Roman wall and perhaps he grudgingly admired it. His people could not build arenas like the one in York. His roads were muddy tracks while theirs were straight and stone edged. They had built temples of marble with intricate tile work for floors while his buildings were timber with beaten earth floors with rushes laid on top. The Romans had gone centuries before and their wonders were decaying now. But they had been marvels at the time.

As he looked across the countryside, he would have known it was time to roll the dice. All of his reign had been spent attacking and defending Scotland. Time and again the English and Danes had tried to capture his land, and time and again he had saved it. Not to fight now would mean they would come again anyway, thinking him weak.

In the end, he had little choice but to fight Edred and Eric Bloodaxe in a brutal, lengthy battle and you can imagine the ferocity of it. The Scots fought like mad, howling devils, as was their dreaded reputation. The Danes and Saxons used swords and spears to cut them down but still the shrieking hordes came, climbing over their dead, their wild hair red with blood.

Malcolm fought defiantly like a fiend as his men were butchered, still screaming, but like his ancestors, he was killed in a shield wall next to their own men, as was Eric Bloodaxe.

For his support, Edred made Oswulf his administrator in Northumbria but by then Edred was a very sick man. By the end of the year, he would also be dead, succumbing to his illness at 32 years old, leaving the first of his two nephews, 14-year-old Edwig, to step up to the throne. With the headstrong Edwig on the throne, life in England would never be the same again.

Malcolm's death did nothing to stop the Vikings. Eight years later, Indulf was still fighting them until his own death at the Battle of Bauds in 962, and once again impatient relatives stepped quickly into the picture. Rivalry instantly resumed and once again, we see cousin fighting cousin to take over the throne for the next 40 years into the future.

During the 10th century, as in previous centuries, there were still dynastic conflicts in Scotland where kings see-sawed between two rival lines of royalty. One descended from Constantine I who reigned between 862 and 877 and the other from his brother Aed who reigned between 877 and 878. Both were sons of Kenneth MacAlpin.

We now come to the year 995 when Malcolm I's youngest son, Kenneth II, was on the throne. Kenneth was not a stupid man. He knew from his ancestors that his own son would probably have to wait to become king until after *his* cousins took their turn before him. The only way to solve that little problem was to change the succession rules by allowing *'the nearest survivor in blood to the deceased king to succeed'* instead of the traditional rules of tanistry. This would mean his own son Malcolm, only nine at the time, would succeed as his heir no matter what.

Kenneth didn't regard himself an old man. He was 60 years old but in good health. All he had to do was stay that way until his son Malcolm grew to be a fine young man. And eight years should do it.

But in the background, we have two young cousins, Kenneth (III) and Constantine (III), who would have seen their future as kings being snatched away from them if Kenneth's plan worked. Kenneth's son Malcolm would take the throne after his father's death and he would a young man of barely 20 years of age. He could have twenty years, maybe more, on the throne and the two cousins would probably never ever sit on it.

There have been many times in history when the drama unfolding is worthy of a Hollywoodesque series and Lady Finella's entrance into history is well known in Scottish legends. As the daughter of the Mormaer of Angus, she had only been quietly present up till then. She secretly nurtured a hate for Kenneth as the man responsible for the death of her only son in battle. So when the two young cousins approached her to kill Kenneth before he had a chance to change the tanistry law, (which would leave the way open for them and push nine-year-old Malcolm to the bottom of the line), she didn't take too long to consider the suggestion. A sudden end to his reign would be revenge enough for her and after all, Scottish kings had a habit of dying suddenly, didn't they? So Lady Finella set herself on a very dangerous path.

This spectacular plan would set the wheels in motion for an engrossing story that would keep evolving for the next 45 years.

Whether folklore or fact, our story begins at dawn on a cold, grey March morning in Fettercairn, Finella's home, where she welcomed Kenneth and his companions at the start of their hunting expedition. That bleak morning, as fog drifted through the trees, Finella saw Kenneth emerge out of the mist as leaves fell softly from the trees.

There is a point of no return in most stories where the characters make their way on stage as the drama is unfolding. For Finella, the stage was set and the timing was perfect. It was an elaborate plan but she had come this far and there was no going back.

Kenneth rode to her gate and she must have been shaking with nervousness and anxiety. It's one thing to plan a murder but it was another thing to actually put that plan into action. Knowing the consequences, it was a huge undertaking when at any time things could go terribly wrong.

Bracing herself, she approached Kenneth to proclaim her loyalty and invited him to visit her residence, whispering in his ear that she had information about a conspiracy. Inside the cottage was a statue, ingeniously connected by hidden strings to a number of crossbows. If anyone touched or moved the statue, it would trigger the crossbows and fall victim to their arrows. Obligingly, Kenneth gently touched the statue and *'was shot through by arrows that sped from all sides, and he fell without uttering another word.'*

Lady Finella would have known she had no hope of escape. She fled towards the coast where she was pursued and cornered by the king's soldiers at the top of a waterfall near St Cyrus. To avoid capture, she threw herself over the waterfall from a height of 150 feet to her death in the valley now called Den Finella as 25-year-old Constantine usurped the throne for himself as Constantine III.

If this period in history up to now was messy and confusing, things were about to escalate because this is where his cousin Kenneth sat back and remembered that he perhaps would never have the throne for himself. Since Constantine was only 25, young Malcolm would be old enough to take the throne for himself when Constantine died and Kenneth would lose out completely.

Barely 18 months later, Constantine III was killed in battle by his cousin, Kenneth, the same one who had gone to Lady Finella for help in killing Kenneth II. With Constantine, the last of the line of Aed to be king died as well as he left no known children.

With Constantine out of the way, Kenneth stepped up to assume the throne for himself as Kenneth III.

You just know Malcolm wouldn't be happy. He waited eight years, until he turned 19, to take his revenge.

On 25th March 1005, in a quiet, highland area of Perth and Kinross called Monzievaird, Malcolm killed both Kenneth III and Kenneth's eldest son Giric II in a battle before usurping the throne for himself as Malcolm II. Kenneth's younger son, Boite, would rather wisely keep a very low profile, either being too young or too smart to attempt taking the throne from Malcolm any time soon. But in the future, Boite's familial line would unknowingly succeed to the throne after all with a very infamous daughter by the name of Gruoch who will marry a man who becomes king. This fabulous story we will see soon.

The son of Kenneth II and Aulgigu of Leinster in Ireland, Malcolm II is referred to as 'The Destroyer'. He was one of several kings within the geographical boundaries of modern Scotland: his fellow kings included the King of Strathclyde, various Norse-Gael kings on the western coast and the Hebrides and the nearest and most dangerous rivals, the Kings, or Mormaers, of Moray.

While Scotland was watching five kings come and go inside 30 years, England was having similar troubles of its own with five kings dying in 40 years. Wave after wave of Viking ships carrying marauders from all parts of Scandinavia and Ireland were arriving and King Ethelred the Unready couldn't keep up with their demands.

It was at this time that King Ethelred's wife died after producing eleven children, of which only four survived. Ready to marry for a second time, Ethelred chose Lady Emma, the sister of Duke Richard II of Normandy, as his bride. His plan was to draw the Duke away from his Viking allies who were using Normandy as a base from which to attack England. The added bonus was Emma was very pleasing on the eye.

Unfortunately for Ethelred, the Viking attacks continued with a vengeance motivated by the dual goals of revenge and complete annihilation of England. Finally in August 1013, a Viking by the name of Sweyn Forkbeard and his son Canute landed at the mouth of the Humber and ransacked, raped and murdered their way through the North, burning women alive, impaling children and suspending men from their private parts. By Christmas 1013, Sweyn simply took over England unopposed while Ethelred was lucky to escape with his life to the Isle of Wight.

Sweyn had only just begun his rule, still beginning the process of organising his new kingdom and finding trustworthy supporters, when forty days later, he was murdered. No one knew who had managed the unbelievable, although everyone knew Ethelred had supporters everywhere. Canute was smart enough to beat a hasty retreat back to Denmark to regroup while Ethelred triumphantly returned to the throne with his wife Emma and their three children.

It only took Canute two years to return with a vengeance but by then Ethelred was an old man and struggling to defend his kingdom. As any Viking worth his salt would do, Canute took full advantage of Ethelred's weakness and moved in, proclaiming himself the King. And on Ethelred's death soon after, Canute took Emma for his bride.

From Scotland, Malcolm watched silently as news filtered in. A clever and ambitious man, he possessed a rare ability to survive in times when earlier Scottish kings fell like flies. Since he was responsible for the death of Kenneth III and his son, there weren't too many left who were brave enough to stand up to him.

So while England struggled, Malcolm was doing what he did best. Surviving. He managed to reign for 29 years when many of his predecessors only managed a few at the best. He was determined to retain succession within his own line except for one major obstacle: unfortunately for Malcolm and his wife, (a granddaughter of a Prince of Norway), what he didn't have was a surviving son and heir, only three daughters. In a time when women were only useful as bargaining tools and still forbidden to hold the throne, all Malcolm could hope to do was marry his daughters to wealthy, influential men and hope they produced male children to continue his line before he himself died.

Bethoc, the eldest daughter, was married to Crinan, Mormaer of Atholl and Abbott of Dunkeld and had three known children. It would be their eldest son Donnchad, anglicised to Duncan, who would become the next king of Scotland through the rules of tanistry as Duncan I.

The youngest daughter, Olith, was married to Sigurd Hlodvisson, Earl of Orkney. Their son Thorfinn Sigurdsson, who would eventually be called Thorfinn the Mighty, was said to be five years old when his father was killed in 1014 in the Battle of Clontarf. Little Thorfinn was then raised at

Malcolm's court and given the title Mormaer, or ruler, of Caithness by his grandfather.

Finally Donada, the middle daughter, was married to Findlaech mac Ruaidri, Mormaer of Moray, who had a son she would name Mac Bethad, anglicised to Macbeth.

By these powerful marriages, Malcolm effectively gathered the lands and riches of Atholl, Moray and Caithness into his family.

And now we come to the story I've been itching to tell. It's complicated and involves three cousins and everyone plays an important role in this complex saga. Although Malcolm II is still alive in my story so far, I am going to jump ahead for a bit to his grandson, Macbeth, and the intricacies of *his* family.

There's a little village of Lumphanan in Aberdeenshire that lies about fifty kilometres to the west of Aberdeen. It's not as celebrated a name in the Macbeth chronicle as Birnam Wood or Dunsinane Hill in Perthshire or Forres in Moray, but in fact it is much more significant because it was at Lumphanan that Macbeth (the historical Macbeth not the Macbeth of Shakespeare's play) met his death in the year 1057.

What Shakespeare did for Macbeth was to make him perhaps the best known, and certainly the most notorious, character in Scottish history but at an appalling cost to historical veracity. Yet he was so skilful in writing his story, so powerful in his characterisation of a noble soul seduced by ambition (and by a ferocious harpy of a wife) that everyone knows it and believes it.

According to Shakespeare, Macbeth was a trusted general of the much-loved King Duncan I of Scotland. With his fellow general Banquo, Macbeth quells an insurrection and defeats a major Viking invasion in Fife. On his way home, on a *'blasted heath'* near Forres, he encounters three witches. The first addresses him as Thane of Glamis (a title he had just inherited). The second addresses him as Thane of Cawdor (which Duncan had just named him although Macbeth did not know it as yet). The third, ominously, addresses him as *'Macbeth! That shalt be king hereafter!'* For Banquo, they promise less in the immediate future but much more to come: *'Thou shalt get kings, though thou be none.'*

Soon afterwards, messengers arrive to announce that Macbeth is to receive the title and possessions of the Thane of Cawdor, who had been a traitor in the rebellion and is shortly to be executed. Macbeth is dumbstruck because two truths predicted had come to pass.

According to Shakespeare, Macbeth now writes a letter to his wife telling her of his encounter with the witches and sends notice that the king himself is coming to stay with them at their castle at Inverness. Lady Macbeth works on her husband's latent ambition and incites him to kill the king, which he does, although unnerved by the deed. Duncan's two young sons, Malcolm, Prince of Cumbria, and Donalbain, fearful of suffering the same fate, flee the country. Macbeth thereupon seized the crown.

Mindful of the witches' prophecy that Banquo will be the progenitor of future kings of Scotland, Macbeth sends hired assassins to kill Banquo and his young son Fleance. Banquo is struck down, but Fleance escapes Macbeth and flees to England, where he fathers a son who much later becomes the first hereditary steward to the King of Scotland. In real life, 'Steward' eventually became the name 'Stewart' (later changed to a pseudo Frenchification 'Stuart'), and Walter Steward, after his services at Bannockburn, was appointed Warden of the Western Marshes and rewarded with a grant of lands which had been forfeited by King John Balliol. He then married Princess Marjorie, the only daughter of King Robert the Bruce by his first wife, and their son, Robert II, began the Stewart/Stuart line of kings in Scotland.

But back to Macbeth.

Macbeth now embarks on a reign of terror. He consults the witches again, and they warn him to beware of Macduff, the Thane of Fife. But they also tell him that *'none of woman born'* will ever harm him, and that he *'shall never vanquished be, until Great Birnam Wood to high Dunsinane Hill shall come against him.'*

Before Macbeth has time to act, Macduff, suspecting that he is next on the king's hit list, flees to England to join Duncan's son Malcolm. In thwarted fury, Macbeth sends his assassins to Macduff's castle in Fife and has Macduff's wife and young family slaughtered.

At the English court, the Scottish refugees, spurred on by Macduff's arrival, assemble an army with English help and invade Scotland. To hide their advance towards the tyrant's lair at Dunsinane Castle, they camouflage themselves with branches cut from Birnam Wood. Macbeth is shaken by the news that the wood seems to be coming to Dunsinane but is even more dismayed when he faces the vengeful Macduff who reveals that he was not *'of woman born'* but had been *'from his mother's womb untimely ripp'd'*.

There is nothing left for Macbeth now but to die valiantly. Macbeth is duly slain by Macduff, who brings the tyrant's head to Malcolm – the future Malcolm III, Malcolm Canmore.

This tale of a witch-ridden, bloodthirsty usurper who lost his head to Macduff is fabulous and we know that Shakespeare was in no way averse to twisting history for political ends. Ten years earlier Shakespeare had played fast and loose with the notorious story of Richard III. No doubt this was done to celebrate the arrival of the first of the Tudors, Henry VII, and in order to please and stay in the good books with his demanding royal patron, Queen Elizabeth. Shakespeare's story bases Richard as the disreputable, ambitious uncle who killed his nephews to usurp the throne. This story as well has come under intense scrutiny as a work of fiction. There is nothing like a good story to keep historical memory alive, however embroidered it might have become.

Now let's come to the historically correct Macbeth.

Macbeth was one of the great Scottish kings and his name in Gaelic, MacBeathadh, means 'Son of Life'. Macbeth's father was Findlaech mac Ruaidri, Mormaer of Moray, and in the 11th century, Moray was an area in the north-east of Scotland and a kingdom in its own right with its own king, Macbeth's father. But although Findlaech had become King of Moray upon the death of his older brother, Máel Brigte, Máel Brigte had two ambitious sons, Máel Coluun and Gille Coemgain, who saw things differently.

The two young men weren't happy about being side-lined by their uncle Findlaech, which would mean their cousin Macbeth would be the next heir to Moray, not them. The way they saw it, they should have been the heirs to the Moray throne, not their father's younger brother and then *his* son. Macbeth's younger cousin, Gille Coemgain, had already set his sights on taking Gruoch, (the daughter of Boite, the younger son of Kenneth III, making her the granddaughter of Kenneth), as his wife since marriage to Gruoch, through her close royal connections to Kenneth III, would take him one step closer to the Scottish throne. What he didn't have to offer Gruoch was a title. But he had a remedy for that.

Before the marriage took place, Gille Coemgain and his elder brother, Máel Coluun, would murder their uncle, (Macbeth's father, Findlaech) and take over as Mormaers of Moray. Being the elder brother, Máel Coluun would then take the throne and after that, Gille Coemgain would take over from him as Mormaer of Moray. Macbeth, younger than both his cousins, was collateral damage. He would have to make his own way in the world or be eliminated too. Problem solved.

Gille Coemgain's marriage to Gruoch was certainly strategic on the part of the powerful Moray family. Marriage to Gruoch and then the birth of their son, Lulach mac Gille Coemgain, meant the Morays held a potential future claimant to the Scottish throne.

Malcolm still had no living sons and the threat to his plans for the succession was obvious. His eldest daughter Bethoc had already given birth to a son Duncan, who by Malcolm's reasoning was the future King of Scotland, not the grandson of a past king that Malcolm himself had annihilated.

But if Macbeth had a cause for revenge on the killer of his father in 1020, Malcolm too had reason to see Gille Coemgain dead. Gille Coemgain's ancestors had killed many of Malcolm's kin, including his brother Dungal in 999, and Gille Coemgain was getting a little too greedy in thinking *he* and his family would have the rights to the throne through a future son of Gruoch.

Malcolm knew what he had to do. If he wanted the way clear for his grandson Duncan, he had to kill Gruoch's cousin Macduff, another grandson of Kenneth III, who was the potential claimant to the throne on Malcolm's death. His second daughter Donada's son, Macbeth, could take the Moray throne back for himself.

The following year in 1021, he did just that.

Let's fast-forward to the year is 1032 where 27-year-old Macbeth was seething in Ireland and planning his revenge for his father's murder. The way Macbeth saw it, he had royal blood in own his veins as Malcolm's grandson through his second daughter Donada so in fact, *he* was the true Mormaer of Moray, not to mention a claimant of the Scottish throne if Duncan were to die without heirs.

From exile, he sent a message to all the families in Moray, who were themselves unhappy with Gille Coemgain's leadership, that he was returning to Moray to kill Gille Coemgain and take back the throne for himself.

Macbeth must have been reading up on his history and the story of the

'McAlpine Treason'. Imagine a great hall one year later with Gille Coemgain and fifty of his men, all happy and inebriated. There would be laughter and singing and the raucous sound would block out the stealthy sounds of Macbeth and his men creeping closer. Waiting for just the right moment, Macbeth stepped forward, blocking the exits, and set the hall alight, burning Gille Coemgain alive along with all of his men. In that instant, Macbeth assumed his father's rank of Mormaer of Moray.

The only minor glitch was Gruoch. As we know, she was herself descended from a royal line and she had just delivered Gille Coemgain's son, Lulach.

For Macbeth, killing Gille was an end to the blood feud in his family. But what Macbeth also saw was a fortuitous opportunity on Gille's death. By marrying Gruoch, and becoming step-father and protector of Gruoch's son Lulach, a child he would raise him as his own, he would effectively strengthen his own claim to the Scottish throne. As an added bonus, Gruoch's royal connections and lands also added to his own somewhat tenuous claim to the wider Scottish throne still held by Malcolm II, who was by now an old man.

Gruoch's feelings about marrying her husband's murderer are unknown, but a desire to protect her young son must have been a significant factor.

Macbeth's personal involvement in the army that marched against his grandfather, Malcolm II, two years later in 1034 is unclear. Perhaps it was out of revenge for Gruoch whose brother MacDuff had been killed by Malcolm in 1021, but no one knows. Perhaps it was as simple as putting the first few steps of his plan into place. What we know is that Malcolm was killed in a battle at Glamis, and Duncan, as planned, succeeded him with a far stronger claim to the throne than his cousin Macbeth possessed. Although arguments were had, Duncan was invested as the King of Scotland at Scone five days after Malcolm's death.

Duncan was not a young man by medieval standards. He would have been around 35 years old, but far from the old man in the famous play. Nor was he murdered by Macbeth while a guest in his castle, as Shakespeare's story goes. In the same vein, Duncan I was not by any means Shakespeare's gentle, much-revered king, rich in years and loved by his subjects. He was in fact a militarily incompetent man and the grandson of a ruthless and despotic king.

Duncan's succession caused widespread anger because apart from tanistry, the ancient custom was succession by election from a group of elders. If that had been allowed to come into effect, Gruoch's son was the correct choice but since he was only a baby, his father, or in Macbeth's case, his stepfather, should rightfully have the throne. Which was exactly what Macbeth thought as well. Besides all that, Duncan had neither the maturity nor the track record to merit the throne. He had clearly inherited his grandfather's ambition, but not his skill. Five years later, Duncan proved his unworthiness by invading the north of England and making a disastrous attack on Durham, followed by making an equally foolhardy attempt to impose his authority on the recalcitrant north of Scotland, in particular the Orkney islands.

This is where his cousin Thorfinn Sigurdsson enters the picture.

Thorfinn Sigurdarsson the Mighty, the Norse Earl of Orkney, is one of the most compelling figures in the great portrait gallery of Norse earls. A huge, powerfully-built, swarthy man, ugly and sharp-featured with a prominent nose, was ambitious, ruthless and very shrewd. He was a born survivor in an age when survival was always precarious. Like Duncan and Macbeth, he was a grandson of Malcolm II through Malcolm's youngest daughter, Olith, created Earl of Caithness and Sutherland by Malcolm II at the age of five in 1014 when Thorfinn's father died at the Battle of Clontarf in Ireland, and thereafter fought his way to control of Orkney by the 1030's. By the time he died, at some future date between 1057 and 1058, he had extended his realm deep into the heartlands of Scotland and over the Western Isles as well, and was recognised as the most powerful ruler in Northern Britain. He was a man of compelling personal authority and after the turbulent years of his early piratical reign, he spent the latter part of his life ruling his realms wisely and benevolently from the palace and church he built on the Brough of Birsay at the northern end of the Mainland of Orkney. His reign was the high point of the golden age of Viking power in the north.

This powerful man wasn't about to let Duncan walk all over him, king or no king, cousin or no cousin. A wise man would have thought long and hard being doing that.

Together with his cousin Macbeth, both with axes to grind, they finally met 39-year-old Duncan somewhere near the village of Pitgaveny, near Elgin, in 1040. The battle was bloody but Macbeth was victorious and was immediately accepted as King of Scots and crowned at Scone, which suggests that Duncan's military failures had antagonised his subjects in the south too.

Gruoch's royal connections were important in bolstering Macbeth's claim to be King of both Scotland and Moray and it may be that in a period of turbulence and uncertainty, the nobility in Scotland rather wisely chose strength over the rights of primogeniture by naming Macbeth the King. Although history has since characterised Macbeth as a usurper, he was rightfully declared King by the people, since Duncan's eldest son, another Malcolm, was barely 9 years old.

Duncan's widow, Sybil, was smart enough to know that the lives of both her boys, Malcolm and Donald, were in danger from Macbeth. She came from a long line of Vikings and she knew what the consequences would be if she hesitated. It was fortunate that she had resources available.

Without waiting, she bundled up her boys with as many possessions she could take with her and escaped to Northumbria to be with her Danish father Siward, Earl of Northumbria, and her two brothers.

The larger than life figure of Siward first appears on the pages of history in 1033 during the reign of Canute. He had grown to be powerful in the north of England, arriving in England in the wake of Canute's conquest, and had entrenched his position in northern England by marrying Elfflaed, the daughter of Ealdred, Earl of Bamburgh, and granddaughter of Uchtred the Bold. And as far as he could see, Macbeth had crossed a boundary that was never to be forgotten. His daughter had been wronged and the lives of his grandsons, Malcolm and Donald, were threatened.

Macbeth may not have been the most compelling King of Scots in the 11th century, but he seems to have been a very capable one. But that doesn't mean things weren't heating up.

Let's backtrack a bit for England to catch up to Scotland.

For all the energy Canute put in to uniting England, when he died one year after Malcolm in 1035, his empire began to crumble. Canute had ruled England for twenty years where he dealt intelligently with situations and always acted with acute political sense. Despite his shaky start, this firm leader was renowned not only for his calculated actions to win support but for his attempts at reconciling the English and the Danes.

Perhaps he was hoping his three sons would follow in his footsteps, but in actual fact, Canute's children were ignorant and coarse Vikings.

Harold Harefoot and Sweyn were sons by a former wife, Elfgifu, while Harthacanute was a son by Emma. Even before Canute was buried, his sons began fighting.

On his death, and while most nobles believed he had left his son Sweyn to rule Norway while both Harold and Harthacanute were to rule England jointly, the rightful heirs to the English throne were in reality the sons of Ethelred and Emma: Alfred and Edward. And Ethelred's eldest son, Alfred, wholeheartedly agreed with them.

From Normandy, Alfred made plans to return to England ostensibly to visit his once-again widowed mother, Emma. Assuredly, his thoughts were with gaining support in order to claim back the throne. After all, he *was* the eldest son of Ethelred and he had a solid right to be the heir to the throne, if you excluded the two sons of Edmund Ironside, both exiled in Europe.

While Macbeth and his cousin Thorfinn, were plotting to rid themselves of Duncan, Magnus I, the son of a former king of Norway, was hell-bent on claiming the throne of Denmark for himself after hearing that Canute was dead. In a panic, Sweyn called for help from Harthacanute to help keep Magnus out of their homeland.

Harthacanute did not want to leave England in his elder half-brother's hands, but he knew he really had no choice. It was either leave England in Harold's hands or let Magnus take the throne of Norway. The whole situation solved itself at Oxford when it was decided that Harold should have all the country north of the Thames with London as its capital and Harthacanute could have the south on his return. With the quarrel sorted, Harthacanute left for Norway with the understanding that Harold would only be the regent of his share of the kingdom during his temporary absence.

At this time, Earl Godwin was the leader of the Danish party in England and he was flexing his own muscles. He could trace his own lineage back to Ethelred I in 871 (surely that counted, right?) and he had six sons of his own to think about. Being a smart man and knowing that the numbers were stacked against him, Godwin soon realised if he wanted to have any influence in government at all, his best interests lay with Harold Harefoot. So Godwin switched sides from Alfred to Harold.

Harold must have felt he had found a kindred spirit in Godwin because very soon, they both began to devise a plan that would exclude both Alfred and Harthacanute from the throne.

Without even being aware of any danger, Alfred landed on the coast of Kent and was welcomed by Godwin with open arms. When they approached the town of Guildford on their way to Surrey, they stopped for the night after the long march. With food and wine in their bellies, all proceeded happily to bed.

The next morning, Alfred was woken early by the sound of confused voices as his men were dragged outside, lined up, tortured and murdered. Alfred was then stripped naked, tied to a horse and led to the Isle of Ely, where he was then blinded with a hot iron. Needless to say, he died soon after from his injuries.

With the succession simplified, Harold Harefoot claimed the throne of England for himself and promptly told his mother, Emma, to leave England immediately. After knowing how Harold killed his half-brother Alfred, one of her sons to Ethelred, she didn't wait to be told twice. She left for Bruges on the next ship.

Maybe the cruelty of the Vikings had scared the population in the past but the fact that Harold had no real bloodline to the English throne did not seem to make too much of a difference to most people. Within two years, Harold was generally accepted as the king. But behind the scenes, Godwin's boys were growing up fast and restless for power.

In Norway, angered and horrified at the treatment of his mother and the murder of his half-brother Alfred, Harthacanute gathered together a force of 62 warships to forcefully assert his claim, demanding revenge and his throne back. He was taking no chances with Harold, planning to arrive as a conqueror with a full invasion force.

Unfortunately for Harthacanute, he was to be denied his revenge. Harold died 'unexpectedly' at the age of twenty-four but while Harold lay dying in Sandwich, a monk reported that Harold grew black as they spoke and the word 'poison' was thrown around. Harold was only one of several youthful kings to die 'unexpectedly' following short reigns. And he would not be the last.

Harold's reign was considered quite peaceful as nothing remarkable happened during his four to five years on the throne. Still, he died little regretted or esteemed by his subjects and was buried before Harthacanute even landed on English soil.

But things were going to change very soon.

When Harthacanute arrived back in England with his mother, his first action was to have Godwin arrested knowing that Godwin was partly responsible for Alfred's death. During his trial where he was being tried for murder, Godwin's defence was that he was merely carrying out the order from Harold himself. After giving a generous gift to Harthacanute, a richly decorated ship with a figurehead of solid gold with a crew of eighty armed men, the charges were suddenly dropped and Godwin escaped punishment and resumed duties as normal.

Harthacanute's second task was to have Harold's body exhumed, publicly decapitated and then thrown into a marsh. A little excessive, but he was a Viking after all.

Harthacanute had always been a quarrelsome man and being the king seemed to bring out the worst in him. He spent most of his time ranting, persecuting and murdering the supporters of his half-brother Harold and was very successful at intimidating his subjects throughout his short reign.

With the influence of Emma, Harthacanute invited his other half-brother, Edward, nicknamed The Confessor, back from exile in Normandy and the three family members seemed happy enough to be reunited.

It was two years later on a bright sunny day in June 1042, that Harthacanute, Emma and Edward attended a wedding in Lambeth. The groom had been a standard bearer for his father and the bride was a courtier. After drinking large amounts of wine and raising a glass to toast the bride, Harthacanute suddenly fell to the ground and died at only twenty-four years of age.

Now there are accidental deaths and there are *accidental* deaths, if you know what I mean, and there was no shortage of discontented candidates to choose from. Keeping that in mind, we should then look to see who would gain the most from Harthacanute's death and we only have one suspect - Emma's son Edward. Edward was brother of Edmund Ironside, younger son of Ethelred, stepson of Canute, stepbrother of Harold Harefoot and half-brother of Harthacanute. With that impressive resume, who was more deserving to have the throne?

With Harthacanute out of the way, Edward's pathway to the throne was clear, although somewhat weak with the Godwins breathing down his neck. So his marriage to Edith, Godwin's daughter, seemed a smart move at a time, especially since Godwin had strengthened his own position by marrying Canute's former sister-in-law. With his wife Edith Godwin by his side as queen and his father-in-law Godwin standing not too far behind him, things looked rosy.

All accounts state that Edith was a kind, gentle woman but from the start, Edward neglected her, much to the anger of Godwin and her six brothers.

At this time in history, there were four young men growing up in a tough world. In Scotland, we have 10-year-old Lulach, Macbeth's stepson to Gruoch. In England, we have Duncan's eldest son, 18-year-old Malcolm, who was learning from his powerful grandfather, Siward, in Northumbria. The powerful Earl of Wessex, Godwin, had many sons, but the eldest son, 20-year-old Harold Godwin, had dreams of taking the throne of England for himself in the near future. And in Normandy, we have Queen Emma of England's great-nephew, 14-year-old William, the illegitimate son of Robert I Duke of Normandy and a tanner's daughter, trying very hard to ignore his nickname of 'William The Bastard'.

According to legend, Robert I, Duke of Normandy, saw the local tanner's daughter Herleva from the roof of his castle tower. The walkway on the roof overlooked the dyeing tranches cut into stone in the courtyard below, which can still be seen to this day from the tower ramparts above. The traditional way of dyeing leather or garments was to trample barefoot on the garments which were awash in the liquid dye in these trenches. Herleva, legend says, seeing the Duke on his ramparts above, raised her skirts perhaps a bit more than necessary in order to attract the Duke's eye. And attract him she did. The Duke was immediately smitten and ordered her brought in through the back door. Herleva refused, saying she would only enter the Duke's castle on horseback through the front gate, and not as an ordinary commoner. The Duke, filled with lust, could only agree. In a few days, Herleva, dressed in the finest clothes her father could provide, was sitting on a white horse, riding proudly through the front gate, her head held high. This gave Herleva a semi-official status as the Duke's concubine.

Later, she would give birth to his son, William, in 1028, who would forever be known as 'William the Bastard' and the future William the Conqueror.

All four young men would play major parts in the near future.

It all came to a head in 1049, eight years after Edward came to the throne while Macbeth was holding his own in Scotland. Macbeth and Gruoch were even confident enough to leave the country, leaving Lulach as their regent in Scotland in their absence, and undertake a lengthy pilgrimage to Rome, an undertaking that would have been unimaginable were they not secure on the throne.

But if things were settling for Macbeth in Scotland, Edward was having a chaotic time in England.

Edward's sister had married Eustace, Earl of Cologne, and the Earl had spent some time visiting his brother-in-law. As Eustace prepared for departure and set off with his numerous attendants to begin the trip home from Dover, they entered the quiet town in full armour demanding that they be given the best accommodation without payment due to their royal connections. One innkeeper firmly stood his ground and refused and it all blew up rather quickly when the armed attendant struck the innkeeper. He in turn, retaliated by killing the armed attendant. Within minutes, word spread to Eustace and in a temper, he and his men galloped to the house, riding over women and children in the streets, surrounded the inn and then killed the innkeeper.

Even in those harsh times, it was a brutal thing to do and the people of Dover were shocked. In a state of absolute fury, they killed nineteen more attendants and wounded many more before blockading off the road to the port where the men were hoping to embark. Eustace beat a hasty retreat back to Edward to inform him of what had happened, demanding that Edward intervene on his behalf and deal out justice. Furious as well, Edward commanded Godwin to take reinforcements to Dover and kill the inhabitants who had slaughtered his brother-in-law's men.

It was the perfect opportunity Godwin had been waiting for. With his sons standing resolutely behind him, Godwin flatly refused. What they hadn't seen coming was Edward's countermove by bringing in an aggressive army and they panicked. While Godwin's sons barely escaped with their lives to Ireland, all Godwin had time to do was gather his possessions together and beat a hasty retreat to Flanders. Unfortunately in the rush to escape, Edith was left behind.

Edward threw a wobbler. Beside himself with anger, Edward unceremoniously sent Edith off to a convent but not before seizing her jewellery. She had been of use to him for a while but he no longer needed her.

With Godwin and his sons out of the way, Edward invited William Duke of Normandy, the illegitimate son of Robert Duke of Normandy who he had lived with while in Normandy, to stay with him and William willingly accepted. But with more and more Normans arriving at court, Edward's popularity hit an all-time low.

Godwin didn't sit on his hands while stewing in Flanders. He spent his time gathering a formidable army and finally, satisfied with the numbers, he sailed to the Isle of Wight to join his son Harold. Together they sailed up the Thames to the cheers from the people.

Edward would have heard the sounds of celebration and he would have known he had no choice but to accept Godwin and Harold back in England again. Unfortunately, it also meant he had to release Edith from the convent and return her jewels.

But if Godwin thought he had won the battle against Edward, he should have taken the time to remember that Harthacanute had died rather conveniently and suspiciously while in Edward's presence. Not too soon later, at a dinner party held by Edward, Godwin had a fit and died. Once again, poison was suspected. With that little problem out of the way, Edward settled comfortably into his throne unopposed.

Malcolm had left his grandfather's court in Northumbria years before and was firmly settled in Edward's court by 1054, planning his revenge on Macbeth. Malcolm had fully supported Edward during the issues with Godwin and Harold, and he wasn't about to let Edward forget that detail.

Together with Earl Siward and Siward's son, Osbjorn, Edward approved an invasion into Scotland. With an eager Malcolm by his uncle's side, they invaded Scotland with a mixed army of Anglo-Saxon Northumbrians and Scots. They reached Dundee apparently unopposed where Siward's army was reinforced by supply ships before moving on to Dunsinane Hill in Perthshire.

Knowing the history of past kings and impatient relatives eager for a chance at the throne, Macbeth should have seen this coming. He barely survived the invasion, unlike Siward's son who died along with 3,000 Scots and 1,500 Englishmen. To save his throne, Macbeth was forced to flee north to his original power base in Moray for safety.

It was a victory of sorts but it was not enough to give Malcolm the throne. Angry and frustrated, he was forced to head back to Edward, while Siward had no alternative but to return to deal with an uprising in Northumbria. One year later, Siward contracted dysentery and died leaving the new earl, Wessex-born Tostig Godwinsson (the half-brother of a Harold Godwinsson) to take over Northumbria.

There was no love lost between the Godwinsson brothers. Over the years, Tostig had been exiled, returned, then exiled again by Edward while Malcolm seems to have been installed as ruler over Strathclyde and the Lothians. But it was never going to be enough for Malcolm. What he wanted was Scotland.

Macbeth and Gruoch did not have any children of their own, but according to the limited records that remain about his reign, there was no sign of tension in the marriage. Old age, the toil of battles against the English and the rising threat from Malcolm, caused Macbeth to return from exile in 1057 to abdicate his throne in Lulach's favour under the unflattering nickname of 'Lulach the Simpleton'.

While Malcolm seethed at the news, English nobles were asking the ageing Edward, who would succeed him at his death since he and Edith had no children.

While Harold Godwinsson insisted it should be him, though how he came to that conclusion is baffling, William the Bastard said *he* had been offered the throne by Edward years before. And he had wholeheartedly accepted.

Edward himself seems to have forgotten all of that because when he heard his nephew, Edward the Exile, was alive and well and living with his family in Hungary, he offered the throne to him if he returned to England immediately. Seeing it as the last chance of an undisputed succession within the Saxon royal house, preparations were made while the young Edward left Hungary with his own son Edgar and two daughters, Christina and Margaret.

The journey took months but eventually they arrived only to be blocked from seeing their uncle by the Godwin boys without any explanation. Two days later, Edward the Exile was dead.

The exact cause of Edward's death is unclear but of course, we can assume he was murdered. By whom is unknown but we do know he had some powerful enemies. It was a time when Harold Godwinsson's power was increasing and the old king, now politically weak, was unable to make an effective stand against the steady advance of the powerful and ambitious Godwin boys. All Edward could do was take young Edgar, Christina and Margaret into his care.

In Scotland, while Edward the Exile was being murdered, Lulach, only on the throne for two months, was being hunted down and killed by Malcom in Strathbogie, the strategic pass between Moray and Strathdon.

All that was left for Malcolm to do was to eliminate Macbeth.

The Peel of Lumphanan is a sort of pudgy hill fortification which the saga writers and chroniclers believe was the likely place where Macbeth and his 400 men were ambushed by Malcolm in 1058. Imagine shadows rushing at you as raindrops as heavy as hail smacked into your chest. Imagine spearheads and axe blades glinting in the light from the moon, shields on their forearms and long hair flowing behind them as a wall of helmets and mail charged at you.

With so few men, there was never going to be any other result except Macbeth's death. He was killed in a desperate final stand rather than a pitched battle and his head was then brought to Malcolm, either on a pole or on a golden platter.

Macbeth's remains were laid to rest in the royal burying ground in Iona, demonstrating that whatever had happened, his contemporaries appreciated his long and successful reign. However, no record exists about what happened to Gruoch.

Malcolm's hold on the kingdom was at last secure. 1 month later, he was crowned at Scone at the age of 27 as Malcolm III and embarked on his 35-year reign as King of Scots.

THE CANMORE DYNASTY

The accession of Malcolm Canmore in 1058 marked the end of what has been called *'the crisis of the MacAlpin succession'*. The Gaelic nickname 'Canmore' means 'Great Chief', but it is frequently translated as 'big head'.

For the first time in history, a Scottish king made the trip to England to visit the king, more than likely to show respect. Edward had, after all, given him the vital assistance he needed to overthrow Macbeth. It did not, however, stop Malcolm from plundering Lindisfarne on his way back to Scotland. His main objective was to seize the lands of Northumbria and Cumbria where there was no recognised border between the kingdoms of Scotland and England.

It was common practice in medieval societies for kings to launch an invasion on a neighbour soon after taking power and the Lindisfarne raid may have been used to boost the stability of a new regime. Since the invasion affected directly only the territory of the rulers of Bamburgh, it is unlikely to have particularly bothered either Edward or Tostig Godwinsson in York (who was on a pilgrimage in Rome at the time) because neither had a good relationship with the Bamburgh family anyway. It left Malcolm free to further extend his territory to south of the Firth of Forth where there were numerous independent or semi-independent realms, including the kingdom of Strathclyde.

With Malcolm now King of Scotland and in his prime and Edward in a state of declining health, Edward saw the perfect opportunity to betroth his 13-year-old niece Margaret, Edward the Exile's daughter, to Malcolm. The marriage, however, would have to wait for Margaret until she was older.

At the time, 29-year old Malcolm accepted the betrothal to please Edward but perhaps had no intention of honouring it. Edward was old in any case and in such brutal times, Malcolm would have been too intent on securing his own kingdom to wait for a thirteen-year-old to grow up. The important issue of succession would have been number one on his agenda and waiting five years for Margaret to grow up was nothing he would even have considered.

The perfect opportunity arose with the death of his cousin Thorfinn in 1060. Thorfinn's widow, Ingibiorg Finnsdottir, a niece of the King of Norway, was an available beauty and it took no time for Malcolm to wed her. She happily left her two sons, Paul and Erlend, both sons of Thorfinn, as the joint rulers of Orkney and within a year, she gave Malcolm his first son, Duncan, followed by two more boys in quick succession.

Edward's death in January 1066 at the age of 62 set in motion a series of disastrous events that would change the history of England forever and for the first time, Scotland prospered while England was in a dramatic state of upheaval and free fall.

At the tender age of 15, Edgar, the only son of Edward the Exile, had no chance whatsoever against the powerful Harold Godwinsson. Although Edgar was the nominated heir, Harold simply took over.

But across the channel, William Duke of Normandy was watching with his full attention focused on the English drama unfolding.

William's claim to the throne was tenuous at best. He was the only son of Robert Duke of Normandy, although illegitimate, and the great-nephew of the English Queen, Emma of Normandy. He could trace his ancestry back to Rollo the Viking and Rollo was no shrinking violet when it came to fighting. But as impressive as his resume was, there wasn't much in the way of bloodline. Although for William, bloodline had little to do with it. Edward had offered him the throne years before and he had accepted. The way he saw it, the throne was his, but he certainly did not have it in the bag.

William went into overdrive laying plans, building ships and assembling an army ready to conquer England. He left his wife Matilda of Flanders at home with six children under the age of 12 and set off for England.

Harold didn't need a crystal ball to know what William was planning and he didn't need one to know his own half-brother Tostig was out for revenge for the bad treatment Harold and the Northumbrians had dished out to him the year before. He also knew Malcolm was giving Tostig asylum, along with offering indirect support to Harald Hardrada in Norway, should he decide to return to England. And since Tostig's wife was Judith of Flanders, an aunt to William's wife Matilda, he knew Tostig would be on Team William.

What delayed William's crossing to England by eight months was not just bad winds and weather, it was the time it took to build his ships. Rather wisely, Harold used the time to assemble troops in England while Tostig spent the summer of 1066 with Malcolm in Scotland, his sworn brother by now, plotting revenge and making contact with Harald Hardrada, persuading him to join up with him to invade York. Tostig then settled in, happy in his cocoon, knowing he had Harald in Norway and Malcolm in Scotland to back him up if needed. He even had Malcolm's two stepsons in Orkney ready to assist him.

William's delay was a Catch 22 situation for Harold. While giving him more time to be ready for the invasion on the south coast, his large army was slowly diminishing from dwindling supplies and falling morale. And then, with the harvest season upon them, Harold made a big mistake. He disbanded his army on 8th September and consolidated his ships in London, leaving the English Channel unguarded.

What followed for Harold was an unfortunate set of circumstances. While William was sharpening his battle-axe in Normandy, Harald Hardrada was heading out of Norway with a fleet of his own ready to invade Yorkshire in the north. And as expected, with him was Harold's younger brother Tostig.

But if Tostig thought Malcolm was going to put himself at risk to help him out in a family squabble, he was sadly mistaken. Malcolm had always refused to engage in a fight and it was pure luck that he refused to get involved in this one as well. He had three young sons under five years of age by this time, and any number of relatives itching to step into his shoes as the

King of Scotland if he died. He knew if that happened, none of his sons would ever be king.

It was late summer when the invaders sailed up the Ouse river before advancing on York. On the 20th September, they defeated a northern English army led by Edwin, Earl of Mercia, and his brother Morcar, Earl of Northumbria, at the Battle of Fulford, outside York. They briefly occupied the city and took hostages and supplies from the city then returned to their ships at Riccall after offering peace to the Northumbrians in exchange for their support against Hardrada's bid for the York throne.

At this time Harold was anticipating the invasion from William in France when he heard of the invasion in the north. Gathering together as many of his nobles and soldiers as he could, Harold raced his English army northwards, travelling day and night to surprise his brother. He made the journey from London to Yorkshire, a distance of about 185 miles, (298 kms), in only four days, enabling him to take the Norwegians completely by surprise. Having learned that the Northumbrians had been ordered to send additional hostages and supplies to the Norwegians at Stamford Bridge, Harold hurried on through York to attack them on 25th September. Until the English army came into view, the invaders were probably unaware that a hostile army was anywhere in the vicinity.

The sudden appearance of the English army caught the Norwegians by surprise. The English advance was then delayed by the need to pass through the choke-point presented by the bridge itself. The Anglo-Saxon Chronicle says a giant Norse axeman, possibly armed with a Dane axe, blocked the narrow crossing and single-handedly held up the entire English army, cutting down up to 40 Englishmen. He was only defeated when an English soldier floated under the bridge in a half-barrel and thrust his spear through the planks in the bridge, mortally wounding the axeman. The delay, however, had allowed the bulk of the Norse army to form a shield wall to face the English attack.

Harold's army poured across the bridge, forming a line just short of the Norse army, then locked their own shields and charged. The battle went far beyond the bridge itself and although it raged for hours, the Norse army's decision to leave their armour behind left them at a distinct disadvantage.

Eventually, the Norse army began to fragment and fracture, allowing the English troops to force their way in and break up the Scandinavian's shield wall. Completely outflanked, and with Hardrada killed with an arrow to his windpipe and Tostig slain, the Norwegian army disintegrated and was virtually annihilated.

So many died in an area so small that the field was said to have been whitened with bleached bones for 50 years after the battle.

All that was left was for Harold to accept a truce with the surviving Norwegians, including Hardrada's son Olaf and Malcolm's step-son Paul Thorfinnsson, allowing them to leave after giving pledges not to attack England again. The losses the Norwegians had suffered were so severe that only 24 ships from the fleet of over 300 were needed to carry the survivors away.

Despite the victory, it was all rather bad timing for Harold. He was breathing a sigh of relief when news reached him of William's unobstructed arrival in Hastings on 28th September. Unaware of Tostig's battle in York, William had settled in and was waiting unopposed for Harold to arrive.

The bad news meant that Harold had to turn around and march his tired army back for another four days to meet William's rested army.

Although Harold was attempting to surprise William, after all it worked at Samford Bridge, scouts found Harold's army and reported the arrival to William who marched from Hastings to the battlefield to confront Harold.

Battles of the time rarely lasted more than two hours before the weaker side submitted. The fact that Hastings lasted an horrific nine hours indicates the determination of both William and Harold. And if Harold and two of his brothers had not been killed shortly before sunset that day, he could have perhaps survived William's final cavalry attacks and recommenced the fight in the morning with fresh backup.

We all know what happened. William the Conqueror won the throne of England and had himself crowned King of England on Christmas morning 1066.

After the conquest, William treated Edgar and his family rather well despite the fact that Edgar had rather optimistically declared himself king-elect after Harold's death. William changed all that quick smart. He tucked the family under his wing, complete with their mother Agatha, and took them back to Normandy before returning to England with them two years later.

But the cosy state of affairs with Edgar and his family being supported by William was about to end.

Everyone knows you don't bite the hand that feeds you. But that's exactly what Edgar did upon his return to England. After a failed revolt of the Northumbrian earls, which Edgar fully supported, he tried to escape back to the safety of Hungary with his mother and two sisters, Margaret and Christina, in an attempt to outrun William's wrath. Their ship, bound for the Continent, was driven off course by gales near Scotland and forced to land in a small bay in Fife.

The story of Malcolm Canmore meeting Margaret of Wessex for the second time has been heavily romanticised. Malcolm's wife Ingjbiorg had recently died, along with one son who died early in life, before Edgar's untimely arrival in Scotland but one of the remaining two sons, Duncan, we will see later on.

This story tells of the 40-year-old Malcolm Canmore, now a widower with two young sons, Duncan and Donald, who rode from his residence at Dunfermline to welcome the royal refugees to Scotland. What he found was that Princess Margaret was no longer a gangly 13-year-old but a beautiful, flaxen-haired, young woman in her early twenties and he instantly fell in love with her. Within a few months they were married.

From Edgar's point of view, his sister Margaret's marriage to Malcolm was a timely political marriage. He would become the brother-in-law to a formidable warrior King of Scots who could provide him with powerful support against the Norman usurpers in the south. For Malcolm, the hopefully fertile Margaret brought not only an alliance with the old royal house of Wessex in England but also a significant dowry in the form of the rich treasure which King Stephen of Hungary had given to Margaret's mother.

When Malcolm married Margaret in 1070 with the hope of expanding his kingdom through children, he hit the jackpot. Margaret turned out to be very fertile, giving birth to six sons, three of whom would reign successively as Kings of Scots: Edgar (1097–1107), Alexander I (1107–1024) and David I (1124–1153). She also delivered two daughters, both of whom married into the English royal house: Edith, the elder, married William the Conqueror's son, Henry, and would become known as the Empress Matilda when Henry eventually became King of England in 1087. Mary, the younger of the two daughters, married Eustace III, Count of Boulogne and their daughter, also named Matilda, would marry Stephen of Blois, (whose mother was a daughter of William the Conqueror), who would usurp the throne of England from his cousin in 1135. Yes, it is complicated.

Marrying Margaret may also have added fuel to Malcolm's ambitions to extend his own kingdom by launching another invasion on Northumbria, allegedly again on Edgar's behalf who was encouraging Anglo-Danish rebellions. He had sought assistance from Sweyn II in Denmark, a nephew of King Canute, and Sweyn, never one to miss out on a fight, assembled a fleet of ships under the command of his sons. The fleet sailed up the east coast of England raiding as they went, and together with Edgar, they took the city of York.

William was having none of all this. It was done under Edgar's name and the ungrateful Edgar, who had spent two years under his protection despite still being a threat to his rule, was about to be taught a valuable lesson.

William gathered his considerable fleet together and marched through the north of England to meet them. While he paid the Danes in York to go home without a fight, the remaining rebels who refused to leave, or meet him in battle, were about to suffer the consequences. The Harrying of the North was about to commence.

Historians vividly record the savagery of the campaign in 1070, implemented during winter, as a huge scale destruction and the widespread famine caused by looting, burning and slaughtering had never been seen before in history. Some have even labelled it genocide. Records from the Domesday Book show that 75% of the population died or never returned.

William stopped at nothing to hunt down his enemies. To his shame, he made no effort to control his fury. He punished the innocent along with the guilty. He ordered crops and herds, tools and food, to be burned to ashes and more than 100,000 people perished of starvation as a result. York still had large areas of waste territory up to 1086.

Perhaps another bonus for Malcolm when he married Margaret was a plausible excuse for attacks into England to *redress the wrongs against his brother-in-law'*. William, on the other hand, took it as a personal threat and marched into Scotland to confront Malcolm.

Like King Constantine before him, when Malcolm saw the size of William's army, he simply refused to fight. The Treaty of Abernathy in 1072 between the two men seemed the only alternative if peace was to be achieved and with William the victor, he had the final say over the terms.

There were a couple of steadfast stipulations. Firstly, he demanded that Malcolm submit to him as his vassal. Secondly, Edgar was to be permanently exiled from Scotland and he and Malcolm's ten-year-old son Duncan by Ingjbiorg were to become William's hostages in the Norman court.

Malcolm agreed to all stipulations, even to handing over his young son to William, but did not consider himself bound by the vassal part. Seven years later, he invaded Northumbria again but this time the English army was led by William's son Robert Curthose. Malcolm once again refused to fight and the treaty was renewed, this time for over a decade.

Malcolm's invasion in 1093 came six years after William the Conqueror's death and was over some calculated insult from his son, William II, known as William Rufus due to both his fiery temper and red complexion. Furious, Malcolm marched south with his own son Edward while Margaret lay seriously ill at home in Edinburgh. This time there would be no leniency. Malcolm was ambushed by Robert de Mowbray, Earl of Northumbria, and killed along with his son Edward.

When news of her husband and son's deaths reached Margaret, she simply gave up. Three days later, with three of her four remaining sons by her bedside, she died and Scotland was in the throes of a civil war.

From his refuge in the Western Isles, where he had been living since Macbeth had killed his father Duncan I, Malcolm's younger brother, now 60-year-old Donald Bán, suddenly appeared with the support of many Scottish nobles and claimed the vacant throne for himself as Donald III.

Donald's taking of the throne was nothing short of a Celtic backlash against the anglicisation of the Scottish court. He stressed that he resented the suppression of the Gaelic language but he also had a vested interest in resurrecting the old process of tanistry which meant it was *his* turn to be the rightful king of Scotland, not a son of Malcolm. The nobles who backed him had also come to resent the English influences associated with Margaret of Wessex and all the associated English who had been with Malcolm, certainly including his four surviving boys.

Donald fully expected the four feisty sons of Malcolm to resist. And he had come prepared for a battle. But instead, what Donald discovered was he had the support from his brother's eldest son to Margaret, 23-year-old

Edmund, and no one knows why Edmund swapped sides. I suppose the juicy carrot of being Donald's heir-designate would have been a serious temptation he just couldn't refuse. Donald's only child was a daughter and rules of primogeniture still applied. To make things more promising for Edmund, Malcolm's eldest son, Duncan, to his first wife, Ingibiorg, had a son, but the 4-year-old William FitzDuncan, born to Ethelreda of Northumberland, was illegitimate.

Rather wisely, 19-year-old Edgar, 15-year-old Alexander and 10-year-old David, beat a hasty retreat for safety to William Rufus at the English court.

There was one other claimant to the throne however who had been almost forgotten: the young man who had been surrendered as a hostage by Malcolm to William the Conqueror twenty-four years earlier. Duncan, Malcolm's first son to Ingibiorg. He had been brought up at the English court and had been formally released and knighted on William the Conqueror's death in 1087 and had become a fully 'Normanised' Celt.

Virtually on hands and knees, 34-year-old Duncan pledged his loyalty to William Rufus and with Rufus' wholehearted support, Duncan marched into Scotland with both a French and English army at his disposal to take the Scottish throne for himself.

Donald was fully aware that Duncan would make plans to take the throne and he wasn't about to sit back and wait for him to arrive. While Duncan marched north, Donald was busy making alliances with disgruntled men who had supported Malcolm.

With such an impressive army, there was no doubt Duncan would be successful. After holding the title of King Donald III for barely six months, Duncan ousted his uncle from the throne and married Ethelreda, the mother of his only son, 4-year-old William, legitimising him.

Unfortunately, there's no happy ending here. Seen by most Scots as an Englishman and a usurper now, Duncan was ambushed and murdered seven months later, more likely by his uncle and his supporters, who miraculously was reinstated to resume his interrupted reign.

Rather wisely I would think, on hearing of Duncan's death, Ethelreda fled Scotland with young William to the safety of Allerdale and to her brother, the Lord of Cumberland. Although he was the now legitimate heir to the throne after his father married his mistress Ethelreda, William would grow up in Cumberland among his cousins. But he would certainly reappear a decade later.

William Rufus was not about to be thwarted by the death of Duncan. He had another claimant up his sleeve. Malcolm's next surviving son after Edmund, Edgar. With the support of his brothers Alexander, David and Ethelred Abbot of Dunkeld, Edgar would be sent at the head of another army and this time there would be no slip ups.

This time, Donald III was soundly defeated, hunted down and captured, blinded and thrown into a dungeon where he eventually died two years later. His nephew Edmund was more fortunate. He was tonsured and sent to a monastery in Somerset where he eventually died as well. His decision to support his uncle had been a disastrous one.

The next few years with Edgar on the Scottish throne passed by in a quiet blur. Known as 'Edgar the Peaceable', there were no uprisings or rebellions during his rule. He never married and had no children but fully supported his sister's marriage to Henry I of England in 1100, the youngest son of William the Conqueror. When Edgar died in 1107 of unknown causes, ten years after taking the throne and at only 33 years of age, he bequeathed his kingdom to his brother Alexander, as Alexander I, except for Cumbria and Strathclyde, which he gave to his youngest brother David with the nod of approval in advance by Henry I.

By then, Henry I had become Alexander's father-in-law. Henry had 'suggested' Alexander marry his eldest illegitimate daughter, 15-year-old Sybilla of Normandy (although he was already his brother-in-law since Henry had married Alexander's sister Edith, now Empress Matilda). Henry had also chosen 39-year-old Maud, Countess of Huntingdon, as a bride for Alexander's younger brother David, a long-time fixture in Henry's court in England since 1100.

Maud was ten years older than David but her pedigree was impressive to say the least. She was the daughter of the Anglo-Saxon Earl of Huntingdon and the granddaughter of Siward, Earl of Northumbria, not to forget she was also the great-niece of William the Conqueror. Through her ancestors, the Counts of Boulogne, she was also a descendant of Alfred the Great of England. But David himself was also related to Siward. His grandmother, Ethelreda, the wife of Duncan I, had escaped Macbeth to her father Siward in Northumbria with her young boys, Malcolm (soon to be Malcolm III after killing Macbeth) and Donald. That would have made Siward David's great-grandfather.

At David's marriage to Maud, David added Maud's vast estates in England to his lands in Cumbria and Strathclyde and by her death in 1131, she had produced four children, although only one child survived to adulthood, a son they called Henry.

Although history states Alexander I was pious, much like his mother and brother Edgar, Alexander's nickname was 'Alexander the Fierce', suggesting he was not a man of peace. Like his father, he was quick to retaliate when poked as on one occasion while Alexander was holding court in Invergowrie and attacked by *'men of the isles'*.

The attackers were said to be from Moray and Mearns and the main offenders were Mael Petair of Mearns and Angus of Moray, grandson of Lulach (of the Macbeth story) who would probably have expected to have a good claim to the throne himself. Both had been suspected of colluding with Donald III in killing Alexander's half-brother Duncan II in 1094 when Donald resumed the throne. Remembering *that* outcome and his brother's fate, Alexander was quick to march north and defeat them. No more is heard about Mael Petair but Angus will reappear later as well in history.

Back in England, Henry I was leading a complicated life although he looked like he had the Midas touch. He owned Normandy. His daughter, 14-year-old daughter Matilda, was married to the Holy Roman Emperor and he had a 13-year-old son and heir, William Aetherling. His elder brother, Robert Curthose, was also safely locked away in Devizes Castle in Wiltshire where he would stay imprisoned for twenty years before being moved to Cardiff Castle, eventually dying at the age of eighty.

His golden touch finished during the winter of 1120 when everything fell apart. His only legitimate son, (Henry had as many as nine illegitimate sons and fifteen illegitimate daughters) had boarded the White Ship, the fastest and most luxurious ship at the time, along with 200 young members of the golden age of Anglo-Saxon nobility elite, including many illegitimate half-brothers and sisters, and sailed out of Benfleur Harbour on its way back to England. The ship was packed with happy, inebriated teenagers hell-bent on celebrating William's coming of age, all heading home for Christmas. Rather fortuitously and suspiciously, left behind as the ship left the harbour, was his cousin, Stephen of Blois, who at the last minute complained of an upset stomach and said he would sail on the next boat.

The ship may have been fast but a well-lubricated crew was probably not the best choice to bring the young prince home. The ship crashed on rocks and a hole was punched in the bow of the ship. As a result, water flooded in.

A vision of terrified teenagers, screaming as they were hurled into the freezing water comes to mind and the heavy brocaded clothing would have soon become heavy, making it impossible to swim or tread water.

The prince's life was the first priority and a life boat was launched. He was already on his way to safety when he heard the cries from his half-sister and it was then he made the fatal decision to turn back and rescue her. However, his sister was not alone. There were other passengers in the water and everyone scrambled to board William's boat. As a result the boat capsized and sank. William along with his sister and various brothers and sisters were drowned.

Henry received the news in horror and as grief overwhelmed him, he must have felt like he couldn't breathe. For all his triumphs during his reign, he failed in the one vital task: to secure the future of the Norman dynasty.

Alexander and David's sister had died two years beforehand so it was a panic decision for 52-year-old Henry to remarry as soon as possible and to a fertile bride. Adeliza of Louvain, the 18-year-old daughter of Godfrey I, Count of Louvain, renowned for her beauty and a descendant of Charlemagne, was chosen. Sadly, the 15-year marriage would produce no children and the only legitimate child remaining was Matilda, Alexander and David's niece. Being a woman, she had an uphill battle in front of her to secure the throne. Eventually, she stood back and let her son Henry take the lead in winning back his throne.

After fourteen years on the throne, Alexander died in 1124 at the age of 46 leaving no legitimate children to Sybilla who died two years previous in 1122, (William of Malmesbury, an English historian in the 12th century, is brutal when he writes about her) and one illegitimate son born two years after Sybilla died. This son, named Malcolm, will also join the queue of those we will hear more about later on.

Alexander's death left the way open for his last brother David to ascend the throne at the age of 40. With four older brothers and one half-brother ahead of him in the queue to the throne, David was never expected to sit on the throne as King of Scots. And he had his troubles from the start.

Despite a childhood spent in Scotland, he had little idea of the culture and society of the Scots, having spent so much of his life living in an English court. Everyone was looking at each other wondering if he could be trusted.

So when Alexander died, the aristocracy of Scotland found they had a choice: they could either choose to elect David as King, or face war with both David and Henry I.

And of course, they chose David.

Almost immediately, Alexander's illegitimate son, Malcolm, chose war.

Malcolm forgot that his uncle David had first-hand experience of Norman military techniques and tactics, not to mention a better understanding of war, so defeat was almost a given. David conquered Malcolm and his followers in two fierce battles and with his tail between his legs, Malcolm escaped back into an area of Scotland not yet under David's control to lick his wounds and look for supporters at the same time as David was crowned King of Scotland.

Malcolm may have been defeated but he wasn't about to be forgotten. Six years later, when David's wife died while he was still in Southern England, Malcolm returned. But this time he came well prepared. With him was King Angus of Moray, the grandson of King Lulach of Scotland, (stepson of Macbeth), David's most powerful vassal, who had a solid claim to the throne himself. Together, the two men seemed invincible.

King Angus had other reasons for siding with Malcolm. Unbeknownst to Malcolm, after defeating David, Angus fully intended to take advantage of the situation and expand his own partially independent kingdom of Moray and become fully independent of all Scottish kings. It was a lovely dream that Malcolm was totally unaware of and I'm sure he would have thought twice about it if he had.

With civil war about to erupt, David had to do something rather quickly or suffer a resounding defeat. What he needed was help of his own.

David's help came in the form of the Lord High Constable of Scotland, whose office traditionally ranks above all titles except those of the Royal Family. He was, after the King of Scots, the supreme officer of the Scottish army and the perfect man to have on his side. In David's absence, the

Constable and the Scottish army marched on to Stracathro to settle the dispute once and for all.

With such an overwhelming enemy, it's no wonder that Angus, along with 4,000 Moravians, were killed while Malcolm barely escaped with his life, yet again.

Malcolm still couldn't let it settle. Four years later, he stubbornly returned for a third bout but this time, he was captured and imprisoned in Roxburgh Castle leaving David to prosper.

But while David prospered, Henry I struggled in England until his death in 1135, leaving his country with no male heir and in the grip of a civil war.

Matilda, Henry's daughter and David's niece, had the obvious claim to the vacant throne and had been nominated as his heir on her father's death bed. But being a woman, it wasn't to be so easy. In later years, there would be queens to serve her country but not at this time in history. A queen was simply not allowed and deep divisions formed as quarrels erupted. Everyone took sides, even though many had already sworn allegiance to Henry's daughter, Matilda, who preferred to be called Maud.

And there was another claimant to the throne. Her male cousin, Stephen of Blois.

Stephen had all his ducks in a row. He was the son of Stephen of Blois, the lucky young man who rather fortuitously was left behind when the White Ship left Benfleur harbour the day the ship sank with Henry's only male heir on board. He was also the son of Adela of Normandy, the daughter of William the Conqueror, making her the niece of Henry I. Placed in the court of Henry I, Stephen rose to prominence and was granted extensive lands when he married the wealthy Matilda of Boulogne, the granddaughter of Malcolm III of Scotland and Margaret of Wessex through their daughter Mary.

Malcolm's two daughters, Mary and Matilda, spent their early years in Romsey Abbey with their maternal aunt, Christina, (Edgar and Margaret's sister), who was the presiding abbess, receiving part of their education. Somewhere around 1093, they were sent to Wilton Abbey, which had a reputation as a centre of learning, to finish their education. Matilda received many proposals for marriage but refused them all. She finally left the monastery in 1100 to marry Henry I of England while Mary would leave to marry Eustace III, Count of Boulogne. It was Mary's daughter Matilda who was now married to Stephen.

Things looked very bright for Stephen but standing in his way to the English throne was his cousin Maud.

To add fuel to the fire, five years after the sinking of the White Ship, Maud's husband died and at only 22 years of age, she was a widow. Clearly, her father told her, she needed a new husband to boost her claim to the throne and for a replacement, he turned to Anjou. In June 1128, 26-year-old Maud married 15-year-old Geoffrey Plantagenet, Count of Anjou, and life would never be the same again.

Geoffrey Plantagenet was an energetic, tall, conceited, ginger-haired teenager with fair skin and good looks but despite that, Maud was very underwhelmed with him. In her opinion, Angevites were barbarians with shocking table manners. And didn't he come from a long line of plunderers and rapists? Rumour had it that his great grandfather had burned his wife in her wedding dress when she had been discovered in a compromising situation with a goat herder.

It turned out the dislike was mutual. They fought incessantly, even to the point of separating for the first couple of years until her father reminded her of her duty to provide her country with an heir.

In 1133, she did just that and delivered a son, which she named Henry after her father. With a grandson and heir to his throne, Henry seemed pleased with life once again. His untimely and unfortunate death two years later, while young Henry was only two years old, changed everything.

The castle and the forest surrounding Lyons-la-Foret was a regular trip planned every year at the same date for two centuries by the Norman dukes and in November 1135, Henry arrived with the full intention of living it up. Even at 68, he still felt strong enough to enjoy the hunt. He arrived the night before with those very thoughts. But during the night he began feeling sick and by the end of the week, he was seriously ill. An Archbishop was called in and three days later, Henry was dead. Food poisoning was suspected but he had eaten the same food as everyone else and no one else had been affected.

Are bells clanging madly in your head?

With something almost like a premonition, Stephen of Blois had already left his wife's country of Boulogne and was crossing the channel on his way to England. Despite his sworn oath to support Maud, he went straight to

London and proclaimed himself king. A few days later, he left for Winchester and seized the royal treasury and had himself anointed as king by the Bishop of Winchester. In one swift move, Maud and her young son were suddenly disinherited.

By all accounts, David's niece, Maud, was remarkable. She was fierce, proud, hard and cynical. But she was pregnant with her third child in Anjou when Henry died and was unable to move as fast as her cousin Stephen who was first on the spot. He also had another advantage. His brother was Bishop of Winchester with a great voice in council and with this backup, the barons stood by him. The speed with which it all happened was mind boggling.

Even with a more impressive bloodline that Stephen, there was no chance that a toddler would be proclaimed King purely by his birth, especially with Stephen's snapping-up-the-throne efficiency. Well, not in this century anyway. And so, Maud and Geoffrey were elbowed aside.

While in the English court, David had spent many years soaking up the Anglo-Saxon ways and backing away from a fight had never been on the English curriculum. As civil war broke out in England between his niece and grand-nephew, David watched with avid interest, biding his time and waiting for the right opportunity to take full advantage of the messy situation. What he wanted was to recover the lost provinces his ancestors had lost, and then tried to recover time and time again.

After mustering a huge army consisting of Pictish Galwegians, men from Moray and other eastern shires, David marched towards York under the pretext of supporting his niece Maud's claim to the English throne. Backing him up was his son Henry of Huntingdon leading his own force of mounted knights and well-equipped men-at-arms from the Borders and Cumbria.

Stephen had his hands full with uprisings popping up all over England so he left the defence of the north to Thurstan, the ageing but militant Archbishop of York. From his pulpit, the call went out for every able-bodied volunteer to repel the Scottish invaders.

When David and his son Henry crossed the River Tees from Durham into Yorkshire they discovered the English army was merely a motley collection of knights, peasants and priests. With this discovery, the plundering and burning increased.

An English chronicler, Henry of Huntingdon, wrote:

They cleft open pregnant women, and took out the unborn babe. They tossed children upon the spear-points and beheaded priests upon the altars. There was screaming of women, the wailing of old men, groans of the dying, despair of the living.
HISTORIA ANGLORUM

THE INVASION BROUGHT out all the deep-rooted English prejudices against the Picts and the Scots as murderous barbarians. What seems to have shocked the English more was the fact that one of their own, a flower of Norman chivalry such as David, should have unleashed such a savage horde to ravage a civilised kingdom. According to the English version, one of David's own Norman-English knights, Robert de Brus, (ancestor of the future King Robert Bruce) whom he had made Lord of Annandale, was so appalled by the brutality that he went over to the English camp. Another of his new Norman friends, Bernard de Bailleul (ancestor of the future King John Balliol) also deserted him.

This time, like his ancestors Constantine and Malcolm before him, David chose not to fight any further. Instead of a battle, David and Stephen's wife Matilda of Boulogne met each other and agreed on a settlement, which had benefits on both sides. David's son Henry was to be restored to the Earldom of Huntingdon and Lordship of Doncaster and if he paid homage to Stephen, he would be given the Earldom of Northumberland as a bonus. The arranged marriage between his son Henry and Ada de Warenne, the daughter of the 2nd Earl of Surrey and a great-granddaughter of Henry I, King of France, would go ahead and King Stephen would include him in his inner circle. David would keep Carlisle and Cumberland while Stephen would retain possession of vital castles such as Bamburgh and Newcastle.

With that, David was satisfied. Temporarily.

It was the arrival of his other niece's in England, Empress Maud and her husband Geoffrey Plantagenet, that gave David an opportunity to do a turnaround and renew the conflict with Stephen. While he and his son retained their previously acquired lands, the juicy carrot of Newcastle and Bamburgh was wiggled in front of him.

And then suddenly everything came to an abrupt stop.

David's only son Henry had been in poor health throughout the 1140's. So when Henry died in 1152 at the age of 38, not too many people were surprised. David, himself in ill-health, was devastated and one year later, David was dead as well.

Unlike the death of Henry I of England, who had died without legitimate male descendants, David's approaching death would not cause a succession crisis. Despite Henry's ill health, his marriage to Ada de Warenne had been a successful one, full of the sound of happy children's feet running through their home in Haddington. The marriage produced seven children: three sons to carry forward his father's lineage and four daughters who would be sure to marry well. The only problem, yet again, was his eldest grandson, Malcolm, was only 12 years old.

While Alexander I reigned, and with no legitimate heirs of his own, he had taken his nephew William FitzDuncan, the son of his brother, Duncan II, under his wing and regarded him as the 'designated heir' by both Henry I and supported by David. But when Alexander died, it is highly likely that he was bought off by David with the lure of being Mormaer of Moray after the defeat of King Angus of Moray who had killed William's father. No just was he ruler of Moray, he also controlled the English lands of Allerdale, Skipton and Craven, making him one of the greatest barons of northern England. But William was now out of the picture since he had died a couple of years previously.

Knowing his time was near, David quickly arranged for his grandson Malcolm to be his successor and his younger grandson William to be made Earl of Northumberland. Donnchad, Mormaer of Fife, was then appointed regent and took the young Malcolm on a tour to meet his future subjects.

There was good reason for haste. Young Malcolm was not without rivals for the kingship and as it happened, David was right to hurry. Months later, he was dead.

With the Mormaer of Fife as his regent, Malcolm shakily took the throne.

At the same time, his cousin Henry Plantagenet, Maud's eldest son, was only one year away from his own throne: the throne of England. With

Stephen's eldest son dead and his second son refusing the English throne and accepting the title of Earl of Boulogne instead, Stephen found himself in the exact same position that Henry I had been in. Distraught, he had no choice but to name the 20-year-old Henry Plantagenet as his heir and within two years, Stephen was dead as well.

Ruling was a balancing act for every king. Weak ones found themselves manipulated by cunning lords while tyrannical ones were disposed of. But successful rulers found the balance that suited the times. England had a few great soldier-kings but none possessed instincts like Henry II.

Two years before Stephen's death, Louis VII was King in France and Henry Plantagenet was a bachelor on the prowl.

Louis VII of France was regarded as the French equivalent of Edward the Confessor in every regard, practicing his devotion by day and doing penance at night. However, his hot-blooded 30-year-old wife, Eleanor of Aquitaine, a reigning princess in her own right, had warmth in her veins and complained that she had married a monk instead of a king.

Eleanor was famous for her beauty and sexuality. At the age of thirteen, she had been an orphan and the sole heir to one of the greatest inheritances of Europe and Louis VII of France had no hesitation in taking her for his bride. She was undoubtedly a catch but both Louis and her life in the French court failed to live up to her expectations.

While she embraced the splendour, her husband dressed and ate like most of the monks she had seen. From the very beginning, the marriage had been doomed. Her scandalous reputation followed her wherever she went and though she gave Louis two daughters, their marriage was in serious trouble. With no male heir, she was aware that she could be replaced at any time with a newer, more docile, version that suited Louis better.

When Henry Plantagenet arrived at court, he was a square-shouldered, sprightly 19-year-old brimming with confidence and overflowing with energy, if you know what I mean. He was impulsive and ambitious and needed little sleep and Eleanor did not waste time coming to a decision. She petitioned Louis for a divorce on the nominal grounds that they were related by blood and two months later, she generously awarded Louis custody of their daughters on the condition that her lands were restored to her. Two months after that, she was married to Henry and at only twenty-two, Henry Plantagenet was Count of Anjou, Count of Maine,

Duke of Normandy, Duke of Aquitaine, Duke of Gascony and Count of Nantes.

With the marriage to Eleanor, half of France passed out of royal control right into Henry's hands. For an ambitious youth, there could not have been a more valuable bride. The marriage was one of the most brilliant political strokes of the age. Henry, later admitting his designs, accepted the admiration of Europe for his audacity. Everywhere men shook their heads at Henry's nerve and the love intrigue that was unfolding.

But with the marriage, Henry found himself threatened from all sides. While England had been struggling to strengthen their ties with France, this marriage did the opposite. King Louis felt slighted, and he certainly had grounds for complaint, as well as Stephen who had disputed Henry's title of Duke of Normandy in the first place. Both were more than a little bit miffed. Then there was the Count of Champagne, the Count of Perche and Henry's own brother, Geoffrey. All of them became spontaneously angry. To add to Louis' anger, within another two months, news reached him that Eleanor was pregnant and the first of her 8 children to Henry, a son, was born. One year later, another son would be conceived and in the future lurked Richard the Lionheart and the tyranny of King John.

When Stephen died, Henry added Lord of Ireland and King of England to his resume.

As everyone fumed, Henry turned his abundant energy towards England. He couldn't have cared less what anyone thought. The Plantagenets had arrived and England was in for a wild ride.

He took his time claiming the throne of England. He arrived two months after Stephen's death with two toddlers under the age of two and a heavily pregnant wife by his side. His first job was to mop up the mess of the English civil war left over from Stephen's reign. He was to find that rebellion hadn't died with Stephen and he was still challenged by powerful nobles who were 'testing the water' as they tried to set limits on his power. Henry's no-nonsense attitude soon put an end to that before it could develop into a more widespread conflict.

When it looked like trouble was brewing in the north, Henry's response was quick. He personally marched into York to confront the earls who were responsible for the tiff. Like his grandfather, Henry 1, this Henry had an outstanding knowledge of the law and he sat on councils whenever possible.

He dressed casually and laughed easily although when opposed, his temper had no boundaries.

But even in a royal family in the Middle Ages, child mortality was high and after the death of their first son William, aged three, they rejoiced months later when their daughter Matilda was born. In rapid succession, two more boys, Richard and Geoffrey, arrived. By 1155, Henry had four healthy children below the age of four with more on the way.

But while Henry II produced child after child in England, he continued to press home to the frail Malcolm in Scotland that Northumbria and Cumbria were not King David's to hand down to him. The lands belonged to England and he was taking them back. Effective immediately. Malcolm could have his Earldom of Huntingdon, but that was it.

Malcolm was in no state to fight about it. Like his father, Malcolm had never enjoyed good health and with the chronic disorder, Paget's disease looming, (typically resulting in enlarged and deformed bones), he decided the safest thing to do was to let the headstrong, aggressive Henry Plantagenet have his own way.

Malcolm was only 24 years old, unmarried and childless, when he died. Much like his father and grandfather, no one seemed too surprised. His younger brother, 22-year-old William, was a much more aggressive character, known as William the Lion, and he stepped up willingly to take his turn at the throne.

William the Lion is one of the least known and most disregarded of Scottish kings despite the fact that his was the longest reign by medieval Scottish monarchy standards. Unlike his religious, frail brother, William was powerfully built, redheaded and headstrong. He reigned for forty-nine years and is strangely unknown compared with his grandfather David I or his successors (his son Alexander II and grandson Alexander III.)

The first nine years, from 1165 – 1174, was a time of comparative peace for William but like most of his ancestors, he quickly gained an obsession with Northumberland and spent much of his time at Henry II's court incessantly badgering Henry about it at every opportunity. When he was constantly refused, he formed a treaty with France and became a key player in the Revolt of 1173 between three of Henry's sons and his wife Eleanor and their rebel supporters. While Henry watched Europe closely for enemies, from out of nowhere his three eldest sons rose up against him, all with axes of their own to grind and urged on by their mother, Eleanor. All of them felt they deserved more titles of their own and the power that went with them. And none of them wanted to wait until his death.

Henry had worked hard to mollify his boys with gifts but he was under no illusion of their capabilities. Or his wife's capabilities.

After eighteen months of fighting, Henry's rebellious family had to resign themselves to his continuing rule although you couldn't quite call it reconciliation.

The year was 1174. England and France are at war and their destinies have never been so intertwined. King Henry's wife, Eleanor of Aquitaine, and his sons, are now on the side of France. As King Henry and King Louis play their war games of cat and mouse, Eleanor was captured and imprisoned by Henry. Allegiances shifted with each battle as the fate of England and France swayed in a delicate balance.

In Scotland, William wasn't finished trying to take back Northumbria by a long shot. He was still struggling to regain the northern counties he'd lost and he meant to have them back at any cost, even if it took a raid in support of continuing the revolt. That year marked the most humiliating year for William. Disregarding the advice of his senior advisers, William put a plan into action.

As a smokescreen, he sent his younger brother, David Earl of Huntingdon, south to the English barons as a supposed sign of his good faith as a smokescreen, while he himself mounted an invasion of Northumbria in Alnwick. He charged the English troops himself, shouting *"Now we shall see which of us are good knights!"*

The result was disastrous. David was quickly taken prisoner while William himself was captured while out riding with a small group of men. Through the early morning mist, a band of cavalry were seen approaching and thinking they were his own men, William happily approached them. Unfortunately for William, they were English knights. By the time he realised his error, it was too late. He was hopelessly outnumbered and quickly unhorsed before being taken prisoner with his legs tied under his horse's belly and taken in chains to Newcastle, then on to Northampton before being transferred to Falaise in Normandy. Henry then sent an army to Scotland and occupied it.

For five long months, William was kept a prisoner until he finally, and reluctantly, signed a treaty accepting England as his overlord and agreed to pay the cost of the English army's occupation of Scotland by taxing the Scots. Into the bargain, William, at 44 years of age, was to marry Henry's 16-year-old granddaughter, Ermengarde de Beaumont, daughter of Henry's illegitimate daughter, Constance Fitzroy. To sweeten the deal, Henry threw in Edinburgh Castle as her dowry and paid for the wedding.

The chronicler Walter Bower described Ermengarde as 'an extraordinary woman', gifted with a charming and witty eloquence. Though William had many lovers before his marriage, the ageing monarch was reportedly never unfaithful to her after their wedding. Even still, it took nine years before their first child, a daughter, was born. Two more children would follow: another girl and a boy they named Alexander, then one more girl. And Alexander became the most protected child in the kingdom.

Neither William and his brother David were satisfied to settle. They always wanted more. They led an army northwards into Easter Ross and established castles north of the Beauly and Cromarty Firths, aiming to discourage the Norse earls of Orkney from expanding beyond Caithness. But in doing so, they ruffled the feathers of Donald Meic Uilleim, a descendant of King Duncan II who briefly took over Ross until his death six years later. William stepped back in and reclaimed Donald's stronghold of Inverness.

As Henry's 50th birthday approached, he was feeling old and his busy life had taken its toll on his body. His legs were bowed from years in a saddle and a femur, fractured years earlier, had never really healed properly. These injuries slowed him down as he limped around his territories during bouts of incapacitating illness.

A clever man might look back and see how much had been altered in the thirty-five years that he sat on the English throne. What had started out as a bright and shining future for the handsome king and his beautiful wife had ended with all of his children fighting like scavengers for morsels of his kingdom. Everyone he had loved, his wife and every one of his sons, had betrayed him.

It was in the midst of this personal grief that Henry died during another rebellion stirred up by his feisty sons in France. In his sorrow, he made no attempt to suggest the succession. As the eldest son, Richard would naturally take the throne anyway. By then, Henry had ceased to even care.

With Richard The Lionheart on the throne, Scotland's misery and stranglehold was relieved a little because Richard had already taken a vow to go on the Third Crusade to Palestine. Desperate for money to finance his adventure, Richard accepted William's offer of 10,000 Scottish *merks* for the annulment of all terms of the treaty. He *did* offer another 15,000 for Northumberland, more than he paid for Scotland itself, but Richard would have none of it.

Despite the Scots regaining their independence, Anglo-Scottish relations remained tense during the first decade of the 13th century when King John succeeded his brother Richard in 1199. Richard had heard of a golden treasure found near a castle of Chaluz on the lands of one of Richard's vassals and always looking for money, Richard moved in to take it for himself.

Greed would be Richard's downfall.e

What he hadn't expected was The Lord of Chaluz trying so hard to stop him. After three days, Richard left his tent armed with only a crossbow, a helmet and a shield and rode arrogantly close to the ramparts of the castle. As Richard stood looking up, he saw a man reach over the top of the rampart carrying a crossbow in one hand and a frying pan from the kitchens as a shield in the other. It is said that Richard took the time to applaud as the kitchen-hand fired a lone shot.

Richard ducked a fraction too slowly and the arrow struck him in the left shoulder near his neck. He tried to pull it out but the arrow snapped, leaving the barb buried inside his body. By the light of a fire, a surgeon would try to take out the shard of metal but as he dug, the wound widened.

As we can all imagine, surgery on a battlefield in medieval times was disastrous. As a result, the wound swiftly turned gangrenous.

Richard knew the end was near and began to set his affairs in order once more. He sent word to his mother and he divided his personal belongings among his friends. As he had no legitimate children, he relented and declared his estranged brother John to be his heir and at the age of 42, ten days after his injury, Richard died in the arms of his mother who had ridden hard to be at her favourite son's side as he passed away.

The character of the man who ascended the English throne is well known. Richard's virtues were likened to a lion after which he was named but there was no animal in nature that combines the conflicting qualities of John. He was a hardened warrior with the subtlety and cunning of a Machiavellian and from time to time during his furious rages, his cruelties were executed with cold, inhumane intelligence. Monks at the time emphasised his violence, greed, malice, treachery and lust and a French writer went as far as to write of his 'madness'.

Things had been pretty quiet in Scotland for William but he had no idea what was in store for him with King John on the throne. Almost immediately, John decided to flex English muscles by marching a large army to Norham near Berwick, in order to exploit the flagging leadership of the ageing Scottish monarch.

By then, William was a relatively old man, in his mid-sixties, and his health was beginning to fail so the easy option of backing down was taken. As well as promising a large sum of money, the ailing William agreed to his three daughters marrying English nobles and when the treaty was then renewed in 1212, William was forced to betroth his only legitimate son and heir, 14-year-old Alexander to John's 2-year-old daughter, Joan. Out of wedlock, William had fathered many children to different women and in the future, their descendants would lay claim to the Scottish throne in 1291, among which would be Roger de Mandeville, Patrick Gailightly and Robert III de Brus.

On a cold December morning two years later, William died and his son, Alexander, now 16 years old, was more than ready to take over.

For the past 200 years, English kings had declared that the land of the Scots belonged to them. The early Canmores, after Constantine, played the game and recognised English authority but England was in for a shock with Alexander succeeding to the throne. Subservience was not his style. As far as he was concerned, he was every bit as good as any English king. Better in fact. Maybe he was brash and arrogant but he was on a mission to take his kingship back, once and for all.

But to do that he had to resolve a dispute with the current king of England: King John.

Northumbria, Cumberland and Westmoreland were lands to which the Kings of England and the Kings of Scotland had both considered their own. To settle the argument, Alexander's ageing father had given England both money and two of his daughters to English nobles to appease them. But England would find that Alexander was nothing like his father. He was determined to take back everything that was rightfully his.

Alexander wasn't the only one with a grudge against John. There was a long line of English barons with grievances against John as well. Their biggest gripe was John's constant request for money to fund his war in France. Which is why Alexander decided to ally himself with the English barons.

The year 1215 was a bad year for John. He had Alexander in Scotland throwing his weight around and in England, the barons had grouped together with one fundamental principle, that Government would be more than the arbitrary rule of one man and the law must stand even above the King. They drew up a short document on parchment and with a handful of resolute men, they set off to present it to King John.

On 15th June, they dismounted without ceremony at Runnymede and met with the him. The Archbishop of Canterbury and several bishops handed over their suggestions. The *"Articles of the Barons"* was read and agreed upon immediately by John and the most famous document in our history, the Magna Carta, was signed in a quiet, short scene. On this document were sixty articles for John to consider and at the bottom, Item fifty-nine, was Alexander's claim to the northern territories: *'I promise to do right by Alexander King of Scots'.*

John duly signed.

Not that he had any intention to stand by his word and uphold the document. John disregarded it as utter foolishness. As soon as the door was shut, he went on his merry way.

A war was about to begin.

The nobles made their first move by seizing Rochester Castle, owned by Stephen Langton, and left unguarded. But John was well prepared. He had stock-piled money and gathered his own men, his most trusted advisers, William Marshal, 1st Earl of Pembroke and Ranulf of Chester. His plan was to isolate the rebels, protect his supply of mercenaries in Flanders, prevent the French from landing in the southeast and win the war through slow but deliberate destruction. For William Marshall's support, John betrothed his newborn daughter Eleanor to William's son who was then aged 25. An impressive effort at multi-tasking, wouldn't you say?

John's campaign started out well. He took back Rochester Castle, named as one of the greatest siege operations in England up to that time. Everybody who had signed the Magna Carta had their hands chopped off first and then they were beheaded. John then split his forces, sending William Longespee, John's illegitimate half-brother, to take the north side of London while he headed north to the estates of the northern barons.

For Alexander, this was too good to miss. He had a golden opportunity to reclaim the borderlines and take back what he saw as rightfully his. With Newcastle in his sights, he headed south into Northern England. First he burnt Newcastle to the ground and then he took Carlyle.

While Alexander tightened his grip in the north, the barons turned to the French for help. King Philip's son, Prince Louis, was the dauphin of France and the husband of John's niece Blanche, so he was as good as any to lead them. The way they saw it, Louis had a claim to the English throne through his marriage to Blanche, as the granddaughter of Henry I, and Louis wholeheartedly agreed with them.

It wasn't just the barons who had reached out to the French. Alexander had thought the exact same thought as well and struck up a deal with Louis guaranteeing him that Scotland would support the French if, in return, they recognised the disputed territories in the north as Scottish territories. Louis was in a great position no matter which way you looked at it.

In one stroke, John had been swept aside and Alexander began his march into England with little resistance to meet up with the French army in Dover. The plan was for Louis to wait in London while Alexander and Louis' army, together with the barons, advanced.

John turned on Scotland with a snarl, *'to chase the red fox-cub back to his lair'*, furious because he was forced to abandon the north and turn south to deal with this fresh oncoming invasion. With enemies on all sides, he had no choice but to retreat. As he withdrew, he watched angrily as many of his military men deserted to the Scots, including his half-brother William Longespee.

What happened next is something that has been rubbed out of the history of English monarchy.

At the request of the barons and with enthusiastic public support, Louis was proclaimed King of England at a mass in Saint Paul's Cathedral. Louis did not have a coronation. There were no bishops left since John had already excommunicated all them so he was merely *proclaimed* king by affirmation only. The coronation would come later, they assured him.

As far as Louis was concerned, he had the throne to himself and he was in. Almost immediately, he began to appoint his friends in France into high English positions.

The barons had looked at everything from all sides but they had not seen that one coming. Although they all spoke French, they were beginning to *feel* English and with the arrival of more and more of Louis' French friends, they panicked.

They had expected to be given more control once they were rid of John but instead; control had merely passed from John to Louis. Worse than that, it had passed on to the French. So they began thinking. John had a 9-year-old son, Henry. Of course, no nine-year-old had ever been a king, but there's always a first for everything, right? And if the young child was to become the king, then one of the barons would have to be the regent and then they really *would* be in charge of everything. But Louis had control of London and the child was at Corfe Castle in Dorset. They would have to get the child to the nearest abbey in Glasgow and crown him quickly. Of course, they didn't really have a *crown* as such. Louis had that. They would have to use his mother's gold neckband instead. And actually, they didn't even have an Archbishop to do the coronation either. Never mind, the Bishop of Winchester was available and he had the keys to the treasury as well. Perfect.

The next thing Louis knew, the 'affirmation' had been withdrawn and he was stupefied. How could you withdraw the offer? he asked. Everything is finally coming to a head, he stated. His armies had gained territories in the southeast of England as well as parts of the north. John was on the defensive after marching from the Cotswolds to Cambridge and had finally arrived in Lincoln. Alexander was invading from northern England and marching south and was set to meet John in battle. In the five months that he had been in the country, he had gained more and more support and was just about to deliver the final blow. He listed all his achievements one by one. At the end of the list, he stated that he was certainly not about to give the crown back to them after everything he had done.

While Louis and the barons argued, the battle between Alexander and John at Lincoln was in full swing. For six hours, the terrible sounds of clashing swords, the screams of men as limbs were either crushed or severed and the cries of dying horses as they were butchered echoed through the city. The streets were said to have flowed with heads, blood and human entrails.

In the end, it was John who was successful. Both the French army and the Scots had been defeated and Alexander was forced to return to Scotland, dejected and destroyed.

As always, fate stepped in to put an end to the dilemma. Negotiations were temporarily put on hold when John contracted dysentery after a bout of overeating, probably while celebrating. Even though he determinately continued west to Wales, losing a significant part of his baggage and belongings including the Crown Jewels sucked in by quicksand in the bogs, his illness grew worse. On 18th October 1216, John died and everything changed yet again.

From Dover, Louis was energised when he heard the news and he began a fresh campaign for the throne. He packed up and headed to London.

But Louis was in for a nasty shock. He arrived fully expecting to be greeted by the same cheers he had received only five months before. To his astonishment, the English were now showering him with arrows and lime to blind him. All of a sudden, everyone was patriotic and for the first time since the Norman Conquest, the French were being described as foreigners who were looting the English.

It was enough to stop Louis in his tracks and with no more than a backwards snarl, he headed back home to France. He'd had enough of the fickleness of the English.

As we know, Louis did not become the King of England and this insult would be well remembered by both Louis and his future generations. John's 9-year-old son became Henry III of England and a new terrifying chapter would begin for England.

At 9 years of age, Henry was the elder of two boys: his younger brother Richard was only 7 years old. The government, who had not supported his father, now flocked to young Henry's side in droves and John's most ardent supporter, William Marshal, 1st Earl of Pembroke, became Henry's regent until he came of age. In Scotland, Alexander had outgrown his usefulness and the barons had decided the 9-year-old child of King John could be swayed a lot easier than a moody Frenchman or an ambitious Scotsman.

The first nine years of Henry's reign were amazing as he made an almost sluggish progress into adulthood. But in that time, an awful lot happened.

At the insistence of his advisers, Henry reissued the Magna Carta removing all references, not even a footnote, regarding Alexander's claim of Scotland. To soften the blow for the Scots, negotiations renewed for

Henry's 10-year-old sister Joan to marry 23-year-old Alexander and within two years, Henry's 9-year-old sister Eleanor, betrothed at birth by their father (who she had never met by the way), married 34-year-old William Marshall, 2nd Earl of Pembroke. By then, Louis had become King Louis VIII of France and then died of dysentery three years later, leaving his 12-year-old son to rule as Louis IX under the regency of his mother Blanche. To top it off, Henry had been victorious in a battle against the French to regain Gascony and his 15-year-old brother Richard had fought valiantly beside him. The victory had given England a valuable and lucrative wine trade and as a reward, Henry gave his young brother the title of Earl of Cornwall as a birthday gift at the beginning of the next year.

All in all, everyone agreed it was a terrific start to Henry's reign.

Passions had gradually cooled over the years so it was not until Henry reached the age of nineteen that he took over the reins of his own government.

As an adult, Henry was a good deal less than average height and like his father, inclined to be plump. He had a drooping left eyelid that covered half of the eye, rendering him a rather sinister appearance and from his earliest years, he seemed almost vague. But if he hadn't inherited his ancestor's strengths, he certainly inherited the Plantagenet temper and pig-headedness and he often flew into rages hurling abuse, even objects, at his ministers. Despite the intenseness of his attacks, he rarely stayed angry for long and he soon lapsed back into a type of lethargy.

It was not until the year 1230 that Henry met Eleanor of Provence. Eleanor was the second daughter of Raymond Berenger, Count of Provence and Beatrice of Savoy. It was about this time that Alexander realised that he was never going to recover Northumberland as a family possession. In the autumn of 1237 he signed an amicable agreement where he renounced all claims to territory south of the Tweed to his brother-in-law. It was an implicit acceptance by England, for the time being at least, of Scotland's right to exist as a free and independent kingdom.

The population of Scotland at this time was only about 300,000 and most of them were poor peasants living in small stone-and-turf houses which they usually shared with any livestock they might have had. Only a small proportion of the population, perhaps 10 percent, lived in the trading towns. New links were being forged with overseas markets and commercial and manufacturing skills were encouraged.

It was a prosperous period of time for Alexander except for one major obstacle. His wife Joan had not delivered a child. At her death in 1238, Alexander immediately applied himself to one of the most urgent functions of medieval kingship: producing a male heir to the throne. The following year, he turned his nose up at England for a bride and married Marie de Coucy, a kinswoman of the French king, instead. In September 1241, she duly bore him a son they named Alexander - the future Alexander III - while Henry and Eleanor in England were up to their third child. But the two kings were barely civil with each other.

The spat with England festered for three years while both armies eyed one another menacingly across the border. No battle ensued but both kings knew something had to be done to reduce the animosity from escalating to outright war. As part of peace negotiations, Alexander's new-born son, Alexander, was betrothed to Henry's infant daughter Margaret, herself only a year older than her bridegroom. By doing this, they hoped a more cohesive coexistence would follow. For Alexander, instead of a fight with England, the time was ripe to extend his authority over the islands to the west to the Hebrides. For too long, in his opinion, they and the Northern Isles, had been subject to the crown of Norway.

King Hakon the Old in Norway had sent a punitive expedition to The Hebrides in 1230 which caused considerable havoc, turning from a furious engagement into a 3-day assault on Rothesay Castle on the island of Bute, in the Firth of Clyde. The Norsemen finally forced their way in by hacking through the castle's thick circular stone walls with their axes despite cascades of boiling lead and pitch raining down upon them from the battlements.

It was only natural that Alexander would want to curb the piratical Islesman so in a peaceful endeavour, he sent an envoy to Norway with the intention of buying back the Western Isles for good. The snub he received in the spring of 1249 sent him in to overdrive. He mobilised a massive expedition by land and sea and set off to crush his enemy.

His first target was Dunstaffnage Castle, the chief stronghold of the MacDougalls, only recently build by Ewen of Argyll. On the eve of the battle, he gathered his fleet in the Sound of Kerrera, the three-kilometre-long fertile island which shelters the Oban coastline. But as his galleys lay at anchor in Horseshoe Bay, poised to launch the assault on Dunstaffnage, Alexander had an ominous dream where three men told him to turn back and that nothing good would come of the battle. One of the men seemed to him to be dressed in royal robes. He looked menacing, ruddy of face, bald and rather stout, of medium height. The second man seemed slender in build and gallant-looking, very handsome and of noble bearing. The third man was much the biggest in build and the most menacing of them all. It was the last of the three that would tell Alexander to turn back. To which he refused.

Whether a dream or a premonition, and whether one believes in either, Alexander did in fact fall ill in Kerrera Sound, either on his ship or on land, in July 1249. On his death bed, I wonder if he was remembering the dream and wondering what would have happened if he'd listened. Hindsight is a wondrous thing.

Unable to progress home, he died there and with his death, his army melted away and dispersed. It would be his 7-year-old son, Alexander, who became the next King of Scotland as Alexander II.

As so often in the past, when a new king is in his minority, there is bound to be an embittered struggle for control between rival parties. And Alexander's minority was no different. One party was led by Walter Comyn, Earl of Menteith and the other by Alan Durward, Justiciar of Scotia. But while they bitterly disagreed on most items, both knew to keep the English king Henry III appeased. And the best way to do that was to uphold the betrothal between the two kings' children made ten years ago.

Barely 10 years old, Alexander III was taken to York in December 1251 to be knighted by Henry III before being married to Henry's daughter, Margaret, aged 11. Henry's only stipulation was that the young couple were not allowed to live together as man and wife and were to be kept under the strict control of tutors and guardians until his daughter reached the age of eighteen.

The seven years dragged on for Alexander as the reins of government were being firmly held by the prop-king nobles, particularly the powerful Comyn family. But when his minority ended in 1259, on his 18th birthday, he quickly put an end to that. He was in the driving seat now and he wasn't about to let anything stand in his way.

For Alexander, reaching eighteen had a dual benefit. It meant that he and Margaret could begin their life together as husband and wife, and one year later, a daughter they named Margaret, was born. It also meant Alexander could resume his father's ambitions in the Hebrides from eleven years before. At aged 21, he laid a formal claim before King Haakon of Norway.

Once again, as with his father, the claim was instantly rejected and the following year, Haakon responded by making a sizeable invasion. Sailing around the west coast of Scotland was Haakon's way of threatening Alexander and once his fleet was noted, he began negotiations again, except this time, they would be on his terms.

Alexander knew his territory well. He knew when the storms would arrive and he knew how badly they could affect a fleet. He also knew that if he could delay the talks until the autumn storms began, Haakon would become weary of delay after delay and simply attack without thinking of the consequences. It was a risky plan but one he was sure would succeed.

As Alexander had hoped, Haakon set sail, planning to attack, and encountered a massive storm that damaged most of his ships. In a hopeless position, Haakon had no choice but to winter at the Bishop's Palace in Orkney leaving him plenty of time to plan his campaign for the next year. Haakon's plan was also a good one, and it had every chance of success, except as usual, fate stepped in. During his stay, he fell ill and died in the early hours of 16th December 1263. The Isles now fell in Alexander's lap.

It took two years for Haakon's successor, King Magnus, to recognise that Norway's supremacy in the Western Isles was no longer tenable. A peace treaty, the Treaty of Perth, was made and in return for Norway to withdraw from the Hebrides and the Isle of Man, the Scots were to pay a lump sum of 4,000 merks of refined silver in four annual instalments and an annual tribute of 100 merks in perpetuity.

Alexander paid the whole sum on the spot.

Things couldn't have been better for Alexander. At the age of 25, he now had a healthy son as his heir and he had singlehandedly, and successfully, enlarged the Kingdom of Scotland where his ancestors had failed. His father and his father's ancestors had fought hard wars for the privilege of ruling Scotland. For years, men died and women wept for their husbands but he hoped that would now be over and the country could rest and be at peace. At the moment, it seemed nothing Alexander did went wrong.

Henry III's death four years later, in 1272, meant his energetic and charismatic elder son, Edward, rose to the throne as Edward I. Alexander found him a congenial enough brother-in-law and the young men were on reasonable enough terms for Edward and his wife Eleanor of Castile to visit the Scottish court several times, to visit Edward's sister.

Although he and his brother-in-law were on good terms, Alexander was under no illusion that the 33-year-old Edward was an experienced leader and a skilful general who had learned the art of war well. Nicknamed Edward Longshanks, he was an intimidating 6 feet 2 inches tall, and the only things that marred his features were a lisp and a drooping eyelid, which had been characteristic of his father. Neither of these impediments affected Edward in the slightest. He could be very persuasive when he put his mind to it.

Alexander knew Edward revelled in war, tournaments, hawking and hunting and when he chased a quarry, he galloped at breakneck speed to cut the beast down. He had also heard that at an early age, Edward showed he had a taste for violence. At one time, Edward had attacked a man, cut off his ear and gouged out an eye. The knowledge of Edward's thirst for violence made Alexander just that little bit more wary of him, brother-in-law or not.

In his private life, the marriage between Eleanor of Castile and Edward was a huge success. As you can imagine, arranged royal marriages were rarely happy, much like Alexander and Margaret's marriage, but this couple were devoted to each other.

Edward and Eleanor were second cousins once removed as Edward's grandfather King John and Eleanor's great grandmother, Eleanor of England, were the son and daughter of King Henry II and Eleanor of Aquitaine. (I know. A lot of Eleanors.) When they married, Edward was 15 and Eleanor was 13.

After three short-lived daughters, Eleanor finally gave birth to a son, John, who was followed by a second boy, Henry, a year later and in 1269 by another healthy daughter they called Eleanor. By then, Alexander's wife had also given him three healthy children: Alexander, Margaret and David.

But in a series of crushing tragedies that would darken the last years of his vigorous and successful reign, Alexander's golden touch was about to come to a heart-stopping end. One year after Edward took the throne of England, after returning from a trip to Fife in 1275, Margaret died at the age of 34.

Although no one could say the marriage was a huge success, Alexander took his time to remarry, seeing no urgent cause to do so at this stage. He had three healthy children and he himself was a strong and healthy man, enjoying life. You see, tragedy hadn't happened yet.

Everything changed six years later in June 1281.

Alexander was still celebrating the betrothal of his only daughter, 20-year-old Margaret to the 13-year-old new king of Norway, Erik II, son of King Magnus, grandson of Haakon the Old, in the hope to ease the tensions that were redeveloping between Norway an Scotland. With the marriage, a more secure future would hopefully unfold for Scotland although Margaret had been against the match since it would mean being married to an adolescent. But Alexander was adamant. She was still unmarried at twenty, which was a remarkably late age for a medieval princess, and it would mean she would be a queen in her own right in Norway.

No one saw the tragedy coming. Alexander's youngest son, David, suddenly fell ill at Stirling Castle at the age of 8 years old and died soon after. The mourning weeds had to be shrugged aside to celebrate his daughter's wedding and coronation in Bergen two months later and 1 year later again, Margaret was pregnant and the celebrations for both her pregnancy and her brother Alexander's marriage to Margaret of Flanders continued in earnest.

It was the 9th April 1283, when Margaret went into labour in Tonsberg. The labour was difficult and long and at not quite twenty-two, Margaret died in childbirth leaving behind a sickly infant daughter, quickly christened Margaret and nicknamed 'Maid of Norway'.

Alexander's brother-in-law Edward sent condolences and there *seemed* a genuine friendship and sorrow between the two kings. After all, Edward knew what it was like to bury children. By then, he'd already buried ten of his own sixteen children.

But still, lurking in the background was the hint of ... something... and Alexander kept his eyes and ears open and alert.

Less than a year later, came the third and cruellest blow for Alexander. On 17th January, 1284, Alexander's eldest son, Alexander, who had been born on the very same day twenty years earlier, died at Lindores Abbey in Fife after a long illness. Young Alexander had been married for just over a year but by April, it was clear his widow was not pregnant.

In the space of nine years, Alexander had lost his wife, two sons and one daughter in quick succession. The only heir to the Scottish throne now was a sickly 3-year-old granddaughter in Norway.

The Canmore dynasty was withering on the vine and Alexander began to panic. Firstly he needed to marry again and father more sons and secondly, he needed to betroth his only grandchild to a suitable candidate.

Then an idea began to form in Alexander's head.

The logic was simple. To unite England and Scotland and to keep the peace, he had to arrange a marriage pact between 3-year-old Margaret and Edward's 1-year-old son. If they could do that one simple thing, the antagonism between Scotland and England would surely cease.

Edward had been watching intently as the tragedies unfolded so you can understand Edward didn't take long to think about it. You see, there was a bonus in the marriage for him. Medieval women were regarded as property and what Margaret owned would instantly belong to his son as soon as they were married. With that little windfall, his son could possibly become the richest man in the world.

In Norway, King Erik was naturally concerned about his young daughter's prospects. She was at the mercy of warring factions and he saw a serious issue that needed to be brought up: the two infants were closely related – Edward I and the Maid of Norway's grandmother were brother and sister – and this would require Papal dispensation.

Not all the magnates were happy to name not only an infant, but a girl, as the future ruler of Scotland. There was no precedent for a female ruler and in any case, many of them felt they themselves had a better claim to the Scottish throne. They comforted themselves with the thought that Alexander, who was still in his early forties, had plenty of time in which to produce another son or two.

Alexander knew he had to remarry again, and quickly. He had not spent his time as a widower alone but the question of succession was now of great importance. The bride he chose was Yolande, Comtesse de Montford, daughter of Robert IV, Comte de Dreux, a vassal of Edward I of England. And on 14th October 1285, they married in Jedburgh Abbey.

Then, on a stormy, windswept night 5 months after the marriage, Alexander III's 36-year reign came to an abrupt end.

Alexander had just finished with business in Edinburgh, intending to ride off from his court and meet up with his new young pregnant wife,

Queen Yolande, twenty-five odd miles away. His advisers begged him not to go because it was such a foul night but Alexander ignored them, insisting on setting out to spend the night with his young wife in the royal castle at Kinghorn on the east coast of Fife. It meant crossing the Firth of Forth in the teeth of a northerly gale heavy with snow, and a hazardous journey on horseback through the stormy darkness. The boatman at South Queensferry at first refused to sail, but complied after being taunted with cowardice. When they landed in Inverkeithing on the north shore, the king was urged to stay there overnight, but he once again refused and took a horse to ride on to Kinghorn, choosing to spend the night in the arms of his new bride.

He never made it.

No one knows what happened that night. The surmise has always been that he became separated from his guides in the darkness. His horse stumbled and lost its footing and at only 45 years old, Alexander was thrown over the cliff and fell to his death. He was found the next day with his neck broken.

Scotland was standing on the threshold of the War of Independence and the only surviving descendant in the direct line of the Canmore dynasty was a tiny, fragile little 3-year-old girl living in Norway and Alexander's widow who was pregnant and in her first trimester. Obviously, plans needed to be made ... in case.

The inheritance of the throne was supposed to pass through the male line. Unfortunately there were no male heirs to pass it on to. Yet. Alexander III had obviously intended to father more children and he was young enough for this to happen before his untimely death. To make the matter more complicated, Alexander had no siblings who lived to adulthood and his father Alexander II had only three sisters. Alexander II had upwards of six half-brothers and sisters, but they were all illegitimate from at least two different mistresses.

One step back in the genealogy line was Alexander II's father, William The Lion, who was the second of three sons of Henry of Huntingdon (David I's only son), the eldest being King Malcolm IV who died unmarried. Their younger brother, David, 8th Earl of Huntingdon, was heir to the Scottish throne until Alexander II was born in 1198 but David died in 1219 leaving behind a wife and three legitimate girls and one legitimate boy who died childless aged thirty. There were at least three illegitimate children but they were out of contention. Another dead end.

One step backwards again from Henry of Huntingdon and we have David I, son of Malcolm III and the brother of Alexander I and Edgar I. Apart from the three sons who became kings already mentioned, Malcolm III had two sons who had both died, and one who became a monk and had died. If the Scots were to look at the only girls in the family tree, we have Malcolm III's daughter, Matilda, who married King Henry I of England, making the King of England the heir to that line. And they certainly didn't want that.

Whatever happened, there was no heir through any male line – "heir-male" as it used to be called. The sisters of Alexander II had all married English Earls – Margaret to de Burgh of Kent, Isabella to Bigod of Norfolk, and Marjory to Earl Marshall. Margaret bore a daughter who died in infancy, the other two marriages were childless. So the next lines were the daughters of Earl David of Huntingdon and Matilda of Chester: Margaret, Isabella and Ada. Girls.

And this is where it gets really interesting.

Margaret was the eldest, and had married Alan, Lord of Galloway. Their marriage produced two daughters: Devorguilla, who married John Balliol of Barnard Castle in Cumbria and Christiana, who married William de Forz. Christiana's marriage was childless, but Devorguilla and John had a son they called John Balliol after his father.

Earl Henry's second daughter was Isabel, who married Robert Bruce, 4th Lord of Annandale. They too had a son, Robert Bruce, and by 1290 he had both a son and grandson, and both were still alive and well.

The third daughter, Ada, married John de Hastings, first Baron Hastings, and they had a son, John. The problem here was Baron Hastings had very little support in Scotland, in addition to being from the most junior line.

Robert Bruce claimed that he should be named King, claiming that he had been named heir to the throne by Alexander II if he had no male heirs, and also that he was the closest living male descendant of Earl Henry. John Balliol claimed that as *he* was descended from the *eldest* line so he should be King.

Balliol and Bruce were political rivals nationally and in the south-west of

Scotland, Balliol was supported by the powerful Comyn family who opposed the Bruces.

To fill the sudden vacuum after the sudden death of Alexander III while the nation waited to see if his young French widow Yolande was pregnant, a committee of six Guardians were elected at Scone one month later comprising of two bishops, two earls (Alexander Comyn, Earl of Buchan and Duncan MacDuff, Earl of Fife) and two Barons (James the Steward and John Comyn, Lord of Badenoch.) The Bruces, although a powerful family in the south-west of Scotland, were not represented. It was a sign of growing political maturity of the nation that prominent leaders could come to such an effective arrangement, despite threatening rumblings of discontent from some leading noble families, especially two who thought themselves legitimate claimants to the throne: the Balliols (supported by the Comyns) and the Bruces.

The nervous uncertainty regarding Yolande and her pregnancy continued for several months. Then their nightmare became a reality. Yolande miscarried her child and in October 1286 the Princess Margaret, The Maid of Norway, was formally accepted as Queen of Scots.

In England, Edward I had put on his velvet gloves and had slipped out of character. He was going about his business very quietly but he was certainly watching with interest. Emissaries had been sent to Edward as a courtesy, he was after all the child's great-uncle, and England had a legitimate interest in the royal affairs of its neighbour. By then, Edward was one of the most powerful and respected kings in Europe. And this is when the question of the Maid of Norway's marriage prospects rose again.

The obvious candidate for the infant queen's hand was still Edward's 2-year-old son, Edward, Earl of Carnarvon, the future Edward II. This match would ensure a stability in Britain it had never experienced in history and Alexander had been smart enough to write to Edward hinting at the desirability of the royal marriage between his granddaughter and Edward's son. Long and painstaking negotiations ensued between England, Scotland and Norway with the Guardians insisting that no matter what happened, Scotland should remain separated from England as a distinct kingdom in any dynastic union. King Erik in Norway once again rose the issue of familial closeness requiring papal dispensation.

At last, three years later in November 1289, all three were ready to subscribe to a preliminary treaty, which was confirmed in the Treaty of Birgham. The marriage settlement guaranteed that Scotland would remain an independent kingdom, separate and divided from England and free in itself without subjection. Should Prince Edward and Margaret die childless, her kingdom would then pass to *her* nearest heir.

That was the intention, anyway.

Even at that early stage, Edward was thinking hard. He added the ominous words: *"Saving always the right of our lord King, and of any other whomsoever, that has pertained to him."* On ratifying the treaty, he insisted on appointing the new Bishop of Durham as his lieutenant in Scotland on behalf of the royal pair and required the Scottish Guardians to obey the bishop.

You can guarantee suspicious looks were flitting around.

In May 1290, Edward sent a ship from Yarmouth to fetch his future daughter-in-law from Norway, bearing gifts of sugar loaves, gingerbread, figs and raisins. King Erik, however, had other ideas. He insisted on using a Norwegian vessel and the English ship returned without her. Four months later, the Maid of Norway set sail from Bergen, bound for Leith.

It was a wild, storm-tossed voyage, and the ship was driven far off course to Orkney, which was till Norwegian territory. From birth, Margaret's health had never been robust and during the voyage she became tremendously sick. She was carried ashore for her safety but soon after, she died in the arms of her maid. Her tiny body was then taken back to Bergen where it was examined by her father before being buried beside her mother.

Margaret, Maid of Norway, had been Queen of Scots for four and a half years and with her death the Canmore dynasty came to a crushing end. The treaty of Birgham was nullified and all thoughts turned to identifying the person who had the best claim to the vacant throne.

As thirteen family members stepped forward to stake a claim for the Scottish throne, Edward in England was digesting the news slowly.

It was a devastating blow for Scotland but it is only in hindsight that we can see just how devastating it truly was. The immediate effect was simply a dynastic crisis. There wasn't just a minority to deal with now, there was a hotly disputed succession to contend with.

Life is full of 'what ifs' and Scotland's history is peppered with many such questions. Take Alexander, Prince of Scotland, for example. Moments before his untimely death, he was the only surviving son of Alexander III and the man who would have been King. The sad fact is that he predeceased his father and left him without an heir.

But what if the younger Alexander had not died and had become Alexander IV, King of Scots? If Alexander had lived, we would probably not have seen William Wallace invent guerrilla warfare. If Alexander's life had not been extinguished, we would not have seen Robert the Bruce in the future assume the throne in 1306. Had Alexander not passed away, we would not have had to endure the reign of John Balliol, 'the Toom Tabard'. Had Alexander lived and inherited the throne, we would perhaps not have seen Edward I take such an interest in the affairs of Scotland.

The events that occurred after young Alexander's death were catastrophic. It caused his father to panic. First his father induced the Estates of Scotland to recognise his granddaughter, Margaret, as his heir-presumptive and she herself became a statistic in the great poll of history. She would have been Queen Margaret, but she was to die before her 8th birthday on her way to Orkney then on to Scotland to assume the throne.

In an attempt to secure a male heir, Alexander III decided to remarry. His marriage to second wife Yolande de Dreux took place on the 1st of November, 1285 and three months later, she was to announce her pregnancy. Sadly, Alexander himself died on the 26th of March, 1286, on his way home to Kinghorn in Fife, anxious to spend another night with the pregnant Yolande. Sadder still, her baby was stillborn in November 1286.

For Scotland, the far reaching effects of the death of both Alexanders cannot be underestimated. For a start, since then, there have been no further King Alexanders - lots of King Jameses - but no more Alexanders. No Gaelic Kings or Queens since Alexander have had any significant Gaelic blood. From John Balliol onwards, the Kings and Queens of Scotland were essentially of Norman descent. If Alexander's line had continued, it is likely that the claim of Robert the Bruce would never have been made, nor needed to have been made. The intervention of Edward I to determine who, from amongst the long list of Scottish Nobles, had the better claim to the vacant throne would have been unnecessary.

If the younger Alexander had become Alexander IV, the Battles of Dunbar and Stirling and Falkirk and Bannockburn would likely never have been fought. Andrew Murray would not have died of his wounds in the months after the Battle of Stirling and Wallace would not have been butchered in Smithfield. With Robert the Bruce unlikely to ever have stepped up to the throne, his succession through the Stewarts (latterly, due to Mary I, Queen of Scots, dalliance with France, known as the Stuarts) would not have occurred. With no Stuarts, there would have been no James VI to become James I on the death of the Virgin Queen, Elizabeth I, and nor would there have been a need for Cromwell to get so upset at the posturing of Charles I, another Stuart. With no Stuarts, there would've been no Jacobites and no Bonnie Prince Charlie.

History would have been unrecognisable.

The reign of the two Alexanders: Alexander II, the son of William the Lion, and Alexander's son, Alexander III spanned most of the thirteenth century. That century came to be wistfully known as a golden age of princely stability and prosperity, especially as it was a prelude to tragedy and to the desperate times of the Wars of Independence.

INSURRECTION

*W*hen the crisis of succession struck Scotland, Edward was a 50-year-old man with an impressive CV. He was Lord of Ireland, King of England and Duke of Aquitaine, tall and handsome but along with the Plantagenet charm he also inherited the Plantagenet vicious temper gene. He was a dominating figure experienced in all the arts of war and peace and committed to strengthening the kingdom he had inherited from his father, Henry III, in 1274.

As England watched, he grew up to become their dashing Crusader, devoted to his Spanish wife, Eleanor of Castile, despite being an arranged marriage and marrying when he was fifteen and she was thirteen. They were rarely apart and he is one of the few medieval English kings not to have fathered children out of wedlock. When she died not long after the Maid of Norway's death, he constructed a series of twelve crosses to mark the places where the funeral cortege would stop on the way to her burial at Westminster.

For three long years after the death of Margaret the Maid, guardians of Scotland dithered endlessly over who would be the next ruler. By 1291, still no choice had been made and it became very clear that the guardians needed help in making a decision.

Perhaps a friendly arbitrator could help? the nobles thought. *Someone with experience who commanded respect? Who else but the King of England*, someone suggested. After all, Edward was family. There was no reason to doubt him. Was there?

Edward was a smart man and he was already taking great interest in the proceedings when the Guardians approached him to arbitrate in May 1291. And of course, he was more than willing to step in and undertake the task. The golden opportunity to interfere decisively in the future of the northern kingdom had fallen into his lap and he was about to take full advantage of it. It must have occurred to him as he sat in his court that this was his best chance to manipulate the situation to his own advantage. All that was needed was strength and determination and he had both.

Ever since he was a young man, it was a deep-seated ambition of his to be king of all the territories north and south. Hadn't he already conquered Wales, the nemesis of every Plantagenet king before him and every one of them since the Norman invasion? It was a time when tales of Arthur and the Knights of the Round Table was a truth, not a romantic story, and Edward had a fixation with the story.

His first attempt at conquering Wales and the Welsh Prince, Llywelyn ap Gruffudd, was when he was a young man and his father, Henry III, was still alive. The campaign had been a complete disaster. Edward had sided against his despotic father during the campaign, together with the barons and his father's brother-in-law, Simon De Montfort, and for his impudence, his father had exiled him to Gascony for two years. Edward's second attempt had been a very different story. He had set out to be the English warrior who defeated the Welsh and he had succeeded. Why not add Scotland to the tally and become ruler of the whole of the British Isles?

As a meeting place, Norham Castle was chosen by Edward with great care. It sat firmly in Northumberland on the banks of the river Tweed, ten kilometres south-west of Berwick. On the English side.

And that's when the Scots smelled a rat.

For Edward, the conquest of Scotland had become entertainment. He had already arrived in full splendour when the Scots stopped just north of the border, wanting him to cross the river and come to them. And of course, Edward would not shift. He wanted *them* to come to *him*. When the Scots reluctantly sent a delegation across the Tweed they were met with a demand that Edward must first be acknowledged as the Lord Superior of Scotland before he would settle the succession as judge. Then they were given three weeks to make up their minds.

The Scots were stunned. Sixty years of peace and now this? To top it off, Edward produced eleven more claimants from prominent families and declared if every one of them didn't acknowledge his overlordship, they could be eliminated from the contest altogether. They argued the point vigorously but Edward was definite.

Within a matter of days, one by one the claimants swore allegiance to him. Others followed his lead and a few days later, John Balliol accepted the inevitable. On 12th June, the Scots finally came to Norham and the lengthy process of adjudication began.

The adjudication of the "Great Cause" dragged on until the competitors were whittled down to a shortlist of two: John Balliol, Lord of Galloway and Robert Bruce, 5th Lord of Annandale, who was in his eighties. A panel of 104 arbiters were appointed – forty each nominated by Balliol and Bruce and twenty-four from Edward's council.

In terms of the claims of the two men, Balliol had the most obviously straightforward claim because of the laws of primogeniture although both men could trace their ancestry back to King David I. But that's not what Robert Bruce, Lord of Annandale thought.

David I's son, Henry, had three sons of his own: one was Malcolm IV, another was William the Lion and the last was David, Earl of Huntingdon who in turn had three daughters, in particular Margaret and Isobel of Huntingdon. Margaret's granddaughter married John, 5th Baron of Balliol and Isobel married Robert Bruce, 4th Lord of Annandale.

There was no love lost between the two men and the animosity went back to Henry III days.

John Balliol was descended from a Picardy nobleman, John de Bailleul, who had been a landowner in England under King William Rufus and whose son, Guy, came to Scotland in the reign of David I, inheriting lands from his father. There was just no money in the package. He was the great, great grandson of David I and to top it off, he was married to Isabella, daughter of John de Warenne, Earl of Surrey (Edward's right hand man). When looking at this pedigree, Edward saw him as an easy choice and Balliol was like a lamb among the wolves.

Robert IV de Brus was descended from an old Normandy family who were given lands in north Yorkshire by Henry I when the family came to Scotland. Then in the reign of David I around 1120 he was granted the Lordship of Annandale. He was the ancestor of a long line of Bruce Lords, most of whom were called, rather confusingly, Robert. Robert Bruce V was born on the family estate in Writtle, Essex and had married Isobel de Clare, the granddaughter of Sir William Marshal, Earl of Pembroke, and had become Constable and Governor of Carlisle and Sheriff of Cumberland. His family had always been loyal to the English kings, mainly due to the fact that most of their lands were in England and not supporting the English meant losing those precious lands and the income they provided. His son, Robert Bruce VI, in turn married the wealthy Marjorie of Carrick and added Carrick in Argyll to his own long list of lands.

Edward's father Henry was having a terrible time with the barons, led by his sister's husband, Simon de Montfort. Henry couldn't hold on to money to save himself, handing out titles and lands to his wife's family, and De Montfort was smart enough to assume control of the government along with a council of nine nobles and began ruling in the name of the king as a parliament. What is surprising, and probably stupid, after having fought so hard to be at the top, De Montfort began dividing the spoils of wars unfairly. He did exactly what Henry had done and gave himself and his sons territories and castles that had been plundered but forgot to reward supporters that had stood by him loyally. By doing so, many barons who had initially supported him now started to take a better look at him. They had expected some sort of recognition for their loyalty but when none came, they began scheming night and day to overthrow him. It was Henry's big chance to take back control of his realm. Finally.

Henry summoned his loyal men to cross the border from Scotland to Lewes in Sussex to fight for their English lands in 1264 and together with Robert Bruce V were John Balliol and John Comyn III of Badenoch, both lords in their fifties, two years his senior and grey-haired men with soft bellies. The division between the enemies extended into families with the Red Comyn's fighting for the Scottish rebels, becoming the Red Comyn's, and the Black Comyn's fighting for England. The colours representing the colours of their banners.

It must have been with watchful unease as Robert Bruce rode down the hill, aware that the enemy beside him might be more dangerous than the one arrayed on the hilltop. A stray blade in the back. A misdirected arrow. Such a thing went against chivalry since nobles did not intentionally kill nobles. But the Comyns had little true noble blood in them, despite their high position.

As the armies clashed, blood flew and flesh opened and the reek of blood swelled as shields cracked and the screams of men and horses rose. De Montfort's men fought valiantly as Henry's ranks floundered and gaps appeared as men fled in disarray.

And then came the dreaded cry. *Retreat! Retreat!*

All around the town of Lewes, torches were burning, flames billowing in the night air giving off a haze of acrid smoke. On the air, horses screamed, too badly injured in the battle to be saved, as they were killed. Above the pitiful screams rose the sound of laughter and song as de Montfort's men celebrated.

In a cell, three men were waiting. From the window, Robert Bruce would have glanced round and seen John Comyn standing by the door and Balliol on the pallet, his head in his hands and knees drawn up to his chest. All men would have been covered in blood and filth and the reek would have been appalling.

The rattle of the latch would have made all three men look up and Robert Bruce would have recognised the person filling the doorway. He had seen him before in Edinburgh and William Comyn, head of the Comyn Clan of Kilbride, hadn't changed much.

The news hadn't been good for Robert Bruce. Simon de Montfort rewarded loyalty to his men and had granted William Comyn two prisoners in return for his service on the battlefield. Of course, William Comyn had chosen his brother and his brother's son-in-law, leaving Robert to negotiate his own terms for ransom from his uncle, Bernard Brus, and cousin, Gilbert de Clare Earl of Gloucester, both supporters of Simon de Montfort, while Henry negotiated terms for the release of his son Prince Edward.

The last thing Robert saw as the three men left the tiny cell, was the smile on John Comyn's face. It was something he would never forget.

One year later, both Robert and his son, Robert Bruce VI, fought at the Battle of Eversham in another attempt to overthrow De Montfort. De Montfort is said to have fought bravely but his last moments were filled with terrible scenes of his men being dragged from their horses and stabbed to death while the smell of blood hung heavily in the air. One son, Henry, was killed and another one, Guy, was captured. It would be Roger Mortimer who would sever De Montfort's head from his body. His feet were cut off, then his genitals, and the last were stuck in his mouth. Lying dead in the summer rain were highborn men and those who had not been killed were wounded and captured. For their support, the Bruce's had acquired lands from the seizure of the rebellious Baron's possessions including Yorkshire, Northumberland and Bedfordshire. You can see why it was in their best interests to support and stay loyal to Henry III and his feisty son Prince Edward. The Bruce's, like the Balliol's, the Comyn's and almost all the other noble Scots houses, owned vast estates in England but without exception such estates were held by the grace and favour of the English monarchs.

Robert Bruce V's big claim was that he was a generation nearer to the throne than his rival, being the grandson of Isobel, the daughter of David, Earl of Huntingdon on his father's side. John Balliol nevertheless saw himself as having the senior claim, being the great, grandson of Margaret, the *eldest* daughter of Earl David on his mother's side. The argument however centred on which was the more important: proximity or primogeniture. And without a doubt, both believed they were the rightful heir.

The most powerful family in Scotland were the Comyns and John Comyn was himself one of the lesser competitors being a descendant going back 200 years to King Duncan I in 1034. He was also Balliol's brother-in-law, having married John Balliol's sister, and there was no love lost between the Comyns and the Bruces. They were in the mix for the throne but not quite as close to the throne as John Balliol and Robert Bruce.

There's no doubt Robert Bruce, 5th Lord of Annandale, was an educated man. He spoke three languages at an early age, having been schooled to speak, read and possibly write in the Anglo-Norman language of his Scots-Norman peers and a portion of his family. He spoke both forms of the Gaelic language, the first of his Carrick birthplace and the second of his mother's family, and the early Scots language. As heir to a considerable estate, he would also have been given working knowledge of Latin giving him and his brothers access to basic education in law, politics, scripture, philosophy and history. All beneficial if you were to be King.

But Robert Bruce was an old man by then, almost eighty at the time of the adjudication. An ancient man by anyone's reckoning, but no less formidable because of that. He was a giant, without a peer anywhere in Scotland or England and he had done everything and been everywhere.

Even in his youth, Robert Bruce was known for his good character and soundness of his word. He fought in the civil war with Henry III against Simon de Montfort and later he rode out on crusade to the Holy Land, representing the old King, because it was his duty. He had always been a true vassal to the Plantagenets, recognising them as his feudal liege. That was the feudal way honoured by the Bruces. Throughout his life, he took great pride in always speaking the truth, no matter what the cost, and no one ever called him a liar. The blood of kings flowed in his veins – pure Norman-French through his mother Isabella who was directly descended from David I whose mother had been Margaret of Wessex, the sister of Edgar the rightful king of England, and who had met by Malcolm III on a beach in Fife after their ship was blown off course on the way to Hungary. After that meeting, Malcolm had fallen in love with Margaret and married her. Robert Bruce himself had served as regent to his young cousin Alexander III during the Kings' minority. In his heart there was no doubt that his loyalty would be rewarded with the throne of Scotland.

The adjudication dragged on through 4 lengthy adjournments and 18 months in total, weighing the pros and cons of each man's claim judiciously and openly. They had two alternatives, each of them sufficiently wealthy in his own right that neither one could be suborned by the promise of riches. One of those two was a towering giant of a man whose physical courage and moral probity, integrity and honour were irreproachable and whose nature and character dictated that he could never be coerced into bowing the knee to anyone with whom he disagreed. The other was made of less solid stuff – equally valid in the strength of his claim to the kingship, but ... less ... in his other attributes.

From King Edward's point of view, it didn't matter who was actually chosen. He had all the claimants in the bag anyway and he had it all stitched up without a single drop of blood being shed. He could choose whoever he wanted. But as far as Edward was concerned, John Balliol was the perfect man for the job. He was more malleable, shall we say. The fact that Balliol had inherited lands from his father but had no money for the upkeep would guarantee keeping Balliol in his place as well.

Catching snippets of gossip, Robert Bruce must have been shocked to hear which way the vote was headed. He had sworn fealty to King Edward but there was no way he was going to do the same to John Balliol if he became the King of Scotland.

Most men would have despaired at that point, especially men of his advanced age, faced with the prospect of losing everything if his enemy John Balliol succeeded to the Scottish throne, and being too old to do anything. Not so Bruce.

In rapid succession he approached Edward, reminding him of his lifetime of loyalty and humbly requesting permission to withdraw his claim to the Scots throne on the grounds of advanced age, and to withdraw into England to live out the final years of his life in peace and quiet. At one thrust, he disarmed all his opponents by providing Edward the perfect answer to the only problem facing him. With Bruce's voluntary withdrawal from the race, no one could ever afterwards accuse Edward of using undue influence in the election of Balliol.

Of course, there was a price for such a sweet piece of collusion. In order for Bruce to be able to retire to England and remain there at peace, he must be able, in good conscience, to reassign his Annandale holdings and his responsibilities to his Annandale folk, in their entirety, including his yet-to-be-valid claim to the Scots throne, to his eldest son, Robert Bruce VI, Earl of Carrick. Edward was glad to accede to that and the first part of Bruce's plan for eventual triumph was in place. By doing this one simple task, the Bruce estates were safe from his enemies, the Balliol's and the Comyn's.

Or so he thought.

As expected, the court adjudicated in favour of Balliol. Robert the Bruce may be one generation ahead of Balliol but Balliol's ancestor had been the elder sister, they stated. Edward gracefully accepted the decision of the court and formally declared John Balliol as the next King of Scots.

The next day, on 17th November, 1292, in the chancel of St Cuthbert's Church in Norham, Edward formally accepted the decision of the auditors and declared John Balliol as the next King of Scots. He then accepted the homage of Balliol for the kingdom of Scotland and three days later Balliol left for Scone to be inaugurated as King of Scots on the royal Stone of Scone.

Bruce was 80 years old when he retired to his castle at Lochmaben and took no further part in politics except for one detail. The next year he set sail for Bergen in Norway for the marriage of his daughter Isabel to King Eric II of Norway, the father of the late Maid of Norway. Her dowry was noted as being precious clothes, 2 golden boilers, 24 silver plate, 4 silver salt cellars and 12 two-handled soup bowls. Within a year of returning to Scotland, Robert died in May 1295 and by October, his son, Robert Bruce, 6th of Annandale and Carrick, clearly acting upon his father's strict instructions but doing so a little reluctantly, in turn surrendered his earldom and his right to the throne to his own son, Robert Bruce, 7th Earl of Annandale and Carrick, who was now only 18 years old, for the same reason his father had, to safeguard their holdings. But it would be his 18-year-old son, Robert, who would be the next in line for the throne, not his father, if anything should happen to Balliol. In the meantime, being extremely cautious, the Bruce lands would be safe in his son's hands and their old enemies would be neutered.

At around the same time, Domhnal I, Earl of Mar, was seeking a strong ally that could help protect his clan from covetous neighbours. When the succession crisis first arose, Domhnal was already amid a clan dispute with John Comyn, his maternal uncle, who was pillaging Domhnal's lands. He was eager to strengthen his clan and he found a natural ally in the powerful Bruce family.

What he had was a bargaining tool: his 19-year-old daughter Isabella. Domhnal saw the young Earl of Carrick as a potential future King of Scots so pursuing a marriage between Isabella and Robert Bruce, to strengthen his position, was a smart move.

Even before the succession dispute, the House of Bruce had sought a political marriage with Clan Mar so this arrangement was perfect. The two clans shared enemies and the marriage could only strengthen each other. If you were a betting person, you'd realise that the Bruce claim to the throne was anything but dead.

Death during childbirth was far from uncommon in the medieval ages. Pregnancy and childbirth was considered perilous and at around nineteen, Isabella was very susceptible. As such, Isabella died delivering her daughter Marjorie the following year.

By then, John Balliol and many Scottish nobles had travelled to Newcastle to swear fealty yet again to Edward. It would be the start of an unhappy four-year reign that would end in humiliation for John Balliol and disaster for Scotland.

There are few details of Balliol's reign. It is clear that much of the authority exercised by the Guardians during the Maid of Norway's minority passed to Balliol and there is evidence that he tried to carry out the functions expected of a king, despite the implacable enmity of the Bruces. But Edward also seemed intent on humiliating him at every turn. Edward usurped the right to hear appeals from Scottish judgements and Balliol was even ordered by the Sheriff of Northumberland to appear before a court in London to account for a wine bill left unpaid by Alexander III.

Balliol found he was up against a king who had the best legal mind in Europe, a man moreover who was fully prepared to use military force if necessary to back up his claims. Edward was constantly telling him what to do and it would have been a brave man who stood up to Edward. Anyone who tried would have had to fight a war over it and John was not that man.

As always, relations with the French were tense. So when King Philip III of France died and his 17-year-old son, Philip IV came to the throne, Edward saw it as the ideal time to begin efforts to try and appease the strained relations. What Edward was to find was that even at this young age, Philip's conniving abilities exceeded his own.

The world was entering a time when France was once again becoming a notable power and the Plantagenets were still too small a family in Europe to be taken seriously. And Philip knew it. If Edward wanted peace, Philip stated, he should hand Gascony back, and if he was *really* serious, Edward was to marry Philip's 15-year-old sister into the bargain.

It was an insufferable humiliation that Edward could not swallow and the proud man promptly began preparing an army.

It was the age-old plan of assembling allies and demanding that Scottish troops help him in his war against France. But in his haste to exert his power, Edward went one step too far. He insisted, without any choice of refusal, that John Balliol raise troops to assist him in his war with Philip V of France and then stand behind him. Together, their combined armies would head off into battle and surely win.

If Edward thought that the Scots had been put in their place, he was wrong. It was a glaring mistake for Edward not to realise that bullying Scotland would only result in their defiance. Without a doubt, it was time for Scottish action.

It wasn't just the slighted Bruces who were disappointed in John Balliol and his inability to stand up to Edward. His own family were frustrated with him and it was John Comyn, his brother-in-law, who finally made the first move. Both their fathers had fought at Lewes under King Henry and it was then the bonds had been cemented. But it was time to do something that did not include familial bonds. Since Balliol could not stop the manipulation and bullying from Edward, since he had allowed Edward to remain as overlord in Scotland, since he had forfeited precious Scottish towns to England, things had to change.

Balliol was told that a meeting of Parliament at Scone had decided to put the direction of affairs into the hands of a Council of Twelve and although Balliol would remain king, he was effectively being side-lined. The real power would now rest with Balliol's main supporters, the Comyn family, and *they* knew what to do.

In towns and villages across Scotland, word spread quickly that John Balliol had been replaced by the new Council of Twelve. Men conversed in worried tones, wondering what would happen now. A few were pleased by the change, blaming Balliol's weakness for the loss of Scotland's liberties and believing the new council would restore their rights. Many more were troubled in light of Edward's bloody conquest of Wales.

As rumours flew, the council organised a delegation to leave Stirling to negotiate a treaty of their own with the French King. The treaty was simple. Should Edward attack France, the Scots would wage war on England. In return, the French would wage war on England if Scotland were attacked. Then they awaited the approach of the new year with bated breath.

This important treaty, named the Auld Alliance (Scots for Old Alliance) would renew time and again in the future, regardless of whether either kingdom was at war with England at the time. The motive would be purely precautionary and would play an important role in the War of Scottish Independence, The War of the Roses and the Hundred Year's War.

As promised, as Edward's army marched into France, the Scots duly marched into England sending raiding parties into Cumberland and destroying towns around Carlisle. Rising through the bottleneck of negotiation, war could only erupt.

Buoyed with the hope of French military assistance as Edward's army marched into France, the Scots raised a national army and assembled at Caddonlea, the traditional site of a Scottish *wapinschaw* (inspection of weapons) four miles south of Selkirk on 11th March.

Significantly, but not surprisingly, the Bruces refused to attend the muster. It was a stark choice: either fight for a king they hated and lose their English estates, or betray their kingdom and lose their Scottish lands.

For Robert Bruce VI, the choice was clear. He had been scathing, telling Balliol's messengers that he would rather lose his lands and his life than lift his sword for the pretender on the throne and as a result their Annandale lands were declared forfeit by John Balliol who then granted them to John Comyn's cousin, Earl of Buchan, head of the Black Comyns.

The Bruces weren't the only Scottish nobles who refused to muster. Their old friend and member of the Alliance at Turnberry, Earl Patrick of Dunbar also declined to fight, as did the Earl of Angus. Both chose to remain loyal to Edward and were summarily disinherited.

What Comyn and Balliol didn't know was that Robert Bruce VI had already been in contact with his old ally Edward who had subsequently made Robert the Governor of Carlisle, keeping all his English lands. Robert Bruce VI then led his family and his men out of Annandale. Bearing as much as they could carry, despite young Robert the Bruce's wife Isabella being five months pregnant, they made their way across the border to Carlisle.

The fuse was lit.

Scotland waited for Edward's response and they didn't have to wait long. With the biggest army ever to be sent north, Edward's sizeable army of 4,000 cavalry and 25,000 infantry marched into Scotland on 1st March 1296. He'd had enough and he was going to show them that he was not a man to do things by half.

By the middle of March, Edward had joined the English army in person as it moved to a new encampment near the village of Brunton, north of Alnwick. Here he celebrated Easter on 25th March and received renewed pledges of fealty from the Bruces (father and son) and other Scottish barons for their lands in Scotland.

In response, Edwards tellingly referred to John Balliol as 'the former

King of Scotland'. To the Bruces it could only have meant that the throne was up for grabs again.

It was the Scots who struck the first blow on 26th March with a strong Scottish force led by John Comyn the younger of Buchan. He attacked Carlisle, which was held by the dispossessed Lord of Annandale and his son, young Robert Bruce, 7th Earl of Carrick, but the formidable fortifications were too strong to be stormed and the attack was repulsed with little difficulty.

It was Edward's turn for the counter-invasion he had been planning all winter. He moved across the border at Coldstream and on 30th March launched a ferocious assault on Berwick, the wealthiest commercial town in Scotland.

He must have looked like a giant as he stared down from the hill overlooking Berwick, which at the time was on Scottish soil. As trumpets blared and drums pounded, the blustery wind would have been blowing his beard wildly, strewn with silvery grey whiskers, and his long hair would have whipped around his face. His handsome, twisted mouth would have been smiling but it would have been the smile of a man who wonders which bug to squash first. As the two armies clashed below, they would have seen him high above them, his hair blowing, mail gleaming and an evil smile on his battle-weathered face against the clear blue sky. He would have been thinking that vengeance was best taken piece by piece.

What occurred was the beginning of one of the most terrible massacres in medieval history. Berwick would never be the same and it was to be a bleak day for Scotland as thousands of corpses were thrown like garbage down wells and into the sea.

For two days, blood flowed from the slain and of the town's 12,500 inhabitants, only 5,000 survived the slaughter. Edward ordered 7500, men and women, to be massacred, the ultimate war atrocity. The local clergy begged for pity but Edward was just warming up. Berwick castle held out, however, until the garrison commanded by Sir William Douglas (who offered himself as hostage) were promised truce and safe conduct from the burning town.

Edward then advanced into the heartland of Scotland at Dunbar and all resistance buckled. English sources claimed that 10,000 Scots were killed, which seems an impossibly exaggerated figure. Dunbar Castle promptly surrendered, followed by Roxburgh, Edinburgh, Stirling and Perth, and many of the leading barons of Scotland, including Atholl, Ross, Menteith and John Comyn the Younger were taken prisoner and sent to the Tower of London. Scotland was paralysed and helpless. Then Edward turned his attention back to John Balliol who had fled with the Comyns after Dunbar.

Balliol had no chance whatsoever of escape. After weeks on the road, he was a visibly broken man with a wasted face and body. Along with the other barons, he was captured and sent to the Tower of London to join the other barons during which time Edward took full advantage of his victory.

Edward was out for a show. At a humiliating ceremony in Montrose a week later, Balliol walked slowly towards the platform where Edward sat waiting. To one side, stood his father-in-law, John de Warenne Earl of Surrey holding a roll of parchment. Crowded behind him were lawyers, royal officials and Bishop Anthony Bek. The Earl of Surrey's gruff voice sounded as he unrolled the document to read the charges against Balliol and as agreed by his surrender, he would now resign his kingdom. When Surrey finished reading, he stepped back, his eyes fixed somewhere distant of his wretched son-in-law. For a moment, Balliol stood uncertain as two knights moved towards him, each holding a dagger, until they began picking at the threads of the red lion adorning Balliol's surcoat.

He had known this was coming. When the head of the lion embroidered on the material was loose, one of the knights gave his dagger to his comrade and took hold of the flap of cloth. With one almighty tug, he ripped downward, tearing the royal arms clean off the surcoat. Balliol staggered backwards, off-balance, his surcoat trailing red threads. Edward had made Balliol the King of Scotland and now he had unmade him.

Balliol was led down the steps of the dais and escorted to the Tower of London along with the rest of the Scottish nobles that had been captured. He was soon moved to a more comfortable house arrest in Hertford and after three years he was released on the condition he would stay in papal custody at one of Pope Boniface's residences.

You have to give Robert Bruce VI some credit for persistence and bravery. Watching the insignia stripped from Balliol, he pushed his way forward and asked to be granted the Kingdom in his stead. Edward's gaze didn't waver or lose its chill. He turned slowly, like a snake before it lunges, the hard lines of his face sharpened by the sun's blaze and his eyes narrowed. For a long moment, Edward didn't speak. When he did, his voice was acid. *'Have we nothing better to do than win kingdoms for you?'* He then turned and left Robert Bruce VI standing alone, stock-still in the middle of the crowds.

Edward had made it plainly obvious he no intention of handing over the throne to Robert Bruce or any other Scottish upstart. Firstly, he made a triumphal trip north as far as Moray Firth where he ransacked the country systematically. The Great Seal of Scotland was ceremoniously broken in two, the Stone of Scone was removed and sent south to Westminster Abbey where it was placed in the chapel dedicated to St Edward the Confessor. The State archives were packed into fifty-three containers and shipped out of the country before Edward ordered the removal of the Scottish crown jewels along with Scotland's strongest symbol of independence, the precious relic of Scotland's only royal saint, the Black Rood of St Margaret.

It was as if he was ticking off items on his list. Next, he left his newly acquired kingdom in the hands of the Earl of Surrey as his Governor before establishing an exchequer at Berwick on the Westminster model. Then he appointed English sheriffs the length and breadth of the country before garrisoning English soldiers in major castles.

It had all taken a bare five months to complete.

From his refuge in the Scottish highlands William Wallace had been watching and seething. The Scots loved their country and they loved their independence and they were nothing if not totally patriotic and it was these final acts that tipped them over the edge.

William had been holding back his raggedy army of men who had been itching for a fight and he wasn't about to hold them back another day. What they lacked in experience they made up for in cold-bloodedness and determination. Wallace was about to show Edward what it was like to face a race of people who were fierce in their patriotism of their country and who wouldn't give up without a fight.

William Wallace belonged to one of the minor knightly families which made up the feudal following of the powerful Stewart family which had been granted the lands of modern Renfrewshire by King David I. The Wallaces seem to have come to Scotland with the Stewarts: the name 'Wallace' may be a corruption of 'le Waleys', suggesting that they could have come from the Welsh Marshes. Little is known of his early life, even the date of his birth is uncertain although most historians accept a date around 1272, which would put him in his mid-twenties when he first 'raised his head' in 1297.

Wallace seems to have fallen foul of the English regime early, around the time of the hearing to decide who would take the throne. When the nobles were compelled to swear fealty to King Edward as their overlord, William's father refused and was outlawed for it. Shortly afterwards, there was a clash between a group of Ayrshire men and English soldiers, supposedly there to keep the peace. Wallace's father came out of hiding to join the mob who were responsible for the deaths of the 5 soldiers and English knights pursued his band until he was captured. William's father was struck down, his legs cut away from under him and left to bleed out on the hillside. It was an appalling way to die and not long after his mother died in abject poverty.

By the time Balliol took the throne, William was living with his uncle, the Sheriff of Ayr, but he already had a great deal of resentment towards the English who had been responsible for the deaths of both his parents.

In Dundee, he is said to have killed, in a street confrontation, a young man named Selby, the 'overbearing' son of the English constable of Dundee Castle. He managed to make his escape but from then on he was an outlaw, a notorious fugitive with a reputation for lethal brawling. Later, when he was fishing on Irvine Water, he is said to have killed a couple of English soldiers who demanded that he give them his catch.

To the English, Wallace was merely a brigand. But it was this that appealed to a deep-seated Scottish resentment of English domination. He was a fully-fledged guerrilla, implacably dedicated to the destruction of the English troops who garrisoned Scotland's towns and castles, with a formidable band of disciplined, battle-hardened followers at his back. He travelled the countryside with his men, murdering Englishmen at every opportunity, attacking and capturing castles apparently at will. What was believed to drive him was a fierce love of liberty for his suffering country, and absolute dedication to the idea of independence for the Scottish nation. He had all the attributes of a born leader: charisma, bravery, nerve, decisiveness and the ability to inspire men to follow him. All the Scottish sources attest to his exceptional strength and size, and some put him at almost seven feet tall, with broad shoulders, hips and strong legs.

The turning point in Wallace's spectacular career came after he secretly married a beautiful young heiress named Marion Braidfoot of Lanark. At the time, Lanark Castle was the seat of an English sheriff, Sir William Heselrig. One day in May 1297, even with a price on his head, Wallace was paying a secret visit to his wife who had recently given birth to a daughter, but because of his uncommonly huge height, Wallace's presence was easily discovered by the soldiery. He and his followers managed to escape after a typically bloody fight but it was Marion and her daughter who was captured and was cruelly put to death, locked up in a house then set alight.

In a murderous fury of grief, Wallace struck back at once. That night, he and his men infiltrated in ones and twos, then formed a surprise attack on the sheriff's residence. They burst into the castle where Wallace hacked Heselrig's body to pieces in his bed. When Heselrig's son rushed to his father's assistance, Wallace killed him too. His men then went on a rampage of slaughter, cutting down every Englishmen in sight. After that, there was no going back for Wallace and his companions. Wallace had arrived and the rebellion had begun in a blood bath.

News of the killing of Heselrig and the massacre of his entire garrison sent shock waves all the way to London. Without giving notice, Sir Henry Percy and Sir Robert Clifford were sent across the border where they surrounded the rebellious nobles and their followers encamped at Irvine on the Ayrshire coast. After lengthy negotiations, the Scots surrendered without a fight on 7th July 1297, giving hostages for good behaviour on condition that they would not have to go to fight for Edward in France. On this agreement, the fight fizzled out with what I can only imagine Wallace thinking it was under humiliating circumstances. Among those who renewed their pledges of loyalty to Edward was young Robert Bruce, 7th Earl of Carrick.

But Wallace was not about to be beaten. After the daring raid on Lanark, Wallace marched south to join forces with Sir William Douglas who had escaped from the Tower after Berwick and was marching south again in open defiance of Edward, reportedly threatening to drive the English out of Scotland singlehandedly.

After another foray in the south-west of Scotland, they moved north with a hand-picked body of men to Scone where the English Justiciar of Scotland, William Ormesby, was holding court and outlawing all those who would not take an oath of fealty to Edward. As Wallace approached Dundee,

Ormesby's troops melted nervously away while Ormesby himself fled to Edinburgh to raise the alarm that bands of rebels were roaming the countryside.

Wallace and Lord Douglas left Douglasdale and marched northwest, leading a large number of men towards Ayr and Irvine, where they were joined by James Stewart, the 5th hereditary High Steward of Scotland, one of the most powerful magnates of the realm. With a this powerful group assembled in Ayr, the Steward's home territories, everyone waited for Edward' reaction.

As expected, Edward was not merely angry, he was apoplectic. More importantly, he was out for revenge. He declared Scotland to be in a state of revolt against himself, its overlord and lawful liege. He was a Plantagenet, the King of England, and his word was law.

In actual fact, he was only saying what his barons wanted to hear. His barons were in a state of near mutiny because of his obsession with war in France and he was very close to losing control of them. And if that meant stating Scotland was in rebellion, then so be it. Saying those words gave him the means to bring the barons back to heel by catering to their greed and lust for a conquest close to home. Scotland provided Edward with the excuse he needed. And that's all the barons wanted to hear.

As for Wallace, his sole purpose in the uprising was to sweep the English out of Scotland in the name of their king, John Balliol. In the Scots eyes, that was noble and patriotic but to Edward and the English people, it was rebellion, plain and simple. As Lord Paramount of Scotland, and that was the indisputable title he awarded himself, Edward in his own mind already outranked a mere Scottish king. He had proved that by arraigning and dispossessing Balliol as a disloyal vassal and stripping him of his kingship. Thus any rising in Balliol's name could only be perceived by Edward as rebellion against his overlordship.

What he wanted was to get over to France with an army, to finish the war and put Philip Capet firmly in his place. That was more important to him than the nuisance of what he perceived as a few rebellious Scots. He had defeated them in a battle at Berwick and he had the greater part of the Scots nobility in his prisons. The problem of Scotland, he reasoned, was largely solved, save for a few local outbreaks.

Edward had been busy with preparations for his expedition to France when he heard the news regarding Wallace and Lord Douglas and he furiously halted preparations. His orders were that Wallace and his men were to be crushed. He chose John Warenne, Earl of Surrey, once again his right-hand-man, as his commander-in-chief to raise an army from the north of England. His job was to give support to Stirling, the key fortress in Scotland, and to deal in any way he saw fit with Wallace who was now besieging another major English-held castle at Dundee. With that, Edward set sail for France satisfied the matter was in hand.

When Wallace heard of the huge army marching north, he broke off the siege of Dundee Castle and sent urgent word to General Andrew Murray in Inverness to come and join him. They met at Perth and together the two generals led their troops on to Stirling, ready to wait the inevitable confrontation with the approaching English army. Wallace was about to show Edward what it was like to face a race of people who were fierce in their patriotism of their country and who wouldn't give up without a fight.

Edward should have left his grievance with France behind him. Instead, on 11th September 1297, John Warenne was to find himself face to face with Wallace on the other side of Stirling Bridge.

Wallace and Murray had arrived at Stirling well before the English did and already taken up position near the Abbey Craig which would give them a clear view of the approaching English army. On the eve of the battle, James the Steward and Malcolm, Earl of Lennox, who were nominally attached to the English army, volunteered to go and talk with the Scots, but their overtures were brusquely rebuffed. Two friars were then despatched to renew the offers of peace, but once again the offers were refused by Wallace.

That evening, Warenne must have stood on the walls of Stirling Castle with the sun setting in his eyes. In the marshy plains below the castle, distant pools of water would have reflected the light. The crimson sky would have been filled with flocks of birds and the air would have been fragrant with the smell of herbs from the garden where the servants worked in the dusk collecting plants for the kitchen. He would have seen people moving through the castle grounds and the grassy stockade below the walls before falling sheer to the flow-speckled meadows that sloped down to the backs of the river. And he would have just made out the wooden bridge over the inky waters below and the lights of Wallace's army blinking at him further on. As he breathed in the smoky air from their fires, he would have turned and given orders for the English army to cross the bridge the next morning for a frontal attack on the Scots before retiring for the night.

At dawn, the morning of 11th September, 1297, the English infantry were preparing to cross the bridge by deploying on the marshy ground on the north side of the rived when they were recalled. John Warenne had not yet risen from his bed. When he eventually arrived, he saw the lightly-armed Scottish army, consisting of Wallace and his band of brigands, glaring at him from the other side of the bridge. Warenne listened in silence as his officers urgently tried to convince him that the bridge would be a death-trap because it was so narrow, especially with Wallace waiting on the other side. They argued that it would take 11 hours to move their entire army across the bridge. In that time, they would be open to attack and totally vulnerable. And what if Wallace met them halfway and attacked before the passage was complete? On the other hand there was a ford farther upstream where cavalry could cross sixty at a time and they could then attack the Scots from the flank while the main army was crossing the bridge. Sound advice but it was rejected.

Warenne was a battle-hardened commander but he made one fateful mistake that day. He refused to listen to his knights. The army would attack on the bridge, he stated.

He must have smiled to himself when he looked back at his own waiting army of 10,000 foot soldiers despite his lieutenant urging him to hurry up. Eventually it was Cressingham, the hugely obese Treasurer of Scotland, who urged Warenne to hurry up since a flanking movement would probably make the Scots retreat and thus prolong the war, which was costing a great deal of money.

Warenne dismissed the cautions of his knights, ordered the horn to be sounded and the massed ranks to be moved towards the bridge.

As the knights had predicted, Wallace watched eagerly as the English troops moved slowly forward. Slow, because no more than two or three horses could ride over it abreast. By midday, less than half the army had reached the halfway point.

On the north side of the river, Wallace could hardly believe his luck. All they had to do was wait. Wallace had little experience as a leader but he had what most good commanders needed. Instinct. He waited for the exact right moment when around seven thousand English soldiers covered half the bridge, the front lines not far from the cavalry, before he gave the signal. A blast from his horn echoed down to his troops below his vantage point on the top of Abbey Craig, making the English troops look up as he spurred his horse down the steep oath from the Craig. Meeting up with their men at the bottom, he and Sir Andrew Murray led the small mounted force along the causeway, riding hard towards the English. Then he hurled the full force of his men at them. Scottish spearmen surged towards the bridge and neither the floundering English horsemen or the panicking foot soldiers could escape.

The Scots had a field day. Warenne could only watch helplessly as nearly half his men were cut to pieces or drowned in the deep waters of the Forth in the space of an hour. Cressingham, who had crossed the bridge confidently at the head of the English knights, was an early victim of spears where he was pulled from his horse and butchered. The English *Lanercost Chronicle* said his body was flayed and his skin used to make a baldric for Wallace's sword.

All across the meadows, to either side of the causeway, lay the bodies of thousands of dead and dying men. The grass had been trampled into a grey sludge, streaked with streams of blood. Men and horses were entwined, a tangle of shredded limbs and clothing. Banners lay in the mud, drowning in blood, and beside them helmets had been battered on to heads, the metal dented and scored by hammer blows or axe strikes.

William's men picked through the bodies, not for signs of life but for spoils. Some of his men who had fought in the battle barefoot now gratefully eased the boots off dead men's feet. Some cut pouch strings from belts or tugged wine skins from saddle packs.

At the head of the bridge, the piles of dead were at their highest, some corpses already consumed by fire, the charred bodies visible in the flames. Stirling Bridge, the key to the north, had been their doom.

According to the English chroniclers, 100 English men-at-arms and 5,000 foot-soldiers perished that day. Meanwhile James the Steward and the Earl of Lennox fell upon the retreating baggage train of the English and plundered it of much of its cargo.

Edward had released the monster and Wallace was the result.

It was a dramatic victory and an achievement of immense psychological importance to Wallace's rag-tag army of Scottish resistance. Not one of the powerful Scottish magnates had been present to lead it. They were either languishing in English prisons or had compromised themselves through their oaths of fealty to Edward. In one frenzied hour, a legend was born and Wallace and his gallant young co-commander Murray were now the *de facto* joint rulers of Scotland, working in the name of John Balliol, their deposed king. The people rallied to them, including most churchmen and some of the least known nobles but there was still work to be done.

The battle had not been won without a cost. Murray had sustained terrible wounds in the fighting and his life hung in the balance for almost two months. By November, his body gave in and he died of his wounds, leaving Wallace to carry on as the sole ruler of the realm.

With bad news after bad news filtering back to Edward, all he could do was to enter into a long series of desperate negotiations with France. It was simply beyond his resources to stay in France and struggle with the Scots at the same time.

The truce with France certainly wasn't what Edward imagined. After five years, Philip was still demanding Edward marry his sister, Princess Margaret, now 20 years old to Edward's 60, as well as making a betrothal between Edward's son, Edward of Caernarfon, and Philip's youngest daughter Isabella. To soften the deal, Philip agreed to hand over a handsome dowry for each girl and with little money left in his pocket, Edward was forced to listen.

Edward knew that time was running out for him. Wallace was proving to be his equal in every way. He was ruthless, brutal and he played dirty. Without hesitating any longer, the marriage took place and very soon afterwards, Margaret declared she was pregnant.

When Edward returned to England, he was to find Wallace was appointed the new Guardian of Scotland. Before he had been angry. Now, with everything he had been forced to give up in France, he wanted absolute bloody revenge. There would be no truce with Scotland and there would certainly be no mercy.

Edward hastened with his whole army, as well as the Welsh army, to Scotland where Wallace waited for him. By then Wallace's position in Scotland seems to have been made official when he was knighted by an unnamed earl. He gained the title of Sole Guardian and styled himself *'Wilhelmes Wallays, Knight, Guardian of the Kingdom of Scotland and Leader of its Armies, in the name of the illustrious Prince, Lord John (Balliol), by the Grace of God King of Scotland'.*

It was too much to hope, however, that all the leading magnates would regard Wallace as someone fit enough to lead the Scottish army. Many regarded him with contempt, perhaps even jealousy. Leading an army was the role of the nobility, they argued, not a low-ranking young upstart.

And that's when Robert the Bruce stepped in.

Initially, despite their resentment towards the English, many were afraid to support him. After all, hadn't he and his family given their fealty to Edward and supported him for many years? Was he a spy now burrowing out Scots to hand over to Edward? He had to work hard and swallow his pride to prove himself and to do that, he had to do what Wallace and the others were doing and win the hearts of his people by winning them back their lands. Gradually, as the weeks went by, more drifted to Robert's company although some were still unsure if they could trust him.

Through Autumn and a bitterly cold winter, he gradually gained their trust. And when his father's lands of Annandale were burned to the ground and his people terrorised, they gradually began to believe his defection was genuine.

Edward wasn't about to let a repeat of Stirling Bridge happen. This time, he was going to be fully prepared. Through the spring and into the hot summer days, he prepared for war. Writs were sent out for the royal court calling men of the realm to serve, from the earls and their retinues down to the poorest infantryman. Crossbowmen were called up as were the archers of Sherwood Forest and commissioners travelled through northern England and the shires of conquered Wales selecting men for the conflict to come. More than 25,000 were ordered to serve as infantry, as well as a large contingent of longbow men from Wales.

Farmers put down their ploughs and blacksmiths put down their hammers to pick up weapons of war. Younger men, drawn by the offer of a wage, came forward eagerly, clutching bows and arrows. Swords were sharpened, helmets cleaned of rust and mail mended. In the middle of summer, the Welsh foot soldiers set out, marching in long lines up the coast and over the mountain barriers of Snowdon, moving slowly and inexorably towards Carlisle and the northern border. The king's officials rode out to granaries, breweries and markets to stockpile sacks of wheat and oats, barrels of wine, beer and mutton. The merchant sailors of the Cinque Ports were kept busy, readying the ships at Dover, Rye and Hythe for the transportation of these provisions and a blockade was established in the Channel to prevent any French vessels from coming to the aid of the Scots.

In time, all supplies were gathered and men conscripted. With the call to arms ringing throughout the shires, Edward moved his seat of government to York. Here he waited stone-faced and silent. The men of England were united in their determination to annihilate Wallace and the peasant army, avenging the deaths of friends and kinsmen who had died on the meadows of Stirling Bridge.

In early June, knights gathered with their lords beneath the walls of their castles, surrounded by squires, banner-bearers and wagons laden with tents and equipment. In towns and villages across the northern counties, men kissed wives goodbye before heading out to join the gangs of soldiers thronging the market squares. Tramping along dusty roads, sweating and complaining beneath steel-blue skies, these companies made their way north to join the army of Welsh foot soldiers gathering on the border. From the south, the ships carrying the host's supplies set sail, sweeping their oars into a dead calm to glide slowly up the coast of England. Far out into the North Sea, towering clouds pulsed with lightning trailed by misty bands of rain. The sailors watched this darkening sky uneasily as they rowed through the airless days.

Despite all the meticulous planning, the logistical organisation of moving such a huge army through hostile territory broke down because the Scots had been busy as well. They had been scorching crops and driving their livestock into the forests. Men and women of the southern shires were told to head north, carrying all supplies. They left nothing for the English to feed upon. The Lowlands of Scotland were left bare. They had devastated their own fields and food stocks in a scorched-earth policy to deprive the invaders of any sustenance and the momentum of the English march began to falter.

The army had to stop a few miles west of Edinburgh to await provisions from ships coming up from Berwick. Most of the ships never arrived because of the bad weather and those that did carried wine, not wheat. Soon the great army was hungry, mutinous and riddled with disease and there were furious drunken altercations between the Welsh archers and the

English foot-soldiers, leading to brawls in which many died, including some priests who had tried to separate the combatants.

Edward's army was in deep trouble. Furthermore, he had no idea what the enemy was up to. For all he knew, the Scots might be planning to mount a massive raid into England in his absence.

On the morning of Monday, 21st July, he was on the point of falling back to Edinburgh to try to feed and calm his demoralised troops, when two Scottish earls (Dunbar and Angus) sent word to his camp that the Scottish army had been sighted within striking distance, only 29 kilometres away, lurking in the great forest near Falkirk. With that he marched towards Falkirk.

That night they rested on the Burgh Muir south of Linlithgow. In case the Scots tried to surprise them with a night raid, the English lay down to sleep in combat readiness, while knights tethered their huge stallions by their sides. At some time during the night, chroniclers say Edward was injured by his charger, breaking two ribs and alarm rippled through the uneasy, wakeful army. To calm his men's fears, the elderly Edward hauled himself into the saddle, strapped and sitting ramrod straight, and gave the order to break camp at once and move on to the enemy.

We can only speculate what went through Wallace's mind when he saw the size of Edward's army advancing through the early morning mist. Did he welcome the chance of a great showdown or was he silently nervous knowing his own army was weary and exhausted?

Whatever his thoughts, Wallace resolutely drew up his army on the slope of a hill on 22nd July 1298, with a forest behind him and a stream with a low-lying boggy meadow in front of him. The nucleus of his army lay in his spearman, trained infantry equipped with 12-foot spears. He also had a corps of skilled archers from Ettrick under the command of James the Steward's brother, Sir John Stewart of Jedburgh. What his army lacked was heavy cavalry, the armoured squadrons of experienced fighting knights that Edward had. When the armies faced each other on the battlefield, there would be a very considerable imbalance in military power as well as numbers.

The Battle of Falkirk was a sharp contrast to Stirling Bridge. This time, Wallace's army was battle-weary and hungry and Wallace was forced to take a defensive position instead of his preferred aggressive one. He was also without his outstanding military commander, Sir Andrew Murray, and he was up against a new and devastatingly effective weapon, the long-range English longbow.

The battle was lost for the Scots almost as soon as the first Welsh arrows began to fall. It was a devastating blow to Wallace who lost trusted friends and loyal supporters in the battle.

The dust of that grievous battle has still not settled 700 years on. From it emerged a legend which has survived down the centuries against all the evidence to the contrary: the idea that Robert Bruce, the future king, had fought on the English side against his own countrymen. According to the Scotichronicon and later a poem named simply named *Wallace*, Bruce himself led the pursuit of the fleeing Scots and had overtaken Wallace whom he told off for his arrogance in trying to oppose the power of the King of England. Wallace's dignified reply was:

"Robert, Robert, it is your inactivity and womanish cowardice that spur me to the liberation of the native land that is legally yours. And indeed it is an effete man even now, ready as he is to advance from bed to battle, from the shadow into the sunlight with a pampered body accustomed to a soft life feebly taking up the weight of battle. It is he who has made me so presumptuous, perhaps even foolish, and has compelled me to attempt these tasks."

With those words, Wallace fled with his men to the safety of the hills.

Robert Bruce was said to be like a man awakening from a deep sleep. The power of Wallace's words entered his heart and he must have begun to realise he was on the wrong side. He was 22 years old and had been bickering with his father for years. Balliol was broken and now deposed and Scotland was without a king. Any oaths given to Edward had been from the vanquished to the victor. Bruce must have realised he was fighting against his own people all along and it would have brought him up short. It must have been a heady volatile feeling because he knew that if he did what his heart told him to do, his father would disown him and his lands would be forfeited and taken by Edward. But then again, Edward was carving up Scotland to suit his own designs anyway. Soon there would be no Scots left in authority. It would have turned his mind to the true course – Scotland.

No amount of imaginative embellishment or justification can disguise the bitter fact that Wallace, the leader who had inspired a whole race of people to fight for independence and nationhood, had failed in his greatest test – and failed disastrously. Wallace took a gamble and lost. Later, Bruce would take a similar gamble and win. Sometimes you have to take the gamble, otherwise you never can win.

Falkirk was Edward's victory and he enjoyed it. Confident that he would soon be told where Wallace was hiding, he went on an orgy of executions.

The defeat at Falkirk presaged the end of Wallace's brief period as the acknowledge leader of the Realm and the Scottish army. Soon afterwards, because of his failure, Wallace resigned his position as Guardian of Scotland, and disappeared from all but a very few of the official records which have survived. No one knows the circumstances of his resignation. Did he feel he had lost the authority which only military success could bestow? Could he no longer stomach the jealous politicking of his noble rivals? For whatever reason, a few weeks after the battle, Wallace stepped down from his frontline position and dropped out of sight into comparative obscurity in Europe, possibly to gain support and the help of an army.

Finally, in the autumn of 1301, John Balliol was released from papal custody and had returned to his ancestral estates in Picardy, France. This must have looked deeply ominous to Robert Bruce: the looming restoration of Balliol (whom he had never recognised as King of Scots) would have meant a restoration of Comyn power in the land as well and the end of his own hopes to achieve the throne. Probably because of this, in January 1302, he turned back to the English side.

His submission was well received by Edward, who was equally concerned about a possible return of Balliol and Bruce seems to have been given a promise – implicit at least – that Edward would support him in his claim to the crown if Balliol were restored to the throne. Bruce's submission to Edward was rewarded by a marriage alliance with Elizabeth de Burgh, a daughter of the Earl of Ulster. This second marriage would bring him much-needed support in Ireland in later years. The immediate effect of his defection meant even his traditional supporters like James the Steward (Stewart) and the Earl of Atholl lost faith in him.

By 1303, Wallace was back in Scotland, having returned from an abortive mission in Europe. There is no evidence that he mustered an army of any strength, although it appears that he took part in some engagements against the English, in particularly a successful foray against an expeditionary English force at Roslin. Castles and strongholds were falling to Edward all over Scotland by then, apart from the pivotal fortress of Stirling Castle, which he bypassed. He was keeping Stirling for a showpiece end to his conquest of Scotland.

Despite Robert's return to the English side, relations between Robert and Edward were wary at best. Then in March 1304 his position in life changed with the death of his father and since the longstanding claim to the throne now reverted to him, his position was made extraordinarily difficult.

Wallace evaded capture for seven years until 5th August 1305, a fugitive hiding in caves and forests as the net closed in around him. On that day, a Scottish knight by the name of John de Menteith, a member of the Stewart family and an uncle of Sir John Stewart who had died with his archers at the Battle of Falkirk, went down in history as an arch-traitor, the man who betrayed and delivered their hero over to English soldiers near Glasgow for the sake of £100 bounty on Wallace's head. Menteith had fought with the Scots at the Battle of Dunbar in 1296 and been imprisoned for his pains, but he had earned his release by fighting for Edward on the expedition to France in 1297. As part of the kings pardon, he was appointed Sheriff of Dumbarton and Constable of Dumbarton Castle in March 1304.

Wallace had no suspicions whatsoever when one of Menteith's nephews attached himself to Wallace's dwindling band. Menteith was a close personal friend of Wallace and Wallace was godfather to two of his children. Wallace trusted him completely. So when he was lured to Glasgow with the promise of a meeting with Robert Bruce, Wallace went willingly. On the way, he was overpowered and taken to Dumbarton Castle in chains then handed over to a professional soldier who had recently been appointed Warden of Scotland south of the Forth. From there he was taken on a 17-day journey, his hands bound behind his back and his feet roped beneath his horse's belly. In every town and village the local people turned out to stare and jeer at the shackled ogre who had plagued their king for so many years. When the procession reached London, he was taken to Westminster Hall and tried for treason.

As an outlaw, Wallace was already a condemned man. There would be no jury, no witnesses and no defence for the charges of treason, murder, spoliation of property, robbery, arson, sacrilege and atrocities and 'horrible enormities' of every kind. His only response was, '*I could not be a traitor to Edward, for I was never his subject.*'

On 23rd August 1305, Wallace was taken from the hall, stripped naked and dragged backwards through the city for more than four miles at the heels of a horse to the Elms at Smithfield. He was hung but released half-alive from the gallows. After he regained consciousness, he was castrated, eviscerated and his bowels burnt before him. Following his bowels, came his lungs and liver and finally his heart, when his long agony came to an end. After that, he was beheaded, his body cut into four parts while his preserved head (dipped in tar) was placed on a pike atop London Bridge. His limbs were displayed, separately, in Newcastle, Berwick, Stirling and Aberdeen.

The brutal execution of William Wallace must have sent a shiver of apprehension through the ranks of the Scottish aristocracy as a dire warning of the penalty for crossing King Edward. As far as Edward was concerned, with the death of Wallace, Scotland was dead as well. What he actually did was the opposite. He had created a martyr who never compromised himself with the English (unlike Robert Bruce) and as far as the Scots were concerned, they had only just started.

The resistance movement led by William Wallace had placed Robert Bruce in a real quandary. Wallace consistently fought in the name of the man he regarded as the rightful King of Scots, John Balliol, who had been deposed by Edward I. The Bruce family on the other hand, felt that their own claim to the throne was stronger than Balliol's. Robert was caught in the difficult dilemma of having to reconcile the conflicting demands of being a vassal of the kings of both Scotland and England. Now in his early thirties, he was planning ahead to when Edward was dead, trying to stay safe on both sides. He was once again out of favour with Edward after the death of his father and as a man with a daughter and a new wife, he was playing a dangerous game.

The vacuum caused by Wallace's death was filled by the appointment of two Guardians. One was Robert Bruce, the other John Comyn, Lord of Badenoch, the Red Comyn, a blood relative of John Balliol.

We know of Robert Bruce's ancestry and claim to the throne but John Comyn was related to many powerful nobles both in Scotland and England

and was letting Edward know that fact. He also had a powerful claim to the Scottish throne through his descent from Donald III on his father's side and David I on his mother's side as well as being the nephew of John Balliol. He wanted his name remembered in history and he wanted it at any cost.

Unbeknownst to Bruce, in a secret agreement with Edward, John Comyn agreed to forfeit his claim to the Scottish throne if the Bruce lands were handed over to him and of course, Edward agreed. With the agreement hot in his hands, Edward planned to arrest Bruce while he was at English court.

Fortunately for Bruce, a friend heard of Edward's deal with Comyn and warned him in the nick of time. Bruce barely escaped the English court in the dark of night, making his way quickly to Scotland. He was on his way to the Church of Greyfriars at Dumfries and he was going to have it out with Comyn once and for all.

Both were ambitious men and they certainly did not get along. In the heat of the argument, Bruce accused Comyn of treachery. Swords clashed and blows were exchanged but in the end, it was Bruce who fatally stabbed Comyn while he was standing before the high altar of the monastery.

The deed was done much sooner than Bruce would have wanted and in worse circumstances than he could have envisaged. Whatever contingency plans he might have had with others had to be brought forward because this was murder. In a church. This sin meant excommunication and expulsion from the Catholic Church and spending eternity in hell. It was a steep price to pay for an impulsive act. But it was done and couldn't be taken back.

There was no time to lose. He had a lot to do before Edward heard the news so speed was needed. Once Edward heard, all hell would break loose.

The Comyn castles in the south-west were seized while Bruce went to Glasgow to make peace with the Church. He made his confession and received absolution for his sin in exchange for an oath that as king he would be obedient to the clergy of Scotland. Then he rode hastily off to be proclaimed king. Six weeks later, he was standing in front of Bishop William de Lamberton at Scone being crowned King of Scots with an alliance of land owners standing firmly behind him. The royal robes and vestments had been hidden from the English but were now brought out by the bishop and draped over Robert. It was no more than he felt was his right. After all, he was a true descendent of the House of Wessex, not a usurper like the Plantagenets or the Normans who had invaded in 1066.

The traditional role of leading the new king to the throne should have been taken by the Earl of Fife, but he was only 16 years old and still a ward of King Edward in England. In his place the Earl's aunt, Isabel MacDuff of Fife, the Countess of Buchan, claimed her familial right to enthrone the king. She led Bruce to the throne and set a simple gold circlet on his head. The young Earl of Buchan was a cousin of the murdered Comyn and his Aunt Isabella's defection to the Bruce cause was a terrible blow to him. Family or not, in the near future it would cost her dearly. Later that year, she was captured by the English and imprisoned for four years in an open wooden cage which was suspended from the battlements of Berwick Castle.

Robert's hurried coronation was the starting signal for the outbreak of civil war in Scotland. When word of Comyn's death reached Edward, he responded with expected brutality. Bruce's usurpation of the throne was the last straw.

Bruce knew full well Edward would retaliate. He had already sent his wife, two sisters and his daughter north for safety under the protection of his brother Neil Bruce and the Earl of Atholl, along with his remaining men and the Countess of Buchan.

But as always, Fate was about to step in.

They almost made it. If it hadn't been for John MacDougall of Argyll, son-in-law of the murdered Comyn and owner of Dunstffnage Castle along the way, they would never have been captured and handed over to the English, forcing Bruce to flee without them.

While Bruce desperately gathered his army together, Edward indulged himself in an orgy of punishments and executions. Bruce's entire family suffered solitary confinement with daily public humiliation while another sister was hung in a wooden cage alongside the Countess of Buchan from the battlements of Berwick Castle. His youngest brother was hung, drawn and quartered.

When Bruce emerged from hiding a year later, it was as a reinvigorated guerrilla leader ready for revenge to take on Edward and his army.

His renewed campaign began disastrously. One division led by two of his brothers headed for Galloway but no sooner had they landed at Loch

Ryan than they were captured and dragged off to Carlisle where they too were hanged and beheaded.

If Bruce had wanted Edward dead in the past, he was determined now. Bruce had learnt a hard lesson delivered by Edward and he would never allow himself to be trapped again. He knew his greatest weapon was his knowledge of the Scottish countryside and he planned to use it to his full advantage. He also knew that with his small ill-equipped army, he could never expect to defeat the English in an open battle.

At 68, Edward was far from well. He was physically shattered from years of warfare and his health was beginning to fail him. By 1306, he was being carried around in a litter. Beside him was his young bride who wanted for nothing and close behind was their two young boys and a daughter. But because he was physically weak didn't mean he was finished. His mind was still strong and he had men who would do the fighting for him.

Determined to crush the Scots once and for all, Edward sent an army into Scotland led by his son Prince Edward, Earl of Caernarfon, while he himself continued on to Lanercost Priory, not far short of the border, where he was forced to rest.

The rest would last nearly 6 months while from his sickbed he directed operations via testy letters to his commanders.

It must have been obvious that Edward had not long to live. Many English nobles were dreading the day because it would mean his weak and ineffectual son, Prince Edward, would be king. Edward had spent years trying to train his son in the art of warfare but he was continually disappointed by him. It wasn't as if his son wasn't as physically impressive as his father, because he was. He had all his father's good points and none of the bad ones. Except for the Plantagenet temper. That little personality trait they definitely shared and they continually clashed. His personality was just not the same as his father's.

On July 7th, 1307, their worst fears happened. Edward died and his son Edward took over as Edward II.

Edward was 23 years old when he came to the throne. He was the oldest surviving son but his character was nothing like his father's. Unlike his father's political marriage, Edward's marriage to Isabella, the daughter of Philippe IV of France, was a disaster from the beginning. She had to endure

Edward's obsession with his 'friend' Piers Gaveston who was just the first of his 'favourites'.

To give Edward his due, he did continue his father's intent to subjugate Scotland to England's will. He was just unable to maintain the impetus. Perhaps we should feel a little sorry for him because his first task as king was to come up against a ruthless war leader like Robert the Bruce at a time when the English people were becoming increasingly resentful of the demands of the 'Scottish War'. But this only went to prove his inability to rule and act.

By the end of August, he'd had enough of Scotland and returned to London. There would be no further expeditions into Scotland for three years during which time Robert Bruce took every opportunity to consolidate his position.

As soon as the English army left, Bruce descended on Galloway in furious retaliation against the MacDougall clan to avenge the deaths of his brothers. Then, leaving his brother Edward in Galloway, he struck north into Argyll to eliminate his enemies in the north.

Bruce's surge into the lands of the MacDougalls set of all the right alarm signals and John MacDougall, lying ill in Dunstaffnage Castle, asked for, and received, a truce. With his rear secure, his next target was the formidable Inverlochy Castle three kilometres north-east of Fort William, guarding the southern end of the Great Glen. By November 1307, Bruce was sweeping onwards to Urquhart Castle on Loch Ness, one of the strongest castles in the north, taking it and destroying it. Inverness Castle surrendered and Bruce had it dismantled to ensure it could not be retaken and used against him. From there, Nairn Castle was razed to the ground at the same time as the Earl of Ross, a key Comyn ally in the north, was frightened into a 6-month truce. Elgin Castle fell soon after and called for a truce.

It was at this point that Bruce fell seriously ill. He was so ill he could neither eat nor drink and his men feared for his life. Bruce and his men withdrew to a defensive position in a wooded bog near Huntly and at this point, on Christmas Day, John Comyn, the young Earl of Buchan, arrived with a strong force. For some reason, Buchan's troops were unwilling to do battle and Buchan withdrew to muster reinforcements. When he returned a week later, Bruce had gone.

That was the turning point for Bruce. Still not yet fully recovered, he destroyed the Earl's castle at Balvenie then moved on to Duffus Castle near Elgin, and Tarradale Castle on the Black Isle.

The final showdown came in 1308. The Earl of Buchan had assembled a large army at Inverurie and Bruce, still being carried around on a litter, was determined to meet the threat head-on. Somewhere on the road between Inverurie and Oldmeldrum the two armies met.

Bruce was helped into his saddle, where he needed two men to hold him upright. The mere sight of him on his charger had an electrifying effect on Buchan's men who took fright and fled while the Earl hurried south to England to seek support.

With the earldom now undefended, Bruce laid waste to the Buchan lands from end to end where all the earl's supporters were put to the sword. Every village was burned and it would be fifty years before the district of Buchan recovered from the terrible harrying carried out by Bruce.

There is no doubt that Edward II's early years on the throne were marked by an inability to act, easing the task of Robert Bruce. Edward's preoccupation with his 'favourite' Piers Gaveston certainly helped. Edward always seemed to be waiting for the right time to strike back but the opportunity never materialised.

When an English expedition into Scotland eventually materialised in September 1310, it was a dismal failure. Starved of the troops he had demanded from his nobles, Edward could do little more than make a tour of an English garrison in the south of Scotland and in November, he retired to Berwick for the winter. When he tried to revive the expedition in the summer of 1311, he was no more successful in raising troops and making progress and he simply retired south in July to face the unrest at home.

By then, Bruce had already started turning the screw and extended his control further south, picking off the English-garrisoned strongholds, one by one. By March 1314, he had recaptured most of the castles in Scotland held by the English and was sending raiding parties into northern England as far as Carlisle. The greatest prize fell into Bruce's hands in 1314. Edinburgh Castle.

Only one key castle now remained in English hands. Stirling Castle.

The year 1314 is remembered for many reasons. It was the year that Robert the Bruce advanced his army to Stirling after a skirmish started between Bruce and Henry de Bohun, the Earl of Hereford's nephew. It was the year that Bruce cut Henry de Bohun's head clean in two with his sword and it was the year that Bruce's army was camped half a mile away by a stream called the Bannockburn that was notorious for flooding and boggy conditions. And it was the year that Edward put his total army of 25,000 men into the field to face Robert the Bruce in battle. The Battle of Bannockburn was about to begin and it was the most wretched and memorable battle in Scottish history.

Edward made a serious mistake by thinking that his superior numbers alone would be an advantage to defeat the Scots. He forgot that 25,000 men took a lot to feed, and his ill-disciplined men had seen little success in eight years of campaigns. Still, he insisted they march and ride towards Scotland to defeat his old enemy. Towards the end of June, they left under Edward's baffling command, sure in the fact that Robert the Bruce would now face the full vengeance of England.

Not only did Bruce have prior warning, he knew the actual day that Edward would come north and fight. It gave him time to think about the size of his force and his strategy. Scotland's army was composed of around 10,000 men consisting of infantry spearman who feared nothing but however fearless and fast they were, how would they cope against the English archers? He needed foresight and he needed to take precautions.

First, he chose a position where he was surrounded by impenetrable woods on one side and the bend of a river on the other. The area covered barely 700 metres but it was a hard spot for the invading army to see. Secondly, his army dug potholes along the side of the road where his men would wait, covered and concealed with bracken, for the attack on the unsuspecting English army. Thirdly, his knights would be waiting at the rear to stop any English soldiers from retreating.

Once his plans were in place, he waited three days until 24th June. The Battle of Bannockburn was about to begin.

There was no way to quieten the incredible noise made from Edward's army of steel-clad horsemen. Bruce could hear them coming from miles away. Unaware of anything except attacking and killing the Scots, Edward thundered down the slope towards Bannockburn. When the English were almost upon them, the Scottish spearmen sprang out of the potholes in an almighty crash just as Bruce had anticipated.

Edward's plan had been for his archers to shoot arrows into the air as

William the Conqueror had done at Hastings. But in the mayhem, they soon found that if they did, they would hit more of their own men than the Scottish infantry. With the English army in terrible disarray, Bruce increased the pressure and sent reinforcements thundering towards them.

From Edward's vantage point, he could see Bruce's army high on the hills roaring towards him and he knew he was in serious trouble. As the Scottish hurled forward down the slope, Edward gave the order to retreat before the bulk of the army could recross the Bannockburn.

Edward barely escaped with his life. As the English army fled over the border, Edward's men managed to drag him from the battlefield after his horse was killed beneath him. Edward's departure from the field was the signal for a general English flight but by then, the battle had turned into a massacre. The Bannock Burn was filled with corpses and the River Forth, meandering lazily past Stirling Castle, filled with dead soldiers. In their panic to escape, the English left behind precious military equipment, expensive armour and gold plate that Bruce made full use of. As a personal bonus for him, he was able to exchange the captured Earl of Hereford for his wife Elizabeth de Burgh, his sister Mary and his daughter Marjory.

It was the worst defeat sustained by the English since the Battle of Hastings in 1066 and Bruce kept the pressure up by advancing further into English territory and further on to Ireland.

John Balliol lived until just after the Battle of Bannockburn but by then Robert was already crowned King of Scotland. But what Robert found was that he had the same problem as John Balliol had, namely that he was not the unanimous choice, and he was opposed by the Balliol/Comyn faction.

It is curious to consider that if we accept that John Balliol was dethroned illegally, he was still the legal King, and Robert Bruce was a usurper (not to mention a sacrilegious murderer) when he seized the Crown. If Edward I was within his rights to dethrone Balliol, (and many question that right), then Robert Bruce was a rebel and the English King was perfectly entitled to install whomsoever he wished on the Scottish throne. Either way, Robert Bruce was the King by force of arms and despite popular perception, and the best efforts of Mel Gibson in the movie Braveheart, William Wallace fought for the restoration of John Balliol to the throne and would never have suggested Robert could be the King.

The matter would not left with the death of John Balliol, however. He had a son named Edward we will see later on.

After Bannockburn, Edward limped his way back to London in humiliating defeat only to find a very different England than the one he left. England was suffering the harshest winter they could ever remember. Floods had swept villages away and massive lakes had formed in low-lying parts. The rain had ruined crops and had plunged England into a horrendous famine. People were starving and had begun to eat anything they could find, resorting to eating pets, rotten corn and on occasion, the bodies of their dead. Disease was even spreading through their precious sheep and cattle. People were close to insanity. His father would have seen the devastation and taken action. Not Edward.

To make matters worse for him, he also found that his cousin Thomas Earl of Lancaster was heading a rebellion against him and with the new threat, Edward left them alone. It was very fortunate timing for Scotland because Bruce, now confirmed as the King, continued his devastation. He continued into northern England time and again, taking Berwick Castle back after several failed attempts, and the devastation was incalculable. He then invaded Ireland and had his brother Edward declared king there in 1316, until he was killed in battle in 1318.

When Edward returned from Bannockburn to find Lancaster in open rebellion, Edward finally snapped. Lancaster was captured and, family or not, he was punished along with his supporters. England would was to know that Edward was as thorough has his father had been.

If there had been any doubt whether Edward could be as ruthless as his father, the horror of Edward's revenge proved it and the realisation shocked the country. Bodies of executed men hung on the outskirts of town, left decaying in the sun as a reminder of what would happen if you crossed Edward the king. The Tower of London buzzed with prisoners who had been either condemned to death and had their sentences changed to life imprisonment, or were simply waiting for their turn to die.

It wasn't just Scotland. Edward also had France to contend with. The French king, Charles IV, his wife Isabella's brother, was taking full advantage of the unrest in England. He marched into Gascony and seized it, and after several bungled attempts to regain the territory, Edward was forced to send his wife back home to France on his behalf to negotiate terms with her brother.

Since things hadn't been going so well with her marriage, Isabella could hardly believe her good fortune. The thought of escaping her husband was simply too good to be true. Before Edward could change his mind, she left for France on the very next ship.

Springtime in Paris is magical but for Isabella, it was more than she had dreamed possible. After taking the time to visit family, she and her brother put their heads together. The plan was for Isabella to tell Edward that she had convinced her brother to make a truce. But first, as a sign of respect to his Uncle Charles, their 13-year-old son, Prince Edward, would have to come to France on a visit. A heartfelt promise was made that she and her son would both return to England by the summer when her brother's ruffled feathers were smooth once more.

After a slight hesitation, Edward reluctantly agreed and sent his eldest son to meet up his mother in France. His youngest son, John, would remain with him in England.

Isabella must have had her fingers crossed when the promise was made because once her son arrived in France, there was no way she was going to leave. By then, she had met an English exile, Roger de Mortimer, Earl of March, and they hit it off straight away. Within months, they were lovers.

It was a huge risk for Isabella to take. Female infidelity was a very serious offence in medieval Europe and both of Isabella's former French sisters-in-law had died as a result of their imprisonment for exactly this offence.

By the end of summer, Edward began to send urgent messages to the Pope and to Charles IV, expressing his concern about his son and wife's absence. All to no avail.

Then he heard the rumour that Isabella had begun a relationship with Roger de Mortimer and he was stupefied.

While Edward panicked in England, Isabella was thoroughly enjoying her stay in the French court and as part of her promise to her cousin Joan, Isabella and Mortimer took Prince Edward with them and travelled north to visit William I, Count of Hainaut. The plan was to betroth Prince Edward to Philippa, Joan's daughter, in exchange for a substantial dowry. This money, plus an earlier loan from her brother Charles, would be used to raise an army.

On 24th September, 1326, Isabella, Mortimer and their modest force set sail to take England for themselves. By January 1327, they had captured her husband in Wales and on 1st February, his 15-year-old son was crowned as Edward III, clearly under the thumb of his mother Isabella and Roger Mortimer.

By then, Robert Bruce knew he was dying. He had been suffering from a serious illness at about the same time that Edward II was dying under 'suspicious circumstances' in Berkeley Castle having been imprisoned there by his wife Isabella, the 'She Wolf of France' and her lover Roger Mortimer. Some chroniclers say Robert had leprosy but it's hard to accept the notion of a fully functioning king, serving in war, holding parliament and court, travelling widely and fathering several children while displaying the infectious symptoms of a leper. Other suggestions are tuberculosis, syphilis, motor neurone disease, cancer or a string of strokes. In any case, he knew he did not have long.

The problem of the succession to the Scottish throne had been a serious concern for many years. When Robert's second wife, Elizabeth de Burgh, was taken captive in 1306, she was still childless. When she was finally released from captivity after the Battle of Bannockburn, no one knew whether she was still capable of child-bearing. In April 1315, parliament enacted a decree that if the King died without a male heir, the crown should pass to his brother Edward. If both brothers died without male heirs, the crown would pass to Marjory, his daughter by his first wife, and her heirs. Shortly after being released from capture, Marjory had married Sir Walter Steward (Stewart) with her father's heartfelt consent and he was feeling confident she would produce male heirs.

Sir Walter's heritage was incredible. His family's ancestral name was Fitz-Flaad and they were reputed to be Norman by culture and training, but Breton by birth. Flaad and his son came to the notice of Henry I in England when Henry was recruiting Breton troops, and Flaad and his son were brought over and were part of the military retinue. Alan's rapid ascent to wealth and power was a symptom of troubled times. An abortive revolt by Robert de Belleme in 1102 had torn apart the Anglo-Norman system of governing the Welsh Marches so with other Breton friends, Alan was given forfeited lands in Norfolk and Shropshire, including some which had previously belonged to Robert de Belleme himself. Robert had proved a threat to

Henry I in both the Welsh Marches and in Normandy, so the king was determined to insert reliable supporters to counterbalance or replace his network of supporters. Alan received more lands since he'd proved his worth, including a large portfolio of lands in Shropshire, Clun and Oswestry and land around Peppering, near Arundel in Sussex, taken from the holding of Rainald de Bailleul, an ancestor of the house of Balliol. These were lands were granted to Rainald by William the Conqueror in recognition of his role as Sheriff of Shropshire but came into Alan's possession as a consequence of his elevation to the position of Sheriff.

As Alan's eldest son, William took over Alan's role of Sheriff of Shropshire on his death as well as the titles of Lord of Clun and Oswestry and Earl of Arundel, becoming the first of the powerful Earls of Arundel. His younger son Walter appears to have arrived in Scotland in about 1136, during the reign of David I, where he served as 'Steward', responsible for the day-to-day running of the king's household. In fact, he served in this capacity for three successive Scottish kings: David, Malcolm IV and William I 'The Lion'.

Walter increasingly witnessed royal charters from about 1150 until King David granted him the stewardship to be held hereditarily for his loyalty to the crown. This meant the title passed from Walter to his son, Alan, to his son, Walter, and so forth until Sir Walter Stewart became the 6th High Steward of Scotland on the death of his father in 1309.

At the age of 21, Walter fought against the English at the Battle of Bannockburn in 1314 where he and his cousin, Lord James Douglas, commanded the left wing of the Scot's army, although due to his youth and inexperience, he was merely the nominal leader. Following the liberation of Robert the Bruce's wife, Elizabeth de Burgh, and his daughter, Marjory, from their long captivity in England, Walter was sent to receive them at the Anglo-Scottish border and conduct them back to the Scottish royal court and one year later, Marjory and Walter were married. Sadly, one year later, she died after a riding accident in her last month of her pregnancy but almost by miracle, her child's life was saved by Caesarean section and named Robert, after his grandfather.

Walter is given the title of 'Forefather of the Stewart clan', later to become the Stuarts during the reign of Mary Queen of Scots. From the moment Walter became 1st High Steward of Scotland, the name invariably changed from Steward to Stewart, turning d's into t's at the end of the surname, becoming the Stewarts. Three generations later, they made it official.

When Edward Bruce was killed in battle in Ireland, parliament assembled to state that, failing legitimate male issue to the king, the heir to the throne was his young grandson, Robert, until the king's wife, Elizabeth, who had so far given birth to two daughters, Matilda and Margaret, delivered a son.

Finally on 1st March 1324, almost 10 years after her release from captivity, the longed-for miracle occurred: she gave birth to twin sons, David and John. Sadly, John died in infancy but David flourished and the succession to the throne was assured.

With the takeover by Isabella and Roger Mortimer until 13-year-old Edward III came of age, Robert was still strong enough to take full advantage of the chaotic situation to launch raids into England. A fragile state of truce still existed between England and Scotland but it was clear it was not going to last. All hell was about to break loose and the most intriguing and complicated era in English history was about to begin.

The Weardale Campaign was a feeble attempt by Roger Mortimer and the newly crowned 15-year-old Edward III, to put the Scots back in their place. The stand-off lasted three days and at the end, the English army marched slowly back home, defeated. That's when Robert laid out his terms in the Treaty of Northampton.

In exchange for £100,000 Sterling, the English Crown would recognise:

- The Kingdom of Scotland as fully independent
- Robert the Bruce and his heirs and successors as the rightful rulers of Scotland
- The border between Scotland and England would be as recognised under the reign of Alexander III.

As a further attempt at a continued peace, he betrothed his 4-year-old son, David, to Joan, the 6-year-old sister of Edward.

Isabel and Mortimer knew a good deal when they saw one. The money was very welcomed and with Joan betrothed to David, peace between England and Scotland was closer than it had ever been. They formally agreed and signed the treaty in the name of Edward III and on 17th July 1328, 4-year-old David was married to 7-year-old Joan.

The ink on the treaty was barely dry when 55-year-old Robert died. He had achieved the almost impossible and Scotland was brimming with self-confidence. After the constant struggle and warfare, Scotland was looking forward to a long period of peace.

But no sooner was Robert in his grave, than it all began to fall apart because now they had Robert's 5-year-old son David on the throne as David II and the governance of Scotland was once again in the hands of Guardians. It was déjà vu from when the Maid of Norway was on the throne.

* * *

DAVID and his child bride took up residence in Turnberry Castle as the Earl and Countess of Carrick and less than a year later, David was crowned King of Scots with Walter Steward acting as his regent. His minority however was to be a troubled one: Edward III would see to that.

Scotland watched warily as Edward made his presence felt in England. For Edward, it was difficult to sit by and wait patiently for his turn on the throne. He was 15 years old but he felt he had already proven himself to be a worthy soldier. So why not a king as well? And his mother, Isabella, agreed.

Westminster Abbey was once again filled to capacity with barons as they watched the crown of Edward the Confessor being placed, with extra padding of course, on the 15-year-old head of Edward. As he stood in front of the throne draped in gold cloth, he swore the same oath his father had made as the banquet hall began to fill with luxuries not to be seen for another fifty years.

Isabella had one more task to complete before she could fully relax. Her son Edward had been promised in marriage to her cousin's daughter, Philippa, and at barely 15, Edward was married to his 14-year-old bride in an opulent ceremony designed to show that English power was definitely not on the decline. Everyone was smiling and everyone seemed happy.

But even at Edward's young age he was calculating. At the next parliament, he watched silently as Mortimer dragged men into court who had been loyal to his father. Among them was his half uncle, the Earl of Kent, accused of treason. Letters were produced and the Earl was duly found guilty and sentenced to death, while his wife and children were sent to prison for life.

It was a savage decision, even for Mortimer, and for a while, there was no one to perform the execution. Eventually, another prisoner whose job it was to clean the latrines was offered his freedom to lop the top off Kent's head. Edmund, another son of Edward 1, suffered much the same fate.

As heads toppled, the questions on everyone's lips were: were Isabella and Mortimer any better than Edward II? Where they perhaps worse?

Edward watched what was happening in silence as he grew into manhood. He had not forgotten the fate of his father or his kin nor had he forgotten how his mother and her lover had used him as a pawn when he was a child. By the age of 17, he was ready for revenge.

Bad news and gossip travels fast and Mortimer had heard the rumours that some friends of Edward were planning to kill him. Of course, at court Edward's friends all strenuously denied it but they knew that the time had come to act with Mortimer watching their every move. Everyone knew what Mortimer was capable of and they had begun to fear for Edward's life as well.

One night as the castle was settling down for the night, Edward, and at least fifteen armed friends including young Henry of Lancaster, moved stealthily through the dark passages deep in Nottingham Castle. Edward's physician had provided him with an alibi for his absence during the evening meal and he'd helped by unlocking the door leading from the hidden passage to the castle keep. From deep within, the young men crept up the steps leading to the royal quarters, now known as Mortimer's Hole. Inside their quarters, Isabella, Mortimer and his two sons, Geoffrey and Edward, as well as three bishops, were silently discussing what to do regarding the very men who were slowly advancing towards the room they were occupying as they whispered urgently.

Suddenly, Edward and his men burst into the room with their swords drawn. Amid the confusion, tables were overturned and two guards were killed while one bishop attempted to escape by throwing himself down the lavatory shaft into the squalid waste below. Mortimer ran for his sword but he was far too slow. He barely made it across the room before he was captured along with his sons and the entire family was escorted to their new home, the Tower.

Isabella waited silently in the dark room for her son to return. Knowing her son's mood, it would have been the longest wait of her life.

For a young man who was out for revenge, simply sending Mortimer to the Tower of London was not enough. Not by a long shot. He had watched his father's humiliation and he wanted Mortimer to suffer every bit as much as his father had suffered. Bound and gagged in Westminster Abbey, Mortimer was accused of usurping royal power along with thirteen other crimes including the murder of his father.

It was the first time his father's murder had been spoken out loud and it was enough for Mortimer to be sentenced to death. Everyone knew he was guilty. He was hung, his lands and titles removed from his family and his body was left on the gallows for two days and nights in full view of the public.

Isabella got off rather lightly, considering her part in the plot. She was simply sent into exile for the next thirty years of her life until her death.

Edward was now his own man, ready to take the reins, and the treaty with Scotland was one of the first things he wanted to rectify. He'd waited a long time for the opportunity to wrest back the gains from Scotland which Robert Bruce had made at England's expense. And as headstrong, implacable and aggressive as his grandfather Edward I had been, Edward clearly resented the Treaty of Northampton signed by his mother and Roger Mortimer on his behalf.

Edward wasn't the only one who regarded the treaty as humiliating. Many fully agreed with him. Even though it was his young sister Joan sitting on the throne with King David, Edward overturned the Treaty, which you can imagine started fresh tempers erupting in Scotland. Barely five years after the signing and a semblance of peace in place, the quarrel with Scotland resumed all over again with a vengeance.

As Philippa produced child after child, Edward was busy making enemies both in Scotland and in France.

In France, King Charles IV had died without a direct heir, opening up a serious problem for France. His paternal cousin Philip was one of the two chief claimants to the throne and the other was Edward himself through his mother Isabella, Charles IV's sister.

The question on everyone's lips in France however was whether the crown could, or should, be passed on to Isabella's son Edward when she had not possessed the crown herself. French nobles were faced with a choice: who would give them more power and independence in their own country - a French King in Paris or a distant English King ruling mostly from London?

Ultimately, as Philip came from the *male* line and Edward came from the *female* line, he was crowned king instead of Edward.

And as you can imagine, Edward had other ideas.

He did not have to wring support from Parliament for an expedition to France. They were all urging him to act. To add fuel to the fire, Edward's sister Eleanor had been betrothed to Philip's son, John, but Philip had reneged and decided his son should marry Bonne of Bohemia instead.

Threats were sent backwards and forwards and Edward steadfastly declared that the French crown was *his* while Philip was just as determined to keep the throne for himself.

In the end, the only solution was to throw England into a war. And so, The Hundred Years War began.

While Edward fumed and fought with France, he was spreading himself pretty thinly in England. It had been 120 years since any king had set foot in Ireland and Edward wanted to be *that* king. Still seething from the French crown being snatched away from him, he was more than ready for another fight with fire in his veins and money in his treasury. He was days away from invasion when news arrived that Scotland had regrouped and were preparing to fight. When he heard, all plans were immediately put on hold. He told parliament there was a change of venue and Ireland could wait. He was going to invade Scotland instead.

Throughout the summer of 1332, battle after battle was fought. Berwick was taken back and then he moved on to Halidon Hill. By his side was his new friend, Edward Balliol. the exiled son of John Balliol, who had arrived back in England from his family estates in Picardy, ready to take the Scottish throne for himself. As support, he had both Scottish and English nobles who had been deprived of their estates by Robert Bruce and of course he had Edward III's full approval.

Balliol had very little time to enjoy being home before a surprise raid on his quarters caught him unawares and sent him scurrying across the border, riding bareback and embarrassingly in his underclothes, to the safety of Carlisle and the English.

The response from the English was immediate. A seaborne invasion of 88 ships made an unopposed landing at Kinghorn and marched on towards Perth where the new Guardian, Donald, Earl of Mar, was ready for them. He had a large army mustered and had taken up position on Dupplin Moor ready to block the advance.

As was usual, the battle began at dawn. The Scots had considerable superiority in numbers and no fewer than twelve earls in their ranks. But they were fighting uphill in blazing sunshine and the rebels were able to absorb the first punishing blows. With an army that seemed like half the size of Scotland, Edward took up a defensive position in the centre as the Scots advanced down the hill. Edward Balliol sat on his horse to his left, his uncle Earl of Norfolk was to his right and beside him was his younger brother, John of Exeter. All men watched intently as Edward's archers shot a vicious hail of arrows on the approaching Scots.

By noon it had turned into hand-to-hand combat, swiftly followed by retreat, and that's when Balliol sent in mounted reserves to finish off the exhausted fugitives. The Earl of Mar was killed along with two earls, several nobleman, sixty knights and nearly 2,000 spearmen while Balliol had lost only thirty men.

The annihilation was complete and terrible and once again it was the English archers who had done the worst damage. It was the worst of Scotland's long, sad litany of military disasters and twenty-year-old Edward III's first and only military engagement on English soil.

Scotland had fallen at the very first blow and Edward Balliol had himself crowned King of Scots one month later. The big problem for Scotland now was it had two kings: the legitimate David II and the usurper Edward Balliol.

As bad as it looked for Scotland, they still had one trick up their sleeves and that was the new Guardian who had replaced the Earl of Mar: Sir Andrew Murray, the son of William Wallace's brilliant general at the Battle of Stirling Bridge. Together with Robert Steward, (David's uncle by marriage - the husband of Robert Bruce's sister Christine) and John Randolph, (the new Earl of Moray), the men led the Scots into the third phase of the Wars of Independence.

If Scotland thought things couldn't get worse, they were mistaken. The nightmare began when Edward Balliol swore fealty to Edward III as Lord

Superior of all Scotland and ceded most of southern Scotland to the English crown while he himself was to rule the north of Scotland in Edward's name.

Scotland was right back where it had been in 1306, a province of England in the grip of civil war with their rightful king, 8-year-old David and his 10-year-old wife Joan, holed up in the impregnable fortress of Dumbarton Castle.

You didn't need to be a clairvoyant to know the two children were in serious danger. As Balliol was re-instated on the throne and declared king with very little support, they were hurriedly whisked away, in the nick of time, to the safety of Boulogne in France. They were greeted with open arms by Philippe VI, a cousin to both children, where they would stay for the next seven years.

On a serious high, Edward spent much of 1333/34 marching north across the lowlands of Scotland before moving on to the Highlands, burning, looting and killing with no purpose in mind apart from exercising his power over his enemies.

With Scotland subdued on one side, the dispute with France was brought back into the limelight. What Edward needed was supporters and resources because by now he was almost bankrupt and floundering badly. Many of his supporters were either given knighthoods or titles as rewards and alongside this new nobility was Edward's eldest son, 6-year-old Edward of Woodstock. In later years, he would be called The Black Prince, not just for his black armour but also because of his diabolical reputation. He was also given the title of Duke of Cornwall, marking him as the next heir to the throne.

It seemed no matter what Edward did, it always turned out to cost him more money. Not wanting to take any responsibility, he became obsessed with the idea that this state of affairs was due, not to his bad management, but due to corruption in his government and he set out on a shocking vendetta to dismiss leading officials from the top down.

First to go was the treasurer, then senior judges. A constable of the Tower was next, followed by leading merchants. The exchequer was fired and it was decreed that all taxes were to be paid straight into Edward's own treasury. He replaced sheriffs then turned on the Archbishop of Canterbury, accusing him of treason. He vowed never to appoint a clergyman as one of his minsters again nor anyone he could not hang, draw or behead if he failed in his service to his king. No one was safe and no one was spared.

It was a grand speech that shifted the blame of the disaster in France from himself to his government and while he ranted, Philippa gave birth to another son, Edmund. While she nursed her new baby, Edward turned his interest back to France where he still believed he had a legitimate claim to the throne through his mother. He decided to stage a major attack on France sailing for Normandy in 1338 with a force of 115 ships and 15,000 men where he quickly defeated Caen. From there, he continued marching across northern France and Scotland breathed a sigh of relief.

Sir Andrew Murray died in the spring of that year and the role of Guardian fell to Robert Stewart (The Steward). He was the 22-year old son of Robert Bruce's daughter Marjory and was eight years *older* than his uncle, King David II. As David's nephew, he was also heir presumptive to the throne since David and Joanna had no children.

Edward was so preoccupied with France, he forgot that David had supporters in Scotland who were never going to give up. While Edward continued marching through France, they obtained the upper hand in Scotland and in 1341, David and Joan returned home to Scotland. At 17 years old, David was ready to take the reins of government into his own hands as he waited for Edward to return to England.

David's return marked a new stage in Scotland's affairs. The Bruce cause seemed more secure with Balliol and his dwindling group of supporters no longer posing a major threat, while on the continent, Edward was deeply embroiled in his war.

David set about restoring his battered kingdom to normality, strengthening his administration, restoring royal revenues, and making a few destructive raids into northern England to get his own back on the absent Edward.

In October 1346 however, he made one raid too many.

Over the past twenty years, Scotland seems to have suffered through battle after battle with England, beginning with Stirling, then Falkirk, Bannockburn and Halidon's Hill. In 1346, they were to face yet another. The Battle of Neville's Cross.

Edward had won a stunning victory over the French at the Battle of Crecy where his archers with their deadly longbows destroyed a larger and more heavily armoured French army. He was besieging Calais when King Phillipe VI called upon Scotland to create a diversion by invading England. To the Scots, the call to invade Northumberland seemed an excellent opportunity of safe plunder. They were confident that the north of England would be a relatively easy target. They were wrong. The Archbishop of York, together with two powerful northern magnates, Lord Ralph Neville and Lord Henry Percy, had mustered an army to meet the Scottish challenge.

Perhaps the Scots were a little hasty in calling the English army a band of 'miserable monks and pig drivers' because helping them out was their old rival, Edward Balliol. He swung into action with a thunderous flank attach which sent both Robert Stewart's battalions to the left and Sir William Douglas' battalions to the right, reeling back into disorder.

When Robert Stewart saw the terrible losses the Douglas' battalions suffered, he withdrew his men from the field, leaving the king's division exposed and stranded. While his men quickly encircled he young king, David fought on courageously but was cornered under a bridge over the River Browney, terribly injured by an arrow in the face. Valiantly, he knocked out the teeth of one of his attackers before he was overpowered and captured then he was carried off to Bamburgh Castle where surgeons from York were brought to treat his serious injuries. Later he was taken to the Tower of London in triumph then moved to Oldham Castle in Hampshire where he would remain his brother-in-law's captive in England for the next eleven years.

Although many great Scottish lords died at Neville's Cross and many were taken prisoner, one Lord escaped from the debacle: David's nephew, Robert Stewart. He made his way back to Scotland unscathed with his own men and a leading supporter, Patrick Earl of March, but his reputation would always be shadowed by this apparent abandonment of his uncle, the king, in his hour of need instead of running to save his own skin.

In the aftermath, the English overran much of southern Scotland with Edward Balliol at their head. But there was little support for Balliol now. He lingered on in the south-west until 1356 when he resigned his claim to the Scottish throne to Edward III personally in return for £2000. He died, childless eight years later.

With David held captive in London, Scotland needed a guardian. Despite the slur, and because David and Joan did not have any children,

Robert Stewart was therefore heir to the throne and the logical choice to run the government, being the son of Robert the Bruce's daughter Marjorie.

Whether that had been Robert Stewart's hope or plan, he wasted no time feathering his nest since he had no way of knowing how long he had on the throne. For the next eleven years while David was held captive, Stewart busied himself using the opportunity to create a formidable and astounding network of power through marriage-alliances and territorial deals throughout Scotland, while collecting earldoms and baronies all over the country. He first married his mistress Elizabeth Mure, legitimising his four sons and six daughters to her, then began marrying each of them to wealthy, powerful men. Margaret, he gave to John, Lord of the Isles, the most powerful magnate in the Gaelic speaking west. Marjorie he gave to John Dunbar, Earl of Moray. Elizabeth married Thomas de la Hay, Lord High Constable of Scotland and Isabel married James Douglas, 2nd Earl of Douglas. Upon the death of his wife in 1355, he then married Euphemia de Ross, the widowed Countess of Moray, and added two more daughters and two sons to his brood. At 1-year-old, his son David to Euphemia, was made Earl of Strathearn and four years later, his son Walter was made Earl of Atholl. As well as his two wives and fourteen children, he also had twelve illegitimate children with several mistresses, making a grand total of twenty-six children.

But while Robert was strengthening his power base and David remained a captive, a far deadlier enemy was marching across the continent while war was holding Edward's attention.

History has no catastrophe equal to the Black Death.

The summer of 1348 was wet. The royal family was maturing and multiplying and even though Edward was only 35 and Philippa was 33, they already had nine children ranging from Edward the Black Prince, who was 18, down to the baby William of Windsor, who was only a few months old. It was the year when their daughter Joan boarded a ship and set sail for France to marry the man of her dreams, the King of Castile, unaware of the terrible danger that lay ahead of her.

When the ship stopped in Bordeaux on the way, the mayor rushed to the docks and told them it was not safe to disembark. A deadly plague had arrived. It had ripped through Cyprus and Italy and had reached Marseille.

For two years, Joan had waited for the moment when she would finally meet her new husband. She'd lived over and over the first embrace and she imagined being swept off her feet and taken to his castle nestling quietly by the sea. She was 13 years old, buzzing with excitement and there was nothing in the world that would stop her from reaching her destination. So the mayor's words of warning were pushed aside.

The character of the epidemic was appalling. The disease itself, with its frightful symptoms, was swift. At the onset, blotches appeared, then the hardening of the glands under the armpit and the groin, followed by the horde of virulent pustules. After that the victim developed a hacking cough that would develop and produce blood then vomiting. Breath, sweat and excrement stank. Delirium and insanity completed the suffering.

Princess Joan never wore her wedding dress made from thick imported silk embroidered with rich strands of gold. She never wore the suit of red velvet with two sets of twenty-four buttons made of silver gilt and enamel nor the five corsets woven with gold patterns of stars, crescents and diamonds. And she never reached her future husband waiting for her in Castile. Joan died horrifically at the same time as her baby brother William of Windsor died in agony in England.

It seemed no one was safe from the disease. No one knew how it spread and no one knew of the different methods of cross contamination. In an attempt to protect themselves, doctors filled a 'beak' containing herbs and placed it over their noses but of course, eventually everyone knew that method of protection was basically useless. Seeing a doctor with this strange contraption on his face sent dread into the hearts of the terrified people. All that could be done was to place a red cross on the doors of infected houses to inform others that the inhabitants had developed symptoms of the Black Death. A whole generation was obliterated as blank spaces appeared on all sides of society and destroyed life. This disease, along with all the other severities of the Middle Ages, was almost more than the human spirit could endure.

Throughout his captivity, David's main concern was how to secure his release. His first major attempt was in 1350, four years into his captivity. David made a deal with Edward which, in effect, pledged the Scottish throne to England in return for his freedom. The basis of the deal was that David was to be released without ransom if the Scottish parliament would accept a new heir-presumptive – one of Edward's younger sons, who was not an heir to the English throne. This son, John of Gaunt, was David's nephew through David's marriage to Joan, Edward's sister. In 1351, David was allowed parole to go to Scotland to try to persuade his subjects to accept the proposal.

Not surprisingly, the main opponent of the proposed settlement was Robert Stewart, who was the current heir-presumptive and in no way ready to step down from the throne of Scotland. This deal would put an end to his own hopes of ascending the throne and his allies carried the day by rejecting the settlement. The decision meant David had to return to captivity or risk outright war with England.

David tried again in 1354, this time with a more limited draft agreement which would obtain his release for a ransom of £60,000, a huge amount to be paid in 9 annual instalments while the Scots were to deliver twenty noble hostages as security. Once again, Robert Stewart seems to have been the stumbling block. Negotiations broke down abruptly when he committed the Scots to another military attack against England supporting France in 1355.

Edward's crushing defeat of the French at Poitiers in September 1356 removed the French card and was the last obstacle to David's release.

It took until 1357, after several protracted negotiations with the Scot's regency council, for a new treaty to be signed. A hefty ransom payable over ten years was organised and ratified by the Scottish Parliament at Scone and in November that year, David returned to Scotland immediately.

On his return, David found a country largely in ruins, devastated by constant internal warfare. His only hope was to try and diminish some of Robert Stewart's powers by promoting his own supporters into positions of territorial strength and secondly, to father sons of his own.

David's wife Joan came back with him after his release but only briefly. It seems Joan had other ideas. They had been married for thirty-four years, unhappy and childless, and within a few weeks she returned to England where she stayed until her death five years later in 1362. During those five years, David consoled himself with an English mistress by the name of Katherine Mortimer.

But there was no happy ending here. Three years into the relation, Katherine was murdered by men hired by the Earl of Angus and according to some sources, the Earl was then starved to death for his trouble.

Katherine was then replaced by a beautiful widow by the name of Margaret Drummond who had already proved her fertility by producing a son to her dead husband. By 1363, it was clear David, by then a widower after Joan's death, was planning to marry Margaret, sure that they would produce an heir, obviating the need of one from England (John of Gaunt) or Scotland (his nephew Robert Stewart). He showered her and her family with titles, lands and offices, all at the expense of Robert Stewart and his family.

It was this major upheaval that prompted the first major crisis of David's reign early in 1363. Perhaps David had been too quick in spending so much money because a coalition of angry barons who resented the king's relentless promotion of his own favourites, and certainly egged on by Robert Stewart and his sons, raised a rebellion against him.

It started with a petition presented to David complaining about the misuse of funds which had been levied to pay for his ransom. These funds, it was alleged, had been frivolously diverted to finance the king's pleasures and to reward his favourites.

Robert Stewart was nothing if not a wily politician. He seems to have realised very early on that he was backing a lost cause and within a matter of weeks, he publicly renewed his fealty to David while David dealt with the other dissident barons one by one.

The rebellion, if that's what it could be called, was an unmitigated failure not to mention a serious setback for Robert Stewart. Not only had his bluff been called, but by his submission to the king he had also alienated the support of fellow barons he had deserted and proved himself someone not to be trusted with the throne. The idea of an English succession, not through Edward III in person but through his son John of Gaunt, was not all that unattractive anymore to many people in Scotland if Robert Stewart was the other candidate.

For the rest of David's life, while making improvements to Edinburgh Castle and building a massive L-shaped tower-house crowning the eastern crags above the grassy edge of Castle Hill, he seems to have been determined to produce an male heir of his own, or to create a new heir-presumptive, anything to stop his nephew inheriting the crown. He even insisted on the marriage of Robert Stewart's eldest son John to Annabella Drummond, Margaret's niece, with the idea that the marriage could produce a male child which would ensure a Drummond-Stewart heir who might eventually ascend the throne if Margaret did not produce a son.

Perhaps David was psychic because Margaret did not produce a male heir. After a while, David seems to have given up hope of fathering a son to Margaret. In 1369, he added a twist to his saga by starting divorce proceedings against Margaret to marry his latest mistress, Agnes Dunbar, sister of the Earl of March. She, too, had children from a previous marriage, proving fertile, and David was still in his prime in his mid-forties. He put through large sums of money for her upkeep and promoted her kinsmen as was now his usual routine. He also insisted on a marriage between Agnes's brother, John Drummond and another Stewart daughter, hedging his bets. Robert Stewart watched helplessly as his own chances of retaking the throne disappeared.

And then, on 23rd February, 1371, everything changed yet again. Practically on the eve of his wedding to Agnes, David suddenly and unexpectedly died in Edinburgh Castle of unknown causes at the age of 47. For me, it was a rather suspicious, convenient death for Robert Stewart if you consider that Agnes was fertile and David was more than willing to produce more children. A male child from the union would have pushed Robert Stewart further down the snakes and ladder board away from the throne.

After all David's machinations and manoeuvrings, the man he had tried so hard to prevent inheriting the throne had simply won by simply surviving. Robert Stewart became King Robert II, the first of the long and tragically unlucky royal Stewart dynasty of Scotland.

In the end, the Bruces won the Great Cause, and through them the Stewarts came to rule Scotland and Great Britain. It is interesting to think what may have happened differently had Alexander III not ridden off in the middle of a stormy March night to meet with his new wife, 728 years ago.

THE STEWART DYNASTY

ROBERT II

Born 1316
Reign 1371 – 1390

In these days, coming to the throne at 55 years of age was late in the stage. Life was hard and Robert Stewart was seen as an elderly man. Nonetheless, he was the first of the royal Stewart dynasty and crowned King Robert II at Scone on 26th March 1371.

Robert was smart enough to know the problems that a disputed succession could produce. His very first act as king, on the day of his coronation, was to name his eldest son, John, Earl of Carrick by his first wife Elizabeth Mure, as his successor. Two years later, an elaborate Act of Succession was approved by parliament which made careful provision for a *male* Stewart succession. It ordained that, in the event of the failure of the direct male line through John, the crown should pass successively to the male heirs of Robert's four other sons: Robert, Earl of Fife, Alexander, the 'Wolf of Badenoch'), David, Earl of Strathearn and Walter, Earl of Caithness and Atholl. At this time, his heir John, who had been married since 1367 had produced two daughters but so far no son, whereas as his next son, Robert, had a 10-year-old son, Murdoch, who was now second in line of succession.

Robert's reputation is even less flattering than his uncle David's was. Perhaps the way to see Robert is as the chairman of the board of a family firmly over-stocked with ambitious and self-seeking siblings, much like Robert himself. Certainly, his family was large enough.

In the early years, he did everything he could to expand the territorial field for his extensive family network with successful marriages and bestowing numerous titles on them and their associated families. In the end, Robert had influence over eight of the fifteen earldoms either through his sons directly or by strategic marriages of his daughters to powerful lords. For some reason, this build-up of Stewart power did not appear to cause resentment among the senior magnates because their territories were not threatened.

A new picture of Robert emerges at this time, a cautious man, intent on providing continuity of a successful government. By then, the economy was doing reasonably well, wool exports were booming and high tax yields enabled him to be generous to his supporters with grants of lands, privileges and pensions. And there was no war with England, nor was there likely to be one as long as the ageing Edward III, now 70 years old, remained on the throne. But that could not be said for Edward's sons. Edward had five surviving sons and every one of them were hot-headed. In the near future, their children would wreak havoc on England in the greatest ever war between cousins. The War of the Roses.

Robert didn't have a crystal ball to see this war between brothers and cousins festering. He would have seen the death of the frail Edward III as a godsend because Edward's eldest son, The Black Prince, had died, leaving Edward's timid grandson, 10-year-old Richard, pushed into an unexpected early reign as the next King of England. A regency led by his uncles was narrowly avoided with a council of men taking over and excluding the ambitions of his eldest uncle, John of Gaunt, already a wealthy man with land and titles under his belt but greedy for more, because basically nobody liked or trusted him. Many were certain he wanted the crown for himself because he was, after all, just one little boy away from him being the king.

Also in the picture were his uncles Thomas of Woodstock and Edmund of Langley, a younger brother married to the sister of John of Gaunt's second wife, making a strong bond between the two brothers. There wasn't much the young Richard could do against three strong and powerful men.

Meanwhile, discontent over increasing taxes was growing heated. If that wasn't enough, as a result of the Black Plague, there was a shortage of manpower giving villains and ruffians the upper hand and an advantage. In a world where the people were supposed to know their place, the old order of service began to waver. English peasants began ransacking their own counties with the flash points being in Kent and Essex. One of the two main issues that set the ball rolling was why the burden of taxes should fall so heavily on the very people who could least afford them. The second issue was whether a noble had a right to keep his servant as a slave with no privileges at all. It was a common enough practice, but was it right?

Finally England erupted and from a turret in the Tower of London, an alarmed 14-year-old Richard watched London burn. Even the breeze would not have been able to take away the stink of the city below. The smell would have been indescribable. During the heavy rain, filth had risen to the surface from the remains of the Roman sewers. On the streets, the slurry would have run past pots of urine and faeces and rushed over animal dung and slop trodden down by more horses and carriages. The English had hardened themselves to the smell but in everyone's heart and mind was memory of a disease that could emerge again at any time.

While Richard watched in horror, tucked away in a closet for his own safety, Henry Bolingbroke, John of Gaunt's son and Richard's cousin, sat silently beside him. However, after the revolt, we see a more confident Richard finally emerge and turn his interests towards Scotland at the same time as Robert was having issues with his heir, John, Earl of Carrick.

John of Carrick had always been an ambitious man. At 43 years old, he was impatient to get his hands on the crown, an age-old story between both British and Scottish kings and their sons. He had established a formidable vice-regal power base in the south of Scotland and was custodian of Edinburgh Castle. Tensions were growing between John and Robert as well as his younger brothers Robert and Alexander.

While the friction continued in England, hostilities increased on the borders with war flaring between border families, especially the Douglas kin-group. Cross-border raiding and skirmishing was once again becoming endemic and war drums sounded throughout the early 1380's as the policy towards Scotland hardened under the new English government under Richard II.

By 1384, everything seemed to happen at once. It was clear a full-scale war was imminent and that the French were willing to send a sizeable force to help Scotland against the English. But at the same time, 69-year-old Robert was pushed aside in a palace coup and his son John succeeded in ousting his father off the throne and was declared Guardian of the Kingdom.

There was nothing Robert could do since John had the support of government. But if John thought it would be clear sailing, he was seriously wrong. As promised, the French had sent a force of knight and men-at-arms and they complained about their billets while the Scots complained about French arrogance and indiscriminate foraging for food. While they bickered, Richard II marched unopposed through southern Scotland with a massive English army, burning the abbeys of Dryburgh and Melrose on their way. When it reached Edinburgh it put the city and St Giles' Church to the torch, before returning in triumph to England.

The French were already feeling disgruntled with Scotland but it was the hasty 3-year treaty Scotland signed with England that sent the disgusted French home, vowing never to return except as allies of the English.

The ease with which the English had walked into Scotland had alarmed the Scots into making the truce but it was equally welcome to England since Richard was now embroiled in a revolt led by his uncle, the Duke of Gloucester. But as soon as the truce period was up, the headstrong border nobles under the leadership of James, 2nd Earl of Douglas, brother-in-law to John, were on the warpath again.

The Battle of Otterburn was about to begin.

It all began with what could be called a simple prank. The eastern prong of the Scots was led by James, Earl of Douglas, while his opponent in the north of England was Henry Percy, son and heir of the first Earl of Northumberland and better known as Henry Hotspur. During the minor skirmishes, James Douglas snatched the silk pennant from Hotspur's lance before galloping as fast as he could back to Scotland. Hotspur swore his standard would never leave England and set off in hot pursuit with a force of about eight thousand lightly-armed troops. He caught up with the Scots in their encampment to the north-west of Otterburn.

Despite Hotspur's men being tired and hungry after their long trek from Newcastle, Hotspur went straight on the attack with fierce hand-to-hand combat. The fighting went on all night with hundreds of men flailing at one another in the fitful moonlight until it soon became too dark for the English to use their most feared weapon, the longbow.

Eventually, Douglas fell, exhausted by his innumerable wounds. His one concern was that his men should not know that he had fallen. His dying wish was to be laid 'by the bracken bush' with his standard raised while his men charged back into the fray shouting the war cry *'A Douglas! A Douglas!'* As dawn broke, Hotspur found himself surrounded. As he looked around and saw between 1000 - 1,500 English casualties compared to only two or three hundred Scots, he knew he was defeated. His words were *'I will only surrender to the man by the bracken bush'*.

Although remembered in folk-lore and ballad as one of the most heroic encounters ever staged between Scots and English forces, there was nothing heroic or grand about Percy's Cross, a 'battle stone' of nothing more than a roughly carved boulder which rested drunkenly in a socket much too large for it.

With the death of James, Earl of Douglas without an heir, the carefully-knitted network of alliances created by the king's son John, Earl of Carrick, began to unravel. With territorial wrangling over the vacant earldom, John found his regional power base rapidly eroding. His accident during a tournament where he was kicked by a horse, left him virtually incapacitated and couldn't have come at a worse time. The council had very little choice but to remove him from the guardianship in favour of his younger, and more ambitious brother, Robert, Earl of Fife, who settled in nicely as the new Guardian.

Robert II died in Dundonald Castle in Ayrshire in April 1390 soon after completing an arduous royal circuit of the north-east. By then, he was 74 years old but still active in his royal duties, although his elder sons, John and Robert, had latterly exercised executive power on his behalf under close scrutiny of the council.

His death left his eldest son John to come to the throne at the age of 50, incapacitated or not. But because of the unhappy association of the name in both England and France, (John II would bring back memories of John Balliol who was John I as well as the tyrannical King John I in England 200 years before), John ascended the throne as Robert III.

ROBERT III

Born 1337
Reign 1390 – 1406

As England edged closer to the cousin's war, the War of the Roses only sixty years away, the Stewart family were having serious problems of their own. Fuming in Scotland was John's younger brother Robert, Earl of Fife, who had taken over the Guardianship in 1388. Despite the fact that his elder brother was undisputedly the rightful heir, Robert was seriously put out by John's ascension to the throne, perhaps seeing his brother as weak as well as taking his name. In addition, their younger brother Alexander, was making his presence felt as well.

Elgin Cathedral, one of the most hauntingly beautiful of Scotland's medieval buildings is called, affectionately, the 'Lantern of the North' but on 17 June 1390, three months after Robert II's death, it fell victim to the fury of the 'Wolf of Badenoch', who turned it into a real lantern of the north by setting it on fire in an orgy of destruction.

The Wolf of Badenoch was Alexander Stewart, Lord of Badenoch and Earl of Buchan, the younger and favourite son of Robert II who has been portrayed as the stereotype of dissatisfied younger royal sons. He was the third surviving son of Robert II by his mistress (later wife) Elizabeth Mure and in 1371, when his father came to the throne, Alexander was showered with lands and titles in Badenoch and the north-east, which he enhanced by marriage to Euphemia, the widowed Countess of Ross. The marriage made him Lord of Badenoch, titular Earl of Moray and Earl of Buchan. His father then appointed him the King's Lieutenant north of the Moray firth, meant to enforce justice in an area driven by feuds and fighting.

In the 1380's he was the most powerful magnate in the northern and western Highlands, conducting a long and acrimonious dispute with John Dunbar, the lawful Earl of Moray, and with the powerful and aggressive Bishop of Moray over authority in the area. He wielded the power of his office with a ruthlessness for which he was censured by the king's council in 1388. To cap it off, he was consistently and flagrantly unfaithful to his wife. Euphemia denounced the marriage as a sham and demanded the return of all the Ross lands, giving the Bishop of Moray an opportunity to censure him again.

Soon after Robert II's death and before the coronation of his elder brother, Alexander erupted from his lair in Lochindorb with a band of *'wyld wikkit Heland men'*. He ransacked Forbes, the second burgh in the earldom of Moray, then wreaked ferocious and symbolic vengeance by burning the cathedral of Elgin, together with eighteen residences of the canons and chaplains.

The destruction ranks as one of the most notorious tantrums committed in medieval Scotland but it did not go unpunished. Alexander was excommunicated by the Bishop of Moray and as soon as his brother was crowned, the king's council forced him to pay hefty reparations to the bishop in order to have the ban lifted so the cathedral could be rebuilt in stages.

Despite his brother's aggression and tantrums, John succeeded his father as Robert III.

The royal succession seemed secure with Robert III. He and his wife, Annabella Drummond, already had a son, David, who was 12 years old and four years later, another son, James, was born. His main ambition and priority as king, was to restore the crown's authority and to safeguard the Stewart succession. He created a power-base for his own precocious son, now the Earl of Carrick, where he could take part in the matters of government.

It took six years for Robert to restore his credibility until one of the most bizarre events of his reign. The Clan Combat on the North Inch of Perth in 1396.

One of the more serious and long-standing feuds in the Highlands at the time was the enmity between Clan Kay and Clan Chattan. To bring the dispute to a decisive conclusion, Robert ordered a public judicial combat in Perth where thirty warriors from each side were to fight to the death. The chosen site was the North Inch, a flat, 32-hectare meadow by the River Tay.

The sixty champions were ushered in to the martial sound of trumpets and bagpipes. No one was allowed body armour but they could carry a sword, a dagger, an axe and a crossbow with three arrows. As protection, they could use a leather shield and no one was allowed to leave the fray.

As the signal to start was given, they all loosened their arrows and flung them at one another.

Throughout the long and bloody afternoon, they hacked and thrust and stabbed at one another until at last, the Clan Chattan men emerged victorious. Eleven clansmen, including the 'guest' clansman who was the giant blacksmith, were still on their feet, although grievously wounded while the last surviving member of the Clan Kay side took to his heels and plunged into the Tay to make his escape.

The government must have hoped that this parody of a medieval tournament would both get rid of the trouble-makers in the glens and break the fighting spirit of the clans. It did neither and the feud continued.

It had become embarrassingly clear that Robert III was barely capable of exercising any kind of authority which the kingdom needed and in a time of deep depression, he called himself *'the worst of kings and the most miserable of men.'* Even historians have characterised both Robert II and Robert III as *'pathetically weak personalities'* and their reigns as *'nineteen years of senility and sixteen of infirmity'*.

Whether it was because of Robert's physical disability or his ineptitude, he created his 20-old son, Prince David, as the Duke of Rothesay, (derived from the ancestral Stewart fortress on the Isle of Bute), and his brother Robert, Earl of Fife as the Duke of Albany. Both were the first royal dukedoms to be created in Scotland and were created as assistance for Robert as he reigned while appeasing the two antagonistic men. It actually did the opposite. It proved to be the setting for what was to become a life-and-death power-struggle between the two men for the control of Scotland.

At first, the two men, uncle and nephew, worked in close co-operation. But by 1399, the General Council ended the ageing King Robert's rule due to his incapacity, and his son David was appointed as the king's lieutenant for the next three years with 'full power and commission of the King', but guided by a council of 21.

This deposition came at the same time as Richard II's deposition in England occurred by Henry IV, his cousin Henry Bolingbroke, the son of John of Gaunt. Henry had returned from exile to lead a revolt against Richard, forcing him to abdicate in Henry's favour. Richard was then imprisoned in Pontefract Castle where he died (probably murdered) by early 1400. As for Henry, he had already taken over as Henry IV and was settling in rather nicely.

If Henry Bolingbroke thought that his violent take-over would end the squabbles, he was sadly mistaken. His rule was definitely not to be a quiet one and his vicious invasion set a more dangerous pattern into motion than he could ever have imagined.

When Henry came to the throne, anyone who had run the risk to support him and put him there now rushed to cement their position in his shaky court. As expected, France regarded Henry as a usurper and they certainly were never going to accept him as the king. He was after all the son of the *third* son of Edward III and there were more rightful claims to the throne than his. For instance, there was Edmund Mortimer. With the Black Prince and his line now gone, the proper heir to the throne should have been through Edward III's *second* son, Lionel of Antwerp. From Lionel's daughter, there was an 8-year-old boy, Edmund Mortimer alive and well in Ireland.

But Henry was a big man with a big army and he was sitting right there in England, not in Ireland, and he was not a little boy.

Without a doubt, Henry was young, charming, brave and a great leader in battle. But without legitimacy, his claim was shabby. Henry was clinging to power by his fingernails and he knew it.

As it turned out, Scotland was having serious problems of their own with rulers. At the time, there were three main families in Scotland, all brawling with each other and all chest beating. All were rich and all had powerful men pushing and shoving each other – the McDonalds, the Black Douglas clan and the Stewarts.

The year 1400 was the year Prince David, Duke of Rothesay, had already taken over the reign from his father and had married into the powerful Douglas family in the Borders. His bride was Mary Douglas, daughter of Archibald 'The Grim', 3rd Earl of Douglas.

It must have seemed a sensible move, to ensure alliance with the warlords who defended the Borderlands against England. But the problem was that David was already married.

In 1395, he had gone through a form of marriage with his kinswoman Elizabeth Dunbar, daughter of the influential Earl of March. However the marriage required Papal dispensation, which had not been sought, and in 1397, the couple were compelled to separate on the understanding that they would be allowed to remarry after a suitable period.

You can only imagine the fury of the Earl of March when he heard of David's wedding to the daughter of the Earl of Douglas. It was nothing but a snub to his daughter and his anger had no bounds. He resigned his allegiance to the Scottish crown and defected to England, to the welcoming arms of Henry IV.

It reignited Henry's urge to march into Scotland, determined to reassert the lingering English claim. Henry was content to press home his advantage and show the Scots that he could march in and take over whenever he pleased and withdraw without any of the burnings and ravaging normally associated with such military incursions. As his huge English army swept unopposed northwards to Leith, the Scots retreated to the relative safety of Edinburgh Castle.

David had lost a great deal of political 'face' by his failure to stem the English invasion at the same time he lost his valuable and influential mentor: his mother. With his father grieving and powerless on the side lines, David began to assert his power as king's lieutenant and heir to the throne much more vigorously. He seized titles and revenues without consultation with his council and thereby began to alarm and alienate his uncle, Robert Duke of Albany.

By the end of 1401, Albany had had enough. As David was leaving St Andrews, where he had been demanding the keys of the episcopal castle, he was 'arrested' by two of his own councillors and handed over to Albany, who imprisoned him in St Andrews Castle. One of David's most powerful supporters, the Earl of Mar (the late queen's brother) was similarly thrown into prison. Albany moved equally swiftly to neutralise any opposition from David's other ally, his brother-in-law Archibald, who had succeeded his father as the 4th Earl of Douglas. For greater security, David was then moved from St Andrews Castle to his Albany's castle in Falkland, wearing russet robes and riding on a mule.

The only question now for Albany was what to do with his nephew. David was the heir to the throne, and certain to outlive his ailing 65-year-old father and he would certainly seek savage vengeance as soon as he was freed or inherited the throne. Albany could only have come to one conclusion: David was simply too dangerous to be allowed to live. He had to be eliminated.

Late March 1402, 24-year-old David died in his uncle's castle and the rumour was he died of starvation. Surrounded by Alban's supporters, a meeting of the General Council in May 1402 made no attempt to charge Albany with treason and asserted that David had died of *'divine providence and not otherwise'*.

Divine or not, it was certainly providential for Albany. With the king declared incapable of ruling, the heir to the throne dead and the new heir being David's 7-year-old brother James, the council had no alternative but to appoint Albany governor of the realm and regent for the young king.

The boy James would not forget the manner of his brother's death when he succeeded to the throne as James I.

Young James Stewart, the king's only surviving son, was now the last frail hope for avoiding the abrupt extinction of the senior line of the Stewart dynasty. It would only take one more 'providential' death for the crown to pass to the Albany family, the male heirs of the king's brother. The king was now confined to his castle on the Isle of Bute, an old man with a long white beard, broken by ill health.

However strong Albany's grip on the kingdom was, it was not quite complete. There was his younger, wild brother Alexander, the Wolf of Badenoch himself, still prowling the northlands unchecked with a pack of warlike sons.

The old king may have been ill, but he wasn't stupid. He could see what was happening and he feared for his young son's life. In 1404, he made him

Earl of Carrick, naming him the heir to the throne, and granted him main Stewart lands, to be held as his own, outside the authority of central government. To safeguard his life, James was then sent away to stay in the safety of St Andrews Castle for two years before sailing further in a row boat to the safety of the Bass Rock, a bare, uncomfortable sanctuary in the waters of the Forth estuary. He stayed there for one month while he waited for a ship to take him abroad. Eventually he was picked up by a merchantman from Danzig, the *Maryenknecht*, carrying wool and hides from Leith to France. Coincidentally, the *Maryenknecht* was intercepted by Norfolk pirates on the way to France and James was carried off in triumph to the Tower of London into the custody of Henry IV of England.

I've never been a big believer in coincidence.

The news hit his father hard. For all his trying, the senior thread of the Stewart dynasty looked doomed. Within days of James' capture, the old king died in his lonely castle and was buried in the comparative obscurity of Paisley Abbey instead of Scone.

With the heir to the throne a captive of England, Scottish parliament had no option but to confirm the dead king's brother, Albany, as governor and regent of Scotland in June 1406. He was to hold that position, unchallenged, until his death in 1420 at the age of 81.

THE ALBANY YEARS

1371 – 1390

For the eighteen years that James was held captive in England, part prisoner part guest, Scotland was ruled by Robert, Duke of Albany. Albany was second in line to the throne, (his brother Alexander, the Wolf of Badenoch, had died the year before James' capture) and his son Murdoch was third. During the reigns of his father (Robert II) and his brother (Robert III) he amassed tremendous wealth, and he liked the good things of life. His most enduring monument was the building of Doune Castle, overlooking the River Teith near Dunblane, as a grandiose fortress-residence.

Although it was pretty certain he had caused the death of his nephew David, there was no evidence to suggest that he tried to engineer a similar fate for James, his youngest nephew. He also did not try particularly hard to have James released from his captivity in England.

Under Henry IV, England did all it could to undermine Albany's regency, calling him a usurper, although Henry IV should have thought a little more about that title 'usurper'. The similarities between Albany's rise to power through David's imprisonment and death and Henry's own ascension to the English throne by having Richard II imprisoned and murdered were mirror-imaged.

By 1410, Henry IV was in a sorry state and unable to even ride his horse.

He had tumours on his face and was described as having *'a rotting of the flesh, drying up of the eyes and a rupture of the intestine'*. The French believed his toes had dropped off while the Scots were adamant that he had shrunk to the size of a child.

Today it is believed that he had leprosy, which can be cured, but in those days there was nothing to be done and his condition would have tested the strongest stomach.

By 1412, Henry was gripping the reins of power convulsively and one year later, he died leaving his 27-year-old son Henry to succeed him as Henry V.

While James remained an English captive, Albany took full advantage of the situation, holding on to his position in Scotland for fourteen years, unchallenged, until his death in 1420 at the age of 81. At his death, his son Murdoch took over at a time when things were hotting up in England.

From the beginning of Henry V's reign, he knew he had to watch his back. After all, there were other impatient family members waiting in a long queue to take his place on the throne, namely the Yorks and the Mortimers. And both families had loads of supporters. But by then, England was tiring of senseless feuds and brawls and Henry was more than ready to wind up the endless squabbling. He didn't have to wait long for his family to make their presence felt. The Mortimers and the Yorks were breathing down his neck.

It would be Henry's lust for war with France that would be his undoing. Henry's final conquest had been Rouen in 1419 when he began serious negotiations with Charles VI, finally signing a treaty with the French king where Charles would disinherit his own son in favour of Henry as the heir and regent of France on one condition. Henry was to marry Charles's youngest daughter, Catherine of Valois, *without* a dowry. Henry could only agree to the marriage and the conditions.

Before agreeing to the condition, Henry perhaps should have looked a little closer at his future father-in-law.

Over the past ten years, Charles VI had been showing definite signs of mental instability. His hair and nails had fallen out and he had occasional bouts of fever when he behaved incoherently. Sometimes he ran from room to room until he collapsed from exhaustion and eventually he was kept in closed shuttered apartments while his voice could be heard wailing and screaming through the walls of the castle. On a journey one day, a page dropped the king's lance with an almighty clang causing the king to draw his sword and swing it around wildly shouting *'Treason!'* He killed five men before he could be stopped. On many occasions, he forgot who he was and at times refused to wash or change his clothes, which resulted in a nasty skin complaint and lice. One time, he insisted he was made of glass and would break if anyone approached him.

His physicians blamed Charles's mental abnormality on his mother Jeanne de Bourbon who had suffered a complete nervous breakdown following the birth of her seventh child. Whatever the diagnosis, the king's condition was catastrophic.

At 18, Catherine was a beauty with delicate features, a small prim mouth and round eyes above high cheekbones. Her slender neck was bent a little to the side as she stood about to marry a battle-hardened warrior. Henry's dark protruding eyes stared at his bride from a face that was clean-shaven, showing scars including the deep one that dated back to when an arrowhead had lodge deep in his cheek and had to be cut out by a battlefield surgeon when he was sixteen.

The carrot Charles was dangling was a delicious one. Kings of England had been fighting their French cousins for centuries in battles for territories, with rare success, and not even the mighty Edward III had managed to come this tantalisingly close to victory. Even the marriage between Edward II and Isabella of France had not been enough to prevent the Hundred Years War. Catherine and Henry's marriage, therefore, was momentous for both families and Henry willingly jumped in with both feet.

But Fate was not going to let Henry go on for much longer. During a return to France one year later, Henry contracted dysentery. His condition was fatal and he knew it. He was an experienced soldier who had seen many men suffer the same fate. He made a detailed will outlining his wishes and died in the royal castle at Vincennes on 31st August two weeks short of his 36th birthday. For Catherine, there would be no fairy tale ending.

Henry did not live to be crowned King of France as he had hoped after signing the Treaty of Troyes and ironically the crazy, sickly Charles VI, survived him by two months.

A baby of barely nine months was set to become the future King of

France and he would become the youngest person ever to become the King of England.

If England thought things had been bad before, they were in for a terrible shock.

Despite James' imprisonment in Henry's prison, he was given a great deal of freedom. He had grown up to be a strong man, a skilled athlete, archer, horseman and wrestler as well as a talented musician. But he was also deeply scarred by the experiences of his childhood. He had endured a brutal upbringing in the exercise of power politics – the desperate insecurity caused by the humiliation of his father and the death of his brother David, not to mention the disgrace of his flight and his capture by English pirates. But then on the other hand, if he hadn't been captured and 'imprisoned', he would never have achieved all these skills and he wouldn't have met, and fallen in love, with Joan Beaufort, Henry's half-cousin.

The original idea of a hostage to keep Scotland in line had been good but nothing of any value had come out of it. If anything, James had had a pretty good time while in captivity. He'd had a good education and Henry V had made sure he understood how the English ran things.

But after eighteen years, and after the death of the Duke of Albany, Scotland wanted him back home. Albany's son Murdoch had taken over but all agreed it was time for James to come home. And considering the amount of money being spent on James, the English couldn't see too many benefits in keeping him in England anyway.

Then an idea struck the two uncles of the baby king, Henry VI. Instead of throwing good money after bad, they could cash in their chips and ransom James back to Scotland for £40,000. As a bonus, they would throw in Joan as James' bride before sending him back to Scotland, minus the 10,000 merks, a Scottish coinage, for her dowry as well. They could make money and create an allegiance with Scotland at the same time. To make sure Scotland held up their end of the bargain, part of the negotiations included twenty-one hostages from the Scottish nobility to be sent from Scotland to England as surety, to stay in England at their families' expense, and to be released or exchanged in the course of the payment of the ransom. In addition, a sum of £4,000 was demanded to cover the costs of the king's eighteen years' enforced residence in England. That money was to be paid in five instalments, but the first would be overlooked as Joan's dowry.

Before too long, Scotland had agreed and James married Joan in a lavish ceremony. The young couple then headed north to Scotland via Brancepeth Castle to the south-west of Durham where James was able to entertain and get to know many of his subjects for the first time, including sixty-four nobles. Early in April, he finally crossed the border into Scotland to resume the active role of king in his own country.

The true life romance of King James and Lady Joan Beaufort was to blossom into a close and enduring marriage. But James had more than love on his mind. He had grown up into a strong and well-built man ready to take over his throne although he was also deeply scarred.

Unfortunately for James, his return to Scotland was not as joyous as he'd hoped. He would have noticed the sly glances and whispers in dark corridors. Many saw him as a stranger, possibly even an English spy after thirty years spent in English company, and Murdoch certainly seconded that.

Whatever their thoughts, he was unconcerned. He was their rightful king, returned to them to take his throne back. What they would soon discover was his overriding ambition to wreak retribution against the Albany-Stewarts who had blighted his early life.

Without waiting for his coronation, James arrested Walter Stewart of Lennox, the son of the former governor, Murdoch, 2nd Duke of Albany. Murdoch was now in his sixties and was the heir-presumptive to the throne until James produced a son. Rather wisely, he had already surrendered his office as governor without demur as soon as James returned from England but his son Walter posed a much greater threat, having never concealed his hostility towards James. He was after all, the heir apparent when his father Murdoch died.

Walter was sent, rather ironically, to the bleak fortress on the Bass Rock where James himself had waited grimly for the ship to take him to France at the age of eleven. This was soon followed by the arrest of the Earl of Lennox, Murdoch's father-in-law.

The first blows had been struck.

JAMES I

Born 1394
Reign 1424 – 1437

James' coronation on 21st May 1424 was attended by bishops and magnates. It was a deliberate display of restored royal prestige where Murdoch himself placed the crown on James' head, despite his son being in detention. The next day in Perth, James summoned a 4-day meeting of parliament to pass a huge agenda of legislation which must make today's parliamentary draughtsmen sick with envy. Laws were made and taxes imposed (James had learnt all about a taxation system in England), and export duties were imposed. Above all, rebellion against the king was outlawed and burgh rents were reserved for the crown. Namely him.

James waited until the next sitting of parliament in the spring of 1425 to make his final assault on the house of Albany. On the ninth day of parliament, he suddenly arrested Duke Murdoch, his wife Isabella and his younger son Alexander. He then dismissed parliament with instructions for it to reassemble at Stirling in the middle of May for the trial of the Albany-Stewarts.

Murdoch's youngest son, James 'The Fat', had managed to escape the royal swoop and was soon encouraging discord in the Lennox area in the west of Scotland. He and his supporters attacked Dumbarton, seized the castle and burned the town to the ground.

Perhaps James had anticipated just such a rebellion in light of the laws passed in 1424. The protest had simply played into James' hand and he was fully justified now to add a charge of treason against Murdoch and the rest of the Albany family.

When parliament convened in Stirling, it set up an inquest of seven earls and fourteen lesser nobles to sit in judgement on the Albany Stewarts. And of course, the king presided. Within two days, he had systematically destroyed the most powerful family in the land. On the first day of parliament, 24th May, Walter Stewart was condemned and summarily executed on the 'Heading Hill' in front of Stirling Castle, the first state execution for more than a century. On the second day, Earl Murdoch was similarly dispatched. Isabella, the Duchess of Albany, was sent into lifelong imprisonment in Tantallon Castle, the formidable fortress which reared up on a rocky headland on the Firth of Forth.

The House of Albany had been destroyed and James' long-nursed vengeance was complete. The executioners axe had delivered three earldoms (Fife, Lennox and Menteith) and their associated territorial rights and revenues to James and it had barely taken a year.

They say revenge is best served cold.

Hindsight suggests that the executions spelled the end of the honeymoon period with his people because from then on there would be increased resentment towards James' rule. Many noble families felt dismayed, and no doubt apprehensive, over the calculated vindictiveness of the king's destruction of the Albany-Stewarts but the ordinary people were also upset at the heavy taxes imposed on them.

But having said all that, his energy never flagged and he worked hard to strengthen his country. He instituted a special court, consisting of representatives chosen from parliament, to consider complaints which could not be decided in the local courts, so that justice would be available to all, rich and poor alike. He also tried to ensure that all litigants, whether men, women or children, had access to a form of legal aid.

In the north and west, however, the 'Highland problem' remained unsolved. Alexander MacDonald, 3rd Lord of the Isles, was in open defiance of the king's writ and of course, James happily stepped in to bring them to heel.

He engineered what was to become a trademark Stewart ploy – a royal kidnapping. In 1428, he summoned the Lord of the Isles and his recalcitrant chieftains to a parliament in Inverness. As they were shown into the Great Hall of the castle, one by one, James had each of them arrested and imprisoned. Three of them were hanged, but the rest, though not Alexander MacDonald himself, were released after a few months in confinement. MacDonald may have been in prison, but his authority was undiminished and James saw no alternative but to release him in order to deal with the continued unrest in the Highlands.

But if James thought he had tamed MacDonald, he was mistaken. MacDonald retaliated with an attack on Inverness, totally burning the town to the ground. Once again, James stepped in, raising an army of 10,000 men who advanced purposefully into the Highlands.

Totally outnumbered, MacDonald finally surrendered and was taken to Edinburgh where, clad only in his shirt and drawers, was placed in front of the high altar of Holyrood Abbey and forced to make abject submission to the king. Then he was once again, imprisoned.

While battling with the Highlands, James mind was constantly on producing a son and heir. Every achievement he made would fail if he didn't succeed with this one task. Joan had given him 5 daughters so far, but no son.

Then in 1430, she gave him twin sons: Alexander and James. Nature is not selective of who should live or die and the eldest of the boys, Alexander, died in infancy. It left James with the younger son, James, as the heir to the throne and a burning determination to produce more sons. In an attempt for a backup, Joan gave James another child, but unfortunately, the child was again a daughter.

The year of 1430 was a triumph for James with the betrothal of his eldest daughter Margaret, 6 years old at the time, to the Dauphin Louis as part of a new alliance with France. It was less of a triumph for Margaret however because in 1436, at the age of 12, she married the 13-year-old Dauphin who would turn out to be a cold and vindictive man, producing a loveless marriage. She would die childless of a fever at the young age of twenty.

By this time, James had lost much of the glamour associated with the young man who returned to Scotland ready to take back his kingdom. He had lost the charm and graceful athleticism of his youth. An Italian diplomat who later became Pope Pious II, visited Scotland and described the king as *'thick-set, very fat, greedy and vindictive in nature'*.

The Christmas season of 1436 was a lavish affair held at the Dominican friary at Blackfriars, a fine old building which stood on the northern edge of the town, outside the burgh walls. During the day, the king would play tennis and in the evening he would play chess, read romances and listen to music. But behind the festivities, there was treachery afoot.

A small but determined group had decided that the only solution to what was perceived as the king's tyranny was his removal. The leaders of the conspiracy were Sir Robert Graham, (the nephew of the Earl of Strathearn who had been sent to England in 1424 as one of the hostages for the king's ransom and who carried a deep grudge against the king), and Sir Robert Stewart, the grandson and heir of James's elderly uncle, Walter Earl of Atholl, Robert III's younger brother. Walter had been suspected of complicity in the death of Prince David, Duke of Rothesay, the heir to the throne in 1402, so he was all too familiar with the politics of royal assassinations. As such, Walter was seen as the brains behind the conspiracy.

On 21st February 1437, the conspiracy moved into gear.

While James and Joan were quietly preparing for bed, Robert Stewart was laying planks across the ditch surrounding the friary and disabling the locks in the house, leaving the doors of the building unbarred. Just after midnight, a small group led by Robert Graham entered the building and made for the royal apartments.

No matter how stealthy you are in the quietness of the night, boards creak and whispers echo. James heard the noise of their arrival and instinctively knew that he was in mortal danger. The windows were barred but he prised up a floorboard with a fire iron and dropped into some sort of drain or sewer which ran under the floor and led to an outlet in the wall by the tennis court. As soon as he was inside the drain, his wife pressed the floorboards back into place. By a supreme irony of history, James had just had the outlet blocked because he was fed up with continually losing balls in the sewer. This small maintenance cost him his life.

It's one of the great 'if onlys' of history. If only he'd left it as it was he would have found it a simple matter to escape through the privy-hole instead of being trapped in the stinking prison below. His only hope was that his would-be assassins would not discover him.

Ten conspirators burst into the royal apartments and in the ensuing scuffle, the queen, in her night attire, was wounded. At first, the intruders could not find the king but after ransacking the rest of the apartments, they discovered the secret egress to the sewer.

Once they gained access to the privy (using saws, levers and axes to get in), the loose plank in the floor was quickly noticed and lifted, revealing James hiding in the muck below. In the darkness and the filth, they descended on him and submerged him before stabbing him sixteen times.

Dressed only in his nightgown and furry slippers, he put up a desperate fight. He disabled the first two men who struck him with their sword but when the others joined in, there was no hope for him.

While the fight was raging, the bleeding and scantily dressed Joan had the foresight to grab 6-year-old James and head for the sanctuary of Edinburgh Castle. She was well aware that the assailants intended to kill her and the heir as well, but when they could not find her, their only thought was to make a getaway before the town was aroused.

Letting the queen escape with her life would cost them very dearly.

The succession was still not assured as there were many factions lurking in the wings to take advantage of the chaos and confusion caused by the king's assassination. In Edinburgh, Joan was safe among her husband's loyal supporters and was able to send them to track down the assassins.

The assassins had no chance really. Sir Robert Stewart was soon captured and put to death with a barbarity said to be appalling even by medieval standards. He had to endure three days of public flogging, wearing a red-hot iron crown on his head, before the executioner's axe brought him merciful release. His death was quickly followed by the arrest of the Earl of Atholl, uncle of James and grandfather of Sir Robert Stewart.

One month after his father's murder, the tiny six-year-old, with a conspicuous vermillion birthmark covering the left side of his face, was crowned James II in Holyrood Abbey in Edinburgh rather than Scone since the trip would have been too dangerous being in Atholl territory. Parliament assembled the same day for the trial of Earl of Atholl but it was a foregone conclusion. The next day he was taken from the Tolbooth in Edinburgh and beheaded.

The jury is still out on James I: whether he was a despicable despot or whether he laid down the foundations of his dynasty. Either way James remains the most enigmatic, some say brilliant, of the early kings of the Stewart dynasty.

JAMES II

Born 1430
Reign 1437 – 1460

When James's father died, Scotland was once again plunged into discord and confusion over a regency for the young king. His mother was determined to lead it but she had precious little support. James I's ruthless attacks on leading magnates had left an extraordinary vacuum in the ranks of the traditional leaders – the earls. Usually there were ten or twelve earls on the Scottish scene. At the time of James's assassination, there were only three (Douglas, Agnus and Crawford) and within two years, the earldoms of Douglas and Angus would be inherited by under-age boys. Two other earls (Sutherland and Menteith) were still being held in England as hostages for James I's still unpaid ransom. The remaining earldoms were vacant and already subject to acrimonious disputes. It was fertile ground for dissension and unrest.

Parliament cautiously appointed Archibald Douglas, 5th Earl of Douglas, as Lieutenant-General but a year later on his death from the plague, a power struggle began in earnest with two new families stepping in

– the Crichtons, namely Sir William Crichton who was Master of the King's Household and Keeper of the key royal fortress Edinburgh Castle, and the Livingstons, namely Sir Alexander Livingston who was, almost out of the blue, appointed keeper of Stirling Castle. Historians have described them as *'bandits, ruffians and opportunists'* as they began a long feud for control of the young king and thereby control of Scotland. The two men played a deadly game of chess in which the young king and his mother were mere pawns on the board of ambition.

Queen Joan could see what was happening and was deeply concerned about her son's safety and future. In the summer of 1439, she managed to smuggle him out of Crichton's care in Edinburgh Castle and take him to Stirling Castle, perhaps hoping the Livingstons would be more amenable. It was while she was at Stirling Castle that she met, and later married, a Scottish nobleman by the name of Sir John Stewart, The Black Lorne, a most trusted ally of the Earls of Douglas, after obtaining a papal dispensation for both consanguinity and affinity.

Livingston's reaction to news of the marriage was as sharp as it was surprising. Without any authority, he locked the couple up in a cell in Stirling Castle. More than anything, because he had overstepped his boundaries, the next General Council four weeks later forced him to release them. But by then, Crichton had responded by kidnapping the young king while he was out riding near Stirling Castle and taking him back to Edinburgh Castle again.

While Crichton and Livingston were fighting it out between themselves about who would take control of the king, a third family, more powerful than either, was making a decisive move to take over the reins of power. The Douglases.

There were two distinct branches of the family operating in the fifteenth century – the 'Black Douglases' and the 'Red Douglases'. To simplify the complex genealogical tangle, the Black Douglases were Earls of Douglas and the Red Douglases were Earls of Angus. Both lines were descended from the 'good' Sir James Douglas (The Black Douglas as he was called because of his swarthy complexion) the hero-lieutenant of Robert Bruce, but the black were descended from the illegitimate son of James Douglas while the Red Douglases (so called because of the colour of their hair) were from the illegitimate son of the 2nd Earl of Douglas who had died a hero in the Battle of Otterburn.

On the death of Archibald Douglas, 5th Earl of Douglas from the plague in 1439, his 15-year-old son William succeeded him as the 6th earl of Douglas. The 8-year-old king James worshipped him and William was equally fond of the boy. Now nearly 'of age' at fifteen, William was poised to become the greatest magnate in the kingdom with 5,000 knights and spearmen at his call. For both Crichton and Livingston, Douglas represented a serious threat, and of course that meant he had to be eliminated.

Working together for a change, Crichton and Livingston invited William to dine with them and the king at Edinburgh Castle in November 1440. The grim occasion they concocted has been known as the 'Black Dinner'.

William and his younger 10-year-old brother David went there trustingly with only one attendant and were received with every mark of friendship. At the table, they were served royally with every delicacy to be found. However, at the end of the meal, a black bull's head was served on a great dish, traditionally the symbol of doom. The young men were seized despite the king's pleas and subjected to a mock trial for treason.

The speed with which the ridiculous trial took place was astounding. The young men and James were then whisked from the hall into the courtyard where an execution block had already been set up in readiness. The helpless young king wept as his friends were beheaded in front of him.

You can be sure this would stay in his heart and mind until he could take his revenge.

But there is another side to this grisly tale. And it's all about greed.

The man who succeeded as 7th Earl of Douglas was James Douglas, known as James 'the Gross' because of his obesity, who had been created Earl of Avondale after the death of James I. He was the great-uncle of the two murdered boys, (does this sound a little like the future Richard III?) but may well have been a willing party to the conspiracy. From his stronghold at Abercorn Castle, he extended the power of the Douglases. By the time he died a few years later in 1443, he had become the most powerful magnate in central Scotland. His successor William, 8th Earl of Douglas, quickly became active in government, exploiting the inherent weakness in the self-seeking coalition of Livingston and Crichton, who by then had been toppled from office and forced to give up control of Edinburgh Castle.

As this drama was unfolding, James reached his 14th birthday, which was when his minority ended, at around this same time that Queen Joan died. Joan had been decisively outplayed in the turmoil and her second husband, Sir James Stewart, swiftly sought safety in England with their three sons.

Despite James' youth, the main issue for him at this time was marriage. Many of his sisters had married into the European aristocracy, (his sister had married the Dauphin of France in 1436), and this paved the way for James to marry a princess of the house of Burgundy, Marie of Guelders, daughter of the immensely wealthy Arnold, Duke of Guelders and niece to Phillip III, Duke of Burgundy, who a member of the Capet and Valois family to which all 15th century kings of France belonged. It was a hugely prestigious match for a Stewart king but it was also a great benefit to the Scottish merchants who were able to establish lucrative new trading links with the continent.

The bride and her escorted sailed for Scotland in 1449 in a convoy of thirteen ships, bringing three hundred men-at-arms. Marie was to receive an annuity of 10,000 gold crowns (£30,000 Scots) and in a lavish ceremony at Holyrood Abbey, Marie was crowned Queen of Scotland. And at that point, 18-year-old James officially became king in his own right.

James had waited a long time for his revenge and it was well-past time. Just like his father before him, his first act was to launch an attack on the Livingston family, bringing an abrupt end to the ascendancy they had enjoyed while he was still in his minority. They forfeited everything and two of them were executed for financial misdemeanours. Crichton seems to have been spared, perhaps because he leant James a considerable loan, and died in 1454 after investing his wealth into Crichton Castle, transforming it into an impressive courtyard castle.

Then he turned his attention to the Douglas clan.

William, the 8th Earl of Douglas, was still in Rome, parading his magnificent train through the courts of Europe, when James made his first move. Irked by this ostentatious display of power, James seized two of his castles. When Douglas returned, he wisely made formal submission to the king and an uneasy truce ensued.

Douglas must have been all too aware of his vulnerability when entered into a mutual alliance with two other noblemen: John MacDonald, Lord of the Isles and 11th Earl of Ross and Alexander Lindsay, 4th Earl of Crawford. And not so unexpectedly, James saw this bond as an act of potential rebellion between the two men, creating a dangerous axis of power between two like-minded men.

In February 1452, James invited Douglas to Stirling Castle for a discussion, giving him a promise of safe-conduct. After two days of protracted wrangling, he openly accused the Earl (probably with justification) of forging links with John MacDonald and Alexander Lindsay and bluntly ordered Douglas to revoke the alliance. When Douglas said he could not and would not, James broke into a fit of temper, shouting, *"Since you will not, I shall!"* He drew his dagger and stabbed Douglas twice, once in the body and once in the neck. His court officials (many of whom would rise to great influence in later years, often in former Douglas lands) joined in the bloodbath, one allegedly striking out the earl's brain with a pole-axe and the rest stabbing him twenty-six times.

It was a particularly odious crime, since safe keeping had been given, so instead of ending the power of the Douglas clan, things progressed to an intermittent civil war for three years. It began with the new 9th Earl of Douglas (James) riding into Stirling with his brother Hugh, Earl of Ormond and 600 men. They nailed the dishonoured safe conduct to a board and dragged it through the street at the tail of a broken-down old horse. Then Douglas plundered and burned the town, formally renouncing his homage to James and offering it to England.

James knew there would be repercussions and he was just waiting to see how far the Douglas clan would go. Perhaps he didn't think they would be so blatant because he retaliated by attempting to seize Douglas lands with such savagery that the Earl of Douglas hurriedly submitted. James graciously accepted but it was just a feint. He wasn't finished by a long shot. He'd only just begun.

Two years later, he launched another attack on the Douglas lands, rolling out the newest firepower available to the monarchy and battered two of the Douglas castles into submission. In the viscous attack, Jams Douglas fled to England while his younger brothers were dealt with at a skirmish at Arkinholm. The Earl of Moray was killed, the Earl of Ormond was captured and later executed and the Lord of Balvenie was driven into exile. Douglas lands were then forfeited and permanently annexed to the crown, along with many other lands and castles.

James had made a spectacular impact. He had destroyed the power of the Black Douglases and in their place had promoted the loyal Red Douglases, namely George 4th Earl of Angus. It was a spectacular year for James only highlighted by the birth of his son, another James, in 1451. Four years later, a second son, Alexander would be born as well. The Stewart dynasty was finally secure.

The successors as kings of Scots never faced such a powerful challenge to their authority again. Along with the forfeiture of the Albany-Stewarts in the reign of James I, the destruction of the Black Douglases saw royal power in Scotland take a major leap forward.

While James was riding himself of the Black Douglases, Richard of York had captured Henry VI at the first Battle of St Albans and had appointed himself Lord Protector of England. This war, called The War of the Roses, would not finish until 1487 on the death of the last Plantagenet king, Richard III. It was basically a terrible family squabble between royal cousins greedy to snatch the crown and the throne of England for themselves away from other family members. These two royal houses, the symbolic red rose of the Lancasters and the equally symbolic white rose of the Yorks, were each making a claim for the throne and it would end in a long and bloody battle at Bosworth with the dead of Richard III. Both were powerful families and both could trace their lineage back to the sons of Edward III.

The rival claims of the Lancastrians and the Yorkists went back to John of Gaunt, Duke of Lancaster (the third surviving son of Edward III) and to Edward's 4th surviving son Edmund of Langley, Duke of York, both of whom had been uncles of the Plantagenet King Richard II.

The conflict began when the Lancastrians seized the throne from Richard II in 1399 and it's truly understandable why people were glad to see the last of him. Three Lancastrian kings followed: Henry IV (r. 1399-1413) Henry V (r. 1413-1422) and Henry VI. Henry VI succeeded to the throne as a nine-month-old infant in 1422 and his minority was governed by his uncle the Duke of Gloucester, which was good news for Scotland because he left them alone while England was steadily losing its possessions in France. Henry VI, a pious young man, the opposite of his warlike father Henry V, married the strong-minded Margaret of Anjou in 1445 and two years later, the Duke of Gloucester was executed.

In the ensuing chaos the Yorkists began building their claim to the throne mainly because poor Henry was subject to bouts of insanity. It was during one of these bouts that Richard Duke of York stepped in at St Albans when the Lancastrians and the Yorks came to blows in May 1455 at the same time James was celebrating being rid of Douglas and the birth of his second son Alexander.

But whether the Yorks were any better than Henry and whether people who lived in those times knew the tragedy that was about to unfold is anyone's guess.

There would be many battles in the War of the Roses during which the throne fell into both the Yorks and Lancastrians camps. By 1460, the Lancastrians were finally deposed, Henry was taken prisoner and Edward Duke of York assumed the crown as Edward IV. In the future, Richard Duke of Warwick would plan for Edward to marry a foreign princess but a silver-haired beauty with the merry laugh by the name of Elizabeth Woodville would snare herself a king and would prove herself more fruitful than Warwick would ever imagine. While Warwick lay unmourned in his grave, killed for his anarchy, the ongoing royal nursery teemed with happy children: two strong sons and a bevy of princesses. It would seem like Edward's hold on the crown was unshakeable and the days of Lancastrians were over.

Not unnaturally, James saw the turmoil in England during the War of the Roses as an opportunity to recover the two major Scottish strongholds that were still in English hands – Berwick and Roxburgh. As Henry VI was being humbled in Northampton in 1460, James was ready to make a decisive move. Within two weeks he had mustered a huge army from all over Scotland. The English expected an assault on Berwick and sent their defences but James's target had been Roxburgh Castle.

James had always been fascinated by artillery but when he was presented with a cannon from the Duke of Burgundy, Marie de Guelders' uncle, in 1457 James was ecstatic. It was called the Mons Meg and was the most advanced cannon of its time. But a cannon of the size and weight of Mons Meg was ponderously slow to move around and could only be trundled about five kilometres a day. Its value was probably more deterrent than actual.

His passion would be his undoing.

In July 1460, he moved to take Roxburgh Castle with the objective to destroy both burgh and castle and thereby dispose of a major base for hostile forays from England. And he took Mons Meg with him.

At the outset, James took the town and levelled it. Then he focused his attack on the castle, deploying his cannons to fire directly at the castle across the Tweed River.

Fate was about to step in. James was standing way to close to the big guns as they were being fired and unfortunately, when one of the guns burst its casing, James was hit by a flying piece of iron and killed instantly.

The man with the fiery birthmark, and personality to match, died at the age of 29 years of age, leaving a nation and his wife with a family of five children: two daughters, Mary and Margaret, and three sons: John, Earl of Mar barely 3 years old, Alexander, Duke of Albany 6 years old and the eldest, James, Duke of Rothesay, 9 years old. Scotland had yet another Stewart boy-king on the throne.

JAMES III

Born 1451
Reign 1460 – 1488

Trouble seemed never far away from Scotland. Once again they found themselves with a king in his minority and in a panic, Parliament hurriedly appointed his mother Marie de Guelders as Guardian of the King's Person with a Regency Council made up of prelates and nobles headed by Bishop William Kennedy of St Andrews.

Not only was Marie a lively, talented and passionate woman, she was also a very wealthy one with a mind of her own. Seeing the Lancastrians, Margaret of Anjou and her husband Henry VI in England as being wronged by their relations, she made welcome and gave sanctuary to them when Edward IV consolidated the Yorkist hold on the crown after a bloody battle in Towton in Yorkshire in March 1461. In return for this hospitality, and the promise of Scottish military support, the exiles surrendered Berwick-upon-Tweed to Scotland with the promise of Carlisle in the future.

Of course, Scotland was ecstatic at the return of Berwick. It had been see-sawing between England and Scotland for over a century and they were happy to welcome it back. The trouble was Bishop Kennedy supported the Yorks.

As a kinsman of young James III, (his mother had been a daughter of Robert III) the Bishop was a brilliant scholar who had been made Bishop of St Andrews at the age of thirty-one. What Bishop Kennedy didn't like was Marie's politicking, finding it not only meddlesome but dangerous. What scandalised him even more than politics was her private life. She had an affair with the Lancastrian Duke of Somerset while he was in exile in Scotland and she lived openly with Adam Hepburn, the Master of Hailes, who was already married. She then switched her support to the victorious Yorkist side, and even discussed with Richard Neville, Earl of Warwick (the future 'Kingmaker') the possibility of marriage to king Edward IV.

Sadly for Marie, she died in December 1463, three years after her husband allowing Bishop Kennedy to take control of government policy. He promptly negotiated a 15-year truce with the Yorkist government, in return for an annual pension from Edward of course, no doubt to ensure that Henry VI would not be allowed into Scotland again. But like Marie, the Bishop did not have long to enjoy the fruits of his diplomacy. He died two years later leaving James without a guardian.

You can only feel sorry for James with his guardians dropping like flies. Luckily, he had turned 13 years old and there wasn't much time for another faction to take control of him before he reached his majority the coming year. But as with his father, when the Livingstons and the Crichtons seized power during his minority, another family was ready to step into the power vacuum: the Boyds of Kilmarnock.

Almost like déjà vu, the following year, while James was out hunting near Linlithgow Palace, he was seized and abducted in a risky *coup d'etat* led by Robert, Lord Boyd of Kilmarnock. The boy was taken to Edinburgh Castle, whose governor and Chamberlain of the Royal Household was Sir Alexander Boyd, Robert's brother. At a parliament in October, the king was somehow induced to say that what had happened had been done with his consent. Parliament could do little except approve a charter whereby Robert Boyd was named as Governor of the King's Person and Keeper of the Fortresses of the Kingdom, giving the Boyds open slather to commence a whirlwind campaign of grabbing whatever they could. Lord Boyd's son Thomas was created Earl of Arran and then married James's elder sister, Lady Mary. It was noted that James wept during the wedding ceremony and it would not be the last time that he would resort to tears in times of stress.

But things were about to come to a full stop. Just before his father's death, an embassy was sent to a meeting arranged by King Charles VII of France between the Scots and the Danes. The intention was to discuss a marriage contract between James's heir, (James III still only 12 years old) and King Kristian I's only daughter, the pious Princess Margrethe of Denmark. The discussions were lengthy as Kristian I haggled and they finally broke down when James died. But when James turned 14 years old, he was of age to be married and the negotiations renewed in earnest.

Kristian I was not one to overlook any source of revenue. A marriage treaty was drawn up where Princess Margrethe would receive the Palace of Linlithgow as well as receive, as a hunting lodge and country retreat, the magnificent Doune Castle near Dunblane.

****

On July 10, 1469, three years later, 18-year-old James married 10-year-old Margrethe, Princess of Norway and Denmark, in a ceremony in Holyrood Abbey. It was happy occasion for James but more so for Scotland because they finally gained the last territories which make up Scotland today: the Northern Isles of Orkney and Shetland. The Northern Isles by then had become heavily Scotticised and the status of Norway had changed considerably.

With that settled, James began his personal reign at the same time as things were heating up in England. The powerful Earl of Warwick (the Kingmaker) in England had swapped sides again and virtually imprisoned Edward IV. When Edward escaped, Warwick tucked his tail between his legs and sailed to France to try and make an alliance with his once enemy, Margaret of Anjou, Henry VI's queen. The juicy carrot he waved in front of her was they could unite and join armies to invade England and Henry could have his throne back.

Edward could see the writing on the wall and fled to Burgundy to raise an army of his own while Margaret celebrated the return of her simple-minded husband to the throne. What she was actually doing was keeping the throne safe for her son Edward to take over when he came of age.

The celebration were brief because Edward's reinforced army arrived and defeated the Lancastrian army firstly at Barnet (where the Earl of

Warwick was killed) and again at Tewkesbury in Gloucestershire a month later, where Henry's son Prince Edward was killed. Margaret barely managed to escape with her life but she wasn't Edward's prize. He took Henry straight back to, humiliating him in public, and that very night, Henry was found murdered in the Tower the next day. Edward then resumed his uninterrupted reign.

James knew he had to stay on good relations with the Yorkist dynasty in England and luckily, Edward's attitude towards Scotland was undecided. At this stage, James was investing in more artillery and displaying considerable confidence, even aggressiveness, just like his warrior father and he knew Edward and his brother Richard would be keeping a close eye on matters in Scotland.

The chance of a more binding relationship with England came in March 1473 when Queen Margrethe gave birth to a son, James Duke of Rothesay (the future James IV), to be followed soon by two more sons later. But it was little James who was the golden egg. At a year old, a marriage was arranged for him with Lady Cecily, the 3-year-old daughter of Edward and the formal betrothal was solemnised in the Blackfriars of Edinburgh a year later. Cecily's dowry was set at 20,000 English marks, a first instalment of 2,000 marks was to be paid immediately, followed by annual instalments of 2,000 and 1,000 marks.

It was good business by Edward because it neutralised any threat from Scotland and left him free to concentrate on France where he still harboured designs on the throne. But in Scotland, the harmony with England, no matter how fragile, did not go down well. James was losing support from the people that mattered - the nobility - especially in the Borders where sporadic warfare with England had become a way of life. But what really irked people was James' lavish spending at a time when the country was suffering from famine, inflation and constant skirmishing. Many thought he was massing money for his personal use and stuffing his *'black kist'* (chest) while still asking for more money from parliament to finance his extravagant outlays on ornaments and clothing for himself, his wife and his favourites. These favourites included men who had intellectual and artistic interests and he had no qualms about feathering their nests as well as his. One favourite was William Roger, an English musician who helped to found the musical tradition in the Chapel Royal at Stirling.

Another was William Scheves, a shirt-maker for the king who ended up as Archbishop of St Andrews. The most notorious was Thomas Cochrane who was said to be a stonemason who acted as James's trouble-shooter in the north-east but only succeeded in infuriating the powerful local nobility. He influenced James in state matters and controlled access to James, charging heftily for the privilege of seeing him. In the crowd of 'hangers-on' were physicians and apothecaries, esquires who were rewarded with extensive lands and baronies, a royal tailor, a fencing master, a royal shoe-maker and an astrologer. With so many with their hands out, government looked to his brothers Alexander Duke of Albany and John Earl of Mar for help.

James was well aware of what his government were up to having been told by his friend Thomas Cochrane, and sometime in 1479 – 80 James did the unthinkable and had his brothers arrested and thrown in prison. John would die in Craigmillar Castle in rather suspicious circumstances, having bled to death in his bath, but Alexander escaped and took refuge in Dunbar Castle. In a fury, James besieged the castle, but Alexander escaped again and made his way to France for help. France however was in no position to help him with his ambitions in Scotland but he knew Edward in England would listen.

Alexander must have forgotten there were three little boys ahead of him in the queue to the throne when he signed a pact with Edward promising to do homage to Edward when he won the crown of Scotland for himself. Maybe that was just a technicality. He even signed himself *'Alexander R, King of Scots'*. He then promised to surrender Berwick and most of the south of Scotland to England and in return, Edward was to commit himself to a full-scale invasion of Scotland to overthrow the existing regime north of the border. The invasion army was to be led by Edward's trusted brother, Richard, Duke of Gloucester (the future King of England) and all of a sudden, war became inevitable and became the greatest crisis to James's reign.

True to his word, Edward's first step was to send a hostile English fleet to patrol the Firth of Forth as well as a massive English army mustered in the north of England. He then demanded the return of Berwick and Roxburgh, given to James' mother for harbouring Henry VI and Margaret of Anjou, and insisted that young James, the Duke of Rothesay, should be delivered to

England by the end of May so that his promised marriage to Lady Cecily could take place.

There was no way on earth James was going to comply with Edward's demands. Especially handing over his son. It was his turn now to muster an army and he turned to his nobles for support. His senior nobles were his three half-uncles (his father's half-brothers when his mother remarried James Stewart, the Black Knight of Lorne) - John Stewart, Earl of Atholl, James Stewart, Earl of Buchan and Andrew Stewart, Bishop-elect of Moray. But the call to arms triggered a remarkable family conspiracy in which even James's queen, Margrethe of Denmark, was personally involved.

It was 1482 and the Scots army was assembled on the Burgh Muir of Edinburgh. At the head of his army, James was marching south to Lauder in Berwickshire while the English army had already moved into Scotland, taking the town of Berwick on the way but bypassing Berwick Castle. Only 48 kilometres away from Lauder, the Scottish nobles found themselves faced with a huge invasion army. Chroniclers have written that the nobles learned that the hated Cochrane had been given command of the artillery so they called a meeting to discuss their position. The ringleader was Archibald, Earl of Angus, nicknamed the 'Bell-the-Cat' who went to James's tent to present him with an ultimatum: either the 'familiars/favourites' were dismissed from positions of command, or the army would not move another step. To which James flatly refused. The lords then decided to take the law into their own hands. They invited Cochrane to meet them and when he appeared, he was wearing gold-painted armour with a heavy gold chain around his neck worth over 500 crowns. It was the final straw for Archibald. He snatched it off, saying that a common rope would suit him better, then held Cochrane while a lynching party went to the king's tent and arrested the other five of James' 'friends'. All were then hanged from the parapet of the bridge over the Leader Water. In a frenzy of vengeance, the invasion all but forgotten, they then seized James and placed him under arrest, marching him straight back to Edinburgh where they kept imprisoned in the castle under the safe keeping of his half-uncles, the earls of Atholl and Buchan.

With no one to stop them, the English army swept into Edinburgh unopposed. Which is where Richard Duke of Gloucester came upon a quandary. The king he had come to depose was already a prisoner in his own fortress and inaccessible without a major siege, for which he was unprepared for and could not afford. James's uncles had the royal seal in the castle and the would-be usurper, James's brother Alexander, now seemed to be in two minds about his promised homage to Edward since he had leap-frogged over his tiny nephews and was in charge.

Richard made the best of an impossible position by extracting a bond for the repayment of Lady Cecily's dowry and went back home, pausing only long enough to capture Berwick Castle. Berwick-upon-Tweed became part of England once again, and has remained so.

The coup, if a coup it was, had gone off half-cocked, but it was one of the great failings of James's reign. After secret 'negotiations", which involved the Queen and his ten-year-old son in Stirling Castle, (oh to be a fly on the wall at that meeting) James was triumphantly released, ostensibly by his brother Alexander, who was appointed the king's lieutenant-general.

Alexander's elevation to power did not last long. One year later, Alexander was in disgrace again, exposed in another conspiracy with England and forced to leave the country. He made a final quixotic return to Scotland a year after that but was beaten up by an angry crowd at a fair. That was enough for him. He went straight into exile in France where he died the following year, mortally wounded in a tournament.

James only just survived the crisis, strengthened by the turmoil engulfing England after the death of Edward IV in April 1483 and the usurpation of the throne by his brother Richard III after his two nephews went missing.

It's fascinating that a king who reigned for less than two years over 500 years ago should still inspire such interest today. Why are we so obsessed with Richard III? Doubtless the fate of his two nephews plays into the mystery. But it's more than that.

There's a sense that he was perhaps wronged by history, that there's a problem that needs to be fixed with his reputation.

Richard was 30 years old when he became King of England. In the years before that, he grew up in the heat of the War of the Roses between the Yorks and the Lancasters during some of the worst years in history. He spent two periods in exile when he was 8 years old and again when he was 18. He fought battles and was a successful soldier despite his scoliosis. He'd been involved in an invasion in France and he led a campaign against the Scots. All of this before he even came near the throne of England. And that man we saw at work in the north, carving out a strong reputation for himself as a champion of justice and equity for the common man, is the same man who is held responsible for the atrocity of murdering his nephews. It's almost impossible to reconcile him with the monster of 1483 that history has bequeathed us.

The more I've read about Richard, the more fascinated I've become and the more questions I have, rather than answers. Almost everything about him is so cloaked in mystery, smoke and mirrors, that two people can read the same evidence and come up with two very different solutions.

From all accounts, he was interested in social justice issues and that made him a bit of a threat to the powers that be in the country at the time and those who benefited from the status quo. And perhaps this plays into why he has such a poor reputation as a child killing monster.

So if the story we have of the Princes in the Tower is so neat and tidy, why has it fascinated us for generations? Why does it inspire heated debate on social media even today, just as it would have done in the taverns in the 15th century England.

It's partly because it was so horrific. It's two small children, twelve and nine, being murdered by their uncle. They are last recorded playing bows and arrows out on the grass under the Tower of London. And then they simply disappeared.

There's a fairy tale element to it. The wicked uncle who steals the throne from his nephews and has them done away with in the middle of the night. It's also partly due to the portraiture that Victorian painters have left for us. The boys are always painted with their lovely flowing blond locks huddled together looking up in the opposite directions as if they are waiting for their murderers to come and finish them off.

In truth, the boys grew up separately. Prince Edward spent his first two years in the Welsh marshes at Ludlow, training how to rule a kingdom. Prince Richard was brought up at London court with his mother and his sisters. The boys would have been virtual strangers to each other. And yet we're sold on the image of them clinging to each other as a single unit in a dark room in the Tower of London, sharing a single, doomed fate.

But it's a mystery and everyone loves a mystery. The fact is, we just don't know what happened to the two princes.

Richard has always been the obvious suspect in the murder inquiry. But how far would Agatha Christie have gone if it was always the obvious suspect who did it?

If you look closely, there are holes in this theory. That the princes disappeared, presumed murdered, is certain. But by whom?

Suspect Number 1. There have been a few names pulled out of the hat and the first one for sure is Richard III. He had the most to gain from their death. But the deaths of the princes would certainly not have been by his own hand. He had people to do that sort of dirty work for him if he so commanded it. And so we move on to Suspect number 2.

Suspect Number 2. No man had done more to place Richard on the throne than the Henry Stafford, 2nd Duke of Buckingham. Yet strangely and suddenly, during the first three months of Richard's reign, Buckingham suddenly changed his allegiance completely and became Richard's mortal enemy. Why did he do that? Was it perhaps his dislike at being an accomplice in what was seen as the usurpation of the throne and the murder of two young children? Perhaps he feared for his own safety? Ah, but then we ask wasn't he of royal blood as well, being a descendant firstly through John Beaufort, son of John of Gaunt, and secondly, through the bloodline of Thomas of Woodstock, Edward III's fifth son? If anything happened to Richard's son, Buckingham's bloodline could be strong enough to claim the throne for himself. Could that have been the real reason? Get rid of the boys, then get rid of Richard and voila, the throne could be his. If discovered, and knowing the York's relish for using the chopping block, it wouldn't have made him feel very safe. Not at all.

So very soon after the coronation, Buckingham changed sides dramatically and no one knows why. What we do know is that his job was one of responsibility and he was in charge of the safekeeping of the boys between June and July. As there were no physical injuries on the small bodies in 1674, suffocation was probably the method of killing them and it was a tried and true means of getting rid of someone you didn't want around.

Suspect Number 3. In the background was Margaret Beaufort, mother of Henry Tudor. No other mother in history, with the exception of Margaret of Anjou of course, seems to have been as dedicated as she was to have her son sit on the throne. But again, she would not have done it herself. There would have been a third party involved.

In 1472 after the death of her second husband, Margaret did the unthinkable and arranged for her own marriage to a prominent widow, Thomas Stanley, 1st Earl of Derby who was in good standing with Edward IV, Richard's brother. By all accounts, the marriage was one of pure convenience. This marriage enabled her to return to the court of Edward and his queen Elizabeth Woodville and she was chosen by Elizabeth to be her daughter's godmother. After Edward's death and Elizabeth's rush to sanctuary in Westminster Abbey, Margaret Beaufort became Anne Neville's lady-in-waiting, (Anne Neville was Richard's wife), even carrying the train at her coronation. Richard had already stripped Margaret of her titles and estates and had given them all to her husband, Lord Stanley, which was a meaningless gesture as he would already have had the rights to her property as her new husband anyway. During all of this (and she must have been absolutely furious), she was actively plotting with Elizabeth Woodville and had betrothed her beloved son Henry to Elizabeth's daughter, young Elizabeth of York. She has been called a formidable opponent of Richard III, habitual conspirator and dedicated promoter of her son's cause.

Within a couple of months of Richard's coronation, Margaret's nephew Buckingham from her previous marriage, (yes it is complicated), raised a rebellion against Richard in favour of Henry Tudor and you can bet she used every bit of her influence on him to encourage the rebellion. She would have promised him anything for his support. I guess my question right now is: why did Buckingham raise the rebellion in favour of Henry and not for the princes since nobody apparently knew they were already dead? Was he the one who gave the orders to kill them? In view of that and the fact that Buckingham had no immediate motive to move against Richard except that he had a claim to the throne himself, what could he hope to gain by attacking the king in such a wild and reckless rebellion after having sworn his loyalty one month previously? My guess is Margaret Beaufort had a hand in it. As a consequence of the failed rebellion, Margaret's current husband, Lord Stanley, was promoted to the position of High Constable in charge of all prisoners in the Tower.

All Margaret wanted was for her son Henry to sit on the throne at any cost. At the beginning of Buckingham's rebellion, she sent word to Henry Tudor who was living in abject poverty in France with Jasper Tudor and told him to gather forces and hurry home. To me, it seems she was pulling the strings and had everything planned and under control.

And here is something else to think about - if Henry Tudor defeated Richard III in battle, Henry would not necessarily become king because the throne would theoretically be restored to young Prince Edward V who *may* be in the tower. However, both princes' removal would leave her son Henry as the prime candidate for the throne.

Suspect Number 4. Henry Tudor had a great need to be king and he was the plausible alternative, but only if the two princes weren't around. Henry was a Welshman, whose grandfather, Owen Tudor had been a page in the court of Henry V and as we know, Owen is reported to have secretly married Henry V's widow, Catherine of Valois. One of their sons was Edmund Tudor, who in turn married Margaret Beaufort.

Perhaps at this stage, I should remind you that Henry Tudor's grandmother Catherine of Valois was the sister of Charles VI of France who had sadly inherited a 'crazy' gene and we saw this gene pop its nasty head up during Henry VI's reign. Although Henry Tudor's claim to the throne was through his mother and the House of Beaufort as far back as John of Gaunt and Edward III, this gene from his paternal French grandmother should not, perhaps, be forgotten regarding future generations and their actions.

It has been suggested by some historians that Richard had stashed the princes in the Tower of London for safe keeping while he ruled in peace. It has also been suggested that it was in fact Henry Tudor, when he was King Henry VII, who had the princes executed between June and July of 1486 when his stepfather was High Constable of the Tower two years later. Richard was long gone by then. It was only after this date that orders went out to circulate the story that Richard had killed the princes. This could easily have been to cover up Henry's own involvement in their murder. It has also been suggested that Elizabeth Woodville knew that this story was false, and so Henry had to have her "silenced" by confining her to a nunnery where she died six years later. All very plausible.

When you think about it, it seems impossible that no one knew what happened to the Princes after they entered the tower. Richard III, Henry VII and Elizabeth Woodville would have had their spies out and all of them would have known the boys' whereabouts and welfare. If both boys had died, the matter could have been discussed and the culprit would have been blamed openly. But neither Richard III nor Henry VII did so with the reason being that if the princes were alive, the boys' claim to the throne was better than either of theirs. The princes would simply have had to go in either case. It's something we will never know and it is history's best-kept secret.

No doubt, we have William Shakespeare to thank for his version of Richard III in a time when Shakespeare would definitely be trying to stay in Elizabeth I's good books, the granddaughter of Henry VII who butchered Richard III and usurped the throne from the Plantagenets.

Fast forward 200 years, and the mystery appeared to be solved when workmen removing a staircase in the white tower stumbled across the remains of two children. King Charles II proclaimed them to be those of the princes in the tower and had them placed in an urn in Westminster Abbey.

Case closed?

Not quite.

In 1933, those remains were exhumed from their urn and subjected to scientific examination. They were unable to age the skeletons or even date them. They couldn't even tell whether they belonged to boys or girls. They found animal bones and all kinds of dirt mixed in from the rubbish pile that those bones had been collected from. So they can't be sure that those are the princes in the urn in Westminster Abbey.

Sorry, back to James in Scotland surviving the crisis.

After Richard's usurpation, James took advantage of England's distractions in 1485 by besieging and capturing Dunbar Castle, ending a long English occupation. Richard had just been defeated at Bosworth by Henry Tudor, Henry VII, who was not deterred from negotiating a 3-year truce with the Scots.

The respite with England did not extend to domestic affairs in Scotland. James's nobles in the Borders grew ever more restless and resentful, demanding reforms. The country was fragmenting into royalists and anti-royalist factions and the anti-royalists were growing stronger all the time.

Even within James's own family circle, problems were looming. In July 1486, Margrethe died in Stirling Castle at only 30 years old, having given James three sons. James and Margrethe had been living apart for some years and the rumour, probably quite untrue, was she had been poisoned by James's counsellors.

James's attitude to his eldest son, James, in later years was strangely hostile, perhaps because of the humiliation in 1482. At any rate, he ignored his heir-apparent and favoured his second son, the Marquis of Ormonde. James was still determined to make strong marriage alliances with England, especially after Henry VII succeeded to the throne, but it was his second son, Ormonde, who was contracted to marry a daughter of Edward IV and James himself who was to marry Edward IV's widow, Elizabeth Woodville. Neither of these fanciful proposals were followed through but they were enough to suggest to his heir that his own future, perhaps even his life, was no longer safe. To top it off, his younger brother was given the dukedom of Ross which must have sent bells ringing in his head.

In 1488, he left Stirling Castle without his father's knowledge or permission and went to ground. By now, the anti-king nobles, Angus and Argyll, and the Homes and Hepburns, had had enough as well. The 15-year-old heir was exactly what they needed to provide a figurehead for revolt. This time, the rebellion was to be conclusive.

In the early months of 1488, James knew he was losing control of his kingdom. Suddenly, he started spending lavishly from his private treasury, throwing money at potential supporters to raise troops for himself. His oldest half-uncle, the Earl of Atholl, for instance received two full chests of money. But it all came too late for him to save his throne.

In June, his son had returned back to Edinburgh Castle, and James fully expected to see him heading a rebellion. James's plan was to leave Edinburgh Castle with as many supporters as he could muster and wait until his son emerged. He would then seize him and put an end to the rebellion.

As expected, the young prince emerged from Stirling Castle with a small rebel force and was surprised near Stirling Bridge, the same scene of William Wallace's victory in 1297. However, Prince James luckily escaped and joined up with the main army of Border rebels farther to the north.

On 11th June, the second and final encounter took place south of Stirling between Sauchie and Bannockburn (later to be known as Sauchieburn) ironically the site of the battlefield of Bannockburn. James was even symbolically carrying the sword of Robert Bruce.

The rebels seemed to have a larger army and their leaders, confident of a victory, all swore an oath before the battle that they would not harm the person of the king. The encounter itself was not so much a battle because no artillery was used, but a series of running skirmishes in which the rebels soon got the upper hand.

And now, fact and fiction become hopelessly entwined. One story states that James left the field unaccompanied, mounted on a great grey charger and abandoning the sword and a treasure chest of £4,000 in gold coin, and headed for the safety of a ship in the River Forth. He got as far as the mill of Bannockburn, but when his horse tried to jump the burn, James was thrown. The miller and his wife found him lying on the ground in his heavy armour, dazed and in pain, and carried him into a nearby stable. He asked for a priest so he could make his confession and the miller's wife ran outside and found a passing stranger who claimed to be a man of the cloth. An alternative version claims that she met a posse of pursuing rebel knights led by Lord Grey who was passing by and asked where the king was. Whatever the truth, this unknown person entered the stable and stabbed the king to death.

The victorious rebels moved swiftly to consolidate their power. One day after his father's death, James issued his first charter. Edinburgh and Stirling castles were secured, as were the late king's money and jewels and the rebel leaders were rewarded with offices of state and posts in the royal household.

The circumstances of James's death remains a mystery. The subsequent parliamentary hearing could only come to the conclusion that the king 'happened to be slain' and his death was just another crisis in the history of Scotland. It marked the end of an era, the end of the Middle Ages and the beginning of the Renaissance in Scotland.

James may not have been the most attractive or heroic of the Stewart kings of the 15th century but he wasn't alone. Historians have had a party with monarchs. Richard III was turned into a monster of depravity and James was depicted as feckless, idle, erratic and vindictive. He broke faith with too many loyal people and rewarded the unworthy. Above all, he had a morbid distrust for members of his own family- rightly or wrongly - and in the end, it was his eldest son who became the indirect instrument of his miserable, lonely death.

JAMES IV

Born 1473
Reign 1488 – 1513

Few monarchs have had a less auspicious start to their reign. 15-year-old James was crowned at Scone, somewhat hurriedly, on 24th June, 1488, the day after his father's funeral at Cambuskenneth Abbey, becoming the first Stewart king to be crowned at Scone since his great-grandfather James I in 1424.

It was a showy occasion because it was the anniversary of Robert Bruce's victory at Bannockburn. The Archbishop of St Andrews, William Scheves, the favourite of James III, did not officiate during the coronation ceremony. The new king was crowned by Robert Blackadder, Bishop of Glasgow.

The minority government had two urgent priorities. The first was to track down as seize as much as possible of the treasure James had hoarded throughout his reign. Ultimately more than £24,000 Scots was recovered, a huge sum, but even that was believed to be only a fraction of the total. The second was to confirm a government which had been responsible for regicide, however unpopular the late king might have been. Murder was still murder and the rebels had to justify their takeover against those who had supported James III. They did this by seizing the administration and arraigning ten of the late king's leading supporters for treasonable negotiations with England. Two new families quickly came to the fore: Patrick Hepburn (Lord Hailes) became Earl of Bothwell, Master of the Household, Keeper of Edinburgh Castle and Admiral of Scotland while Alexander Hume became Lord Hume, Warden of the east Marches, Keeper of Stirling Castle and Chamberlain for life.

Despite being only 15, James quickly proved to be very wise. He left the running of his government to Patrick Hepburn, 1st Earl of Bothwell and William Elphinstone, Bishop of Aberdeen who became Keeper of the Privy Seal and one of James's closes advisers and ambassadors throughout his reign. Together they established a new privy council that annulled many of the previous forfeitures, becoming known as the 'healing parliament'.

Almost immediately, an insurrection, of basically supporters of James's father, broke out against the new government. James's supporters quickly defeated the major rebellion led by the Earl of Lennox and Lord Lyle, laying siege to Crookston, Duchal and the Lennox stronghold of Dumbarton castle at enormous cost using huge artillery pieces like Mons Meg, and defeating a rebel army at Gartloaning in Stirlingshire. All just one year after his coronation.

His minority was to last until his 21st birthday in March 1494 when he was able to start his own personal rule but up until then, he was still receiving lessons in hawking and the chase, formal tournaments, lessons in several languages including Latin and French and of course Flemish, German, Italian, Danish and a little Spanish. He also spoke Gaelic.

He had become a virile, handsome young man and as a teenager during his minority, he was 'fed' a succession of lovers by those in power who saw political advantage in encouraging his sexual intrigues with their relatives. His first affair was in 1492 with Marion Boyd, a niece of Archibald Douglas, Earl of Angus, a close confidant and card-playing companion of James. The affair lasted three years during which the Earl of Angus rose high in royal favour. Marion bore James his first two illegitimate children – Alexander Stewart, who would be appointed Archbishop of St Andrews at the age of 11, and a daughter, Catherine. The affair came to an end in 1495 when James married Marion off to someone else.

The second mistress was Margaret Drummond, daughter of the first Lord Drummond, one of the royal justiciars. This affair lasted two years, where she was publicly installed in Stirling Castle and bearing him a daughter also named Margaret. In 1497, he sent her back to her father suitably rewarded.

The third and most durable of James's affairs was Janet Kennedy, daughter of John, Lord Kennedy, and mistress of Archibald, 5th Earl of Angus. Rumour had it that Archibald fell out of favour with James over Janet because he was dismissed as Chancellor and put under house arrest on the Isle of Bute for ten years. In 1501, Janet bore him a son he called James, Earl of Moray who we will hear much more of in the future. James's womanising continued after his marriage in 1503, showering gifts on the last of his public mistresses, Isabel Stewart, daughter of James, Earl of Buchan who bore him a daughter, Janet.

All of these alliances, despite the number of illegitimate offspring that occurred, were only a side-line. The important question was, who should he marry?

Efforts to find James a suitable bride began when James was only one year old where his father negotiated a marriage with Cecily, the daughter of Edward IV. This fell through during the crisis of 1482 when England invaded Scotland and James was imprisoned by his nobles in Edinburgh Castle. Another English bride was suggested in 1484 with Richard III of England – Anne de la Pole, one of Richard's nieces – but Richard's defeat and death at the Battle of Bosworth the following year put paid to that scheme as well.

Given the anti-English sentiment after James's death in 1488, an English marriage was out of the question. Four years later an envoy was sent to France to seek both a bride and a treaty. Again, without success.

Relations with England were still very uncomfortable, to say the least, so not only harbouring and welcoming the 'pretender' Perkin Warbeck, who claimed to be the younger of the two murdered 'Princes in the Tower', sons of Edward IV and nephews of Richard III, was perhaps not the smartest thing James had ever done. He even gave Perkin a daughter of the Earl of Huntley as a bride. Warbeck was simply a pawn in the rivalries between England and Scotland as Henry VII struggled to consolidate his Tudor hold on the English throne.v

James used Warbeck as an excuse to raise the stakes by assembling his army and all his heavy artillery into England where he spent a fortnight plundering Northumberland. When an English army began to muster at Newcastle, James simply withdrew, having made his point. Henry responded by declaring war on Scotland but just before he could invade, an armed insurrection of men from Cornwall and Devon who were marching on London at alarming speed caused him to halt. He was forced to divert his troops back to London and of course, James went back on the attack again. He trundled all his artillery, including the Mons Meg, to the border where he bombarded Norham Castle for a week before returning home.

It was just a push and shove gesture as much as anything but James had proved himself to be a brave, and very popular, warrior-king who was not afraid to take on the military might of England. He could claim to have fought Henry VII to a frustrated standstill and had taken his place at the top of European diplomacy.

The outcome, strangely enough, was a treaty between James and Henry which included the marriage of his eldest daughter Margaret to James, of which the dowry was £10,000 Sterling (about £35,000 Scots).

The roof of the Great Hall of Edinburgh Castle was completed by James just in time for the marriage, decorated with roses and thistles, meant to symbolise the marriage between the Scottish thistle and the Tudor rose, and sealed with a Treaty of Perpetual Peace between the two nations in 1502. It was a fateful moment in Anglo-Scottish relations for although nothing had been further from the minds of the treaty-makers at the time, it would eventually lead to the union of the two crowns exactly one century later, when a great-grandson of the marriage, James VI of Scotland would become James I of England.

The wedding at Holyrood has been called the greatest display of pomp and ceremony of pre-Reformation Scotland and no expense was spared. The festivities went on for five days with a succession of banquets, pageants, dancing and the courtyard of Holyrood Palace rang to the sounds of jousting that lasted for three days.

Despite the 'treaty of peace', the marriage failed to secure more than a brief honeymoon peace with England. It also very nearly failed to produce a son who could inherit the Stewart throne. James's first legitimate child, another James, was born in February 1507 and with both queen and son very ill, James set off to make an arduous eight-day pilgrimage on foot to the shrine of St Ninian in Galloway, 190 kilometres from Edinburgh. Even this spectacular act of piety failed to save the life of his child who died a year later. One year later, the queen gave birth to a daughter who died shortly afterwards and then a second son one year on again who was christened Arthur, but who died the following year as well.

At last in 1512, after ten years of marriage, another son – again named James – was born. This son would survive to be James V, but only just. Young James would be followed by another daughter who died early in 1513 but in the summer of 1513, the queen would announce she was pregnant again.

At the time, the reign of James was in full flowering of Renaissance ideas and many European monarchs had nothing but praise for James. James kept a large and colourful court full of leaned men who spoke in at least six different languages. He was fond of organising impressive jousting tournaments and kept a menagerie of lions and other exotic wild beasts, all part of the Renaissance ideal of conspicuous royal expenditure. He befriended scholars and poets and one Italian scholar and abbot who was given a laboratory in Stirling Castle in which to carry out researches in alchemy, in an attempt to change base metal into gold. This man had also attempted to fly from the battlements of Stirling Castle to France on a pair of huge homemade wings but he was attacked by birds and plummeted to earth, landing in a dung heap.

As well as writers, James was involved in setting up a printing works in Scotland, granting patents to two Edinburgh burgesses to import and establish a printing press. His interest in education flourished because of this, creating a more broadly-based education system. All his barons were ordered to put their eldest sons to grammar school from the age of eight or nine, to remain there until they had acquired a basic education and mastered Latin, and then spend three years studying art and law – on the pain of £20 penalty. He sent his own illegitimate sons, Alexander and James to study at Padua. He was very much the king who brought justice and peace to his country.

Traditionally, Henry VIII of England is regarded as the 'Father of the Royal Navy' but James has every right to be considered for that title as well. He was quick to recognise the need of a fleet of warships to be made available for the protection of his realm and during his reign, he built or bought or seized no fewer than thirty-eight vessels for the crown.

In his father's lifetime, James had seen the menace of an English fleet in action. The invasion army of Richard Earl of Gloucester and James III's treacherous brother, Alexander Duke of Albany, had been supported by a sizeable fleet led by the massive *Grace Dieu* that sailed into Leith unopposed.

This only highlighted the vulnerability of Edinburgh to attacks by sea as well as land. In 1491, parliament agreed to build a fortress on the island rock of Inchgarvie, at the narrows of the Firth of Forth by Queensferry and at the turn of the century, James made the construction of a Royal Scottish Navy a principle policy. He imported shipwrights from France and shipped in two massive timer keels which could not be procured in Scotland. The first of these keels was used for the pride of his early fleet, the *Margaret,* named after his bride and launched from a new dock in Leith in 1506. Her main armament consisted of a large cannon and four smaller guns.

His most memorable achievement was his flagship, the *Great Michael* which took four years to build under the supervision of French shipwrights and launched in October 1511. She was the most powerful warship afloat at the time, between forty-five and fifty-five metres long, and weighed about a thousand tons and cost a staggering total of about £30,000. By comparison, Nelson's *Victory* was fifty-six metres long. The *Great Michael* was armed with twelve bronze cannons on either side and carried a crew of three hundred.

Now we come to the great tragedy of Flodden Field, a battle which need not, and should not, have occurred.

The reason for the battle lies buried in the bewilderingly complicated political situation of Europe at the time. The fragile Treaty of Perpetual Peace which had been signed in 1502 as part of the marriage contract between James and Margaret Tudor did not last after the death of her father, Henry VII in 1509, and the accession of her aggressive brother, Henry VIII.

The main problem was the growing strength of France under Louis XII and of Spain under Ferdinand and Isabella, which caused acute concern in every chancellery in Europe. Scotland, allied by marriage and treaty to England, was still deeply involved in an even long-standing treaty and alliance with France: the Auld Alliance made by John Balliol, not that it did Scotland much good.

In 1511, Henry joined a 'Holy League' against France formed by Ferdinand and Isabella of Spain, Pope Julius II and Venice. To counter this threat,

Louis of France prevailed upon James to renew the 'Auld Alliance' and for each to come to the other's aid if one were attacked.

Then in May 1513, Henry did what everyone expected. He invaded France and King Louis invoked the terms of the Scottish alliance, sending an envoy with money, arms and experienced captains to help James to train a Scottish army.

James probably did not want war. He was married to Henry's sister and his wife was pregnant again. He also had only one surviving son and that son was still an infant. Peace with England had brought prosperity.

But he must have been tempted by the chance to demonstrate Scotland's importance in the international power-politics of the day and his sense of chivalry must have been aroused by the gift of a gold-and-turquoise ring from the Queen of France and a letter calling him her champion. She appealed to him to *'take three paces into English ground and break a lance for my sake'*. It was not meant to be a full-blown invasion of England but a diversionary tactic to take the pressure off France. James also leant his fleet, including the *Great Michael*, which Scotland would never see again.

It all began in July 1513 when James sent envoys to Henry VIII giving notice of his intention to invade Northumberland. To counter the Scottish threat during his absence in France, Henry entrusted his northern command to the highly experienced military commander, 70-year-old Thomas Howard, Earl of Surrey. Compared to the Earl of Surrey, James was a military amateur. What is more important, James had no particular strategy except to create a disturbance in the north of England.

The army James mustered was the best-equipped ever to invade England and numbered at least 25,000 men. About 7,500 Highlanders were by his side as his ability to speak Gaelic had made him genuinely popular among them. He also had the best of his nobility, including eighteen earls, twenty barons and hundreds of knights, all ready and willing to fight beside him.

On 22nd August, after Henry had rejected an ultimatum from James, the Scottish army crossed the Tweed at Coldstream and encamped on English soil. James had brought an enormous artillery train of 17 heavy siege guns pulled by 363 oxen and 7 horses with 95 drivers and 216 labourers to clear a route across the moors with picks and spades.

His first action was to lay siege to Norham Castle on the Tweed and five days later, his cannon pounded it into surrender. The Scots now turned their attention to nearby Etal Castle which surrendered at once, then Ford Castle where James stayed for a few days. Legend would later claim that he wasted time there on a dalliance with the daughter of the lady of the castle, Lady Heron.

On 4th September, the Earl of Surrey assembled his army at Alnwick, 19 kilometres away. It was inferior in numbers to the Scots by some twenty thousand men but it included 1,200 marines from the English fleet which had been brought to him by his eldest son along with 22 artillery pieces.

Surrey was concerned that the Scottish army would slip back into Scotland after causing a diversion without even fighting so he appealed to James to fight by 9th September at the latest. James accepted the challenge and moved his troops to Flodden Edge, an impregnable feature rising above the bleak and windswept Millfield plain to a height of about 150 metres. It was a natural fortress and Surrey instantly realised that it could not be stormed from the south. He struck camp and moved his army around the Scottish flank, bringing him to the north of their position. It caused a little confusion in the Scottish camp and the next morning when Surrey crossed the river Till at Twizel Bridge to take up position at Piper's Hill, the Scots made no attempt to interfere since the English were at their most vulnerable. Instead, they redeployed along the ridge of Branxton Hill and waited while the English grouped into battle formation on the other side of the low-lying stretch of boggy ground between the two armies.

On the Scottish side, James was in the centre, to his left was a division led by the earls of Crawford, Erroll and Montrose and further out a division led by the Earl of Huntly and Lord Home. On the right were the Highland division led by the earls of Lennox and Argyll. The Earl of Bothwell kept a division in reserve at the rear.

At 4pm the battle began. The Scottish gunners were less experienced than their English counterparts and were unable to discharge their guns sufficiently while the English cannonade was devastatingly effective. Soon the Scottish guns fell silent and the English cannon methodically raked the flanks of standing Scottish spearmen.

To avoid being scythed down, the Scottish Borderers under the Earl of Home on the left wing swept into the attack, driving the English right from the field. They then formed up in a position to menace the English flank but inexplicably, took no further part in the action.

James, thinking that the battle was practically won, placed himself at the head of his own division and led them in a charge at the English centre. It was a reckless, unpardonable mistake, leaving the army and his generals effectively leaderless and with James in the lead, like an ordinary knight, the Scottish infantry went charging downhill, but came to a muddy halt at the base of the hill. With their momentum gone, they had to start lumbering up the slippery slopes towards the English ranks in the face of heavy artillery fire. Soon they were encircled.

The Scottish right under Lennox and Argyll and the reserve division under Bothwell were scattered by a surprise cavalry attack from the flank and with that surprise attack, James and his infantry divisions must have known they were doomed. But they still fought on courageously.

There is a story that tells of James launching himself against the banner of the Earl of Surrey towards the end of that bitter day and fell only a spear's length away, scythed down by the earl's retainers. He fell with a deep gash in his neck and shoulder, one of his hands hanging by a shred of skin. His last wound was an arrow through his open mouth fired at close range.

At dusk, after three hours of furious fighting, up to 15,000 Scots lay dead, including 40-year-old James, his illegitimate son Alexander, Archbishop of St Andrews, two bishops, eleven earls, fifteen barons and 300 knights. The body of James was so mutilated that it was not recognised until the following day.

In the minds of historians, Flodden represents the end of the most successful kingship, the most successful reign of the late medieval period that was brought to an end by the retaliation of a vengeful king, Henry VIII, for their association with France. James IV stands as the culmination of Stewart kingship which had started off in a shaky fashion in 1371. Flodden was simply one of the many border raids which went terribly wrong, a battle itself that was not intended. It was also a mistake because the portable cannon, James's best firepower, was on his fleet in France, helping the King of France.

He left behind a pregnant wife and a 17-month-old boy, James, and Scotland was back once more with an infant-king and a state of turmoil.

The tragic loss of the king and much of the nation's men should have meant an end to battle. Unbelievably, even after two centuries of war, the flight was far from over.

JAMES V

Born 1512
Reign 1513 – 1542

Twelve days after the death of his father at Flodden, Prince James was crowned James V at Stirling, conducted by James Beaton, the new Archbishop of Glasgow since Robert Blackadder was one of the many who had died at Flodden. James was barely seventeen months old.

Instead of a calamitous destruction of the Scottish nobility at Flodden, the nation had not disintegrated because many of the earls and barons were fortunate enough to have produced male heirs. Satisfied at his success at Flodden and totally uncaring of the pain he had caused his sister, Henry VIII fixed his sights firmly on France and made no attempt to follow up the victory with a full-scale invasion of Scotland.

According to her husband's will, 25-year-old Margaret Tudor was to be the child-king's guardian for as long as she remained unmarried, although this didn't automatically make her regent. The Scots were very wary of Margaret from the outset, being Henry's sister, and eyes soon turned elsewhere in a search for a more suitable guardian for the king and governor of the country.

The man who was favoured for the task was John, Duke of Albany, the son of James III's brother Alexander who had made the failed attempt to depose his brother with English help in 1482. Alexander had fled to France in exile where he died three years later but not before he produced a son, John, who became the new Duke of Albany. John's mother was French and he grew up in France, served in the French Army and spoke no English whatsoever. But although he was a French subject, he was James II's grandson and James IV's cousin, making him the next in succession to the Scottish crown after James V. In the autumn of 1513, the General Council agreed that Albany should be invited to come to Scotland as governor with the backing of French soldiers and munitions and that the 'Auld Alliance' should be renewed. Again. Albany arrived in Scotland in May 1515 and took up residence in Dunbar Castle where according to the terms of his regency, he was entitled to keep a French garrison.

Within a year after James IV's death and soon after the birth in April of her short-lived second son, Alexander, Margaret Tudor suddenly married the 24-year-old Archibald Douglas, 6th Earl of Angus, thereby invalidating her claim to be her son's rightful guardian and forced to yield the custody of James and his baby brother to Albany. The couple moved to England but the marriage which had seemed capricious enough at the time, soon broke up in a long and acrimonious public separation but not before she produced a daughter, Margaret. In the future, Margaret would marry Matthew Stewart, 4th Earl of Lennox and produce a son they would name Henry Stuart, Lord Darnley, who we will see much more of later in the story.

As to be expected, the next few years of Scottish politics were to be punctuated by squabbles over the custody of young James and led to a choice between magnates who supported a closer alliance with France and those who saw more safety in an association with England. Politics in Europe were complex and France and Spain were vying for supremacy and Scotland was always in danger of being side-lined.

The main stabilising influence in these confused years was surprisingly the Duke of Albany. As an 'outsider', he was able to make the most of the situation though a cross-section of the nobility in the General Council and he proved himself to be resolute and tolerant and played the skilful diplomatic at the European table. As requested, he negotiated the renewal of the 'Auld Alliance' with the Treaty of Rouen although the Scots were understandably wary of committing military adventures against England in support of France. That had been a disaster that they were still trying to come to terms with.

Disregarding their qualms, Albany brought a large French expeditionary force to Scotland but it turned into posturing rather than active hostilities, despite the English raiders burning Kelso and Jedburgh. The Franco-Scottish army advanced to the border but the Scots, no doubt remembering Flodden, were unwilling to risk another full-scale invasion of England. One year later, clearly in a huff, Albany returned to France, taking his French troops with him and never returned.

By this time, after her disastrous marriage, Margaret Tudor had been allowed back into Scotland on the promise of good behaviour as an honest and loyal Scotswoman, regaining the guardianship of her 12-year-old son. Her young son Alexander had died suddenly while in Albany's care and many suspected he had killed the small child so he could retain the heir apparent status. James was invested with crown, sword and sceptre, attended by a bodyguard of two hundred men-at-arms sent by his uncle Henry VIII of England, who seems to have been in a fit of infrequent benevolence. But Margaret's eventual divorce from the Earl of Angus in 1527 caused a rift with her brother Henry VIII who, at this stage, was still disapproving of divorce. Probably more to the point, Henry was busying himself with building up a pro-English party in Scotland, led by her estranged husband the Earl of Angus, so her divorce couldn't have helped his cause.

James's minority ended one year before the divorce in 1526 on his fourteenth birthday but his step-father still had control of James by a bold *coup d'etat*. A sensible scheme had been devised whereby James' safekeeping was to be entrusted to four groups of magnates in a rotating regency, three months at a time. The first group was led by the Earl of Angus along with his kinsman the Earl of Morton and young James' tutor Gavin Dunbar, Archbishop of Glasgow. The scheme quickly fell apart when the Earl of Angus simply refused to hand James over when the time came for him to pass him to the second group. The Earl promptly appointed himself a Chancellor and Keeper of the Privy Seal and packed the royal household with his own relatives to ensure the king was kept under constant close supervision. James remained in custody for two years, a virtual prisoner, despite a failed attempt at a rescue outside Linlithgow during which time the Earl of Lennox was killed.

James' imprisonment continued until the summer of 1528, soon after his 16th birthday, until his dramatic escape from Falkland Palace when he slipped his supervisors and rode all night to Stirling Castle, to his mother's keeping. A group of leading noblemen, including the Earls of Argyll, Arran, Bothwell, Eglinton, Montrose, Moray and Rothes, closed ranks around James in open opposition of Angus.

You just know Angus wasn't about to be exonerated. One month later, the young king and his supporters rode into Edinburgh with a bodyguard of 300 spearmen and feeling rightfully nervous, Angus resigned his position of Chancellor and withdrew to Tantallon Castle and fortified it. James was then ready to rule.

It had been a strange childhood for James. His father would hardly have been remembered and he lost a baby brother, Alexander, while he was still a toddler. He had been caught up in an endless tug-of-war between his mother and his stepfather, whom it seems he did not like at all, and he had endured the familiar trauma of emotional neglect amid grand surroundings which was so often the lot of royal children.

Understandingly, James's first act in his personal rule, more than likely at his mother's urging, was to get parliament to arraign his stepfather for treason, along with several of his closest kin, including the earl's sister, the Countess of Glamis. After a flurry of raids on other Angus strongholds, James laid siege to Tantallon Castle in October, which was ongoing for three weeks but failed to force a surrender. In order to isolate Angus from his English support, the Scottish parliament managed to negotiate a five-year truce with England in April 1529 to force Angus to surrender. I can only assume Henry was totally consumed with his efforts to divorce Catherine of Aragon while wooing the coquettish Anne Boleyn at the time, perhaps signing the truce in order to focus his attention on his own personal problems instead of annoying Scottish skirmishes. With no help coming from England, Angus was forced to surrender Tantallon Castle and was allowed to retire into exile in England where he became a pensioner of Henry VIII. His estates in Scotland were forfeited and all his Douglas kinsmen were disgraced.

For many years, seasonal cross-border raiding had become a way of life for many Borderers and the Armstrongs of Liddesdale had been a law unto themselves for many years, even going so far as to state they acknowledged neither the authority of King of Scots or King of England. James promptly descended his force on the border lands of the West Marches which had been the cause of endless contention. His main target was Johnnie Armstrong of Gilknockie.

The story of the swoop on Liddesdale and the manner of Armstrong's death became the subject of a poignant ballad which claims James enticed Armstrong to a peace-meeting at Caerlenrig with fifty unarmed followers and then broke his word by having them arrested. A rather familiar tale when it comes to the Stewarts. Johnnie Armstrong and most of his accomplices were taken outside and summarily hanged. Only half a dozen were spared.

James had failed to deliver the killer-blow against his stepfather but many of Angus' kinsmen and supporters were not so lucky. Of those who had been arraigned with him for treason, many were granted pardons for their 'crimes', 146 people in all. Others were not so lucky. Three individuals were executed for the treasonable crime of conspiring to kill the king: John, Master of Forbes, Sir James Hamilton of Finnart and most notoriously of all, Janet Douglas, Countess of Glamis, one of four sisters of the forfeited Earl of Angus and sister-in-law to John, Master of Forbes. Janet Douglas has come down in history as a horrific victim of royal vindictiveness and royal greed.

The Master of Forbes, who had been in constant trouble with his neighbouring landowners, was found guilty of patently trumped-up charges of plotting to shoot the king and was hanged, drawn and quartered on 14th July 1537, an English form of execution previously unknown in Scotland. His extensive lands, of course were forfeited to the crown.

Sir James Hamilton of Finnart was the illegitimate son of the 1st Earl of Arran and thus tainted by his connection with the Douglas clan. More importantly, he was a key member of the royal household, the royal architect and principal Master of Works. He supervised the building works of Falkland Palace, Linlithgow Palace, Edinburgh Castle and Stirling Castle but his contribution to Scottish architecture did not save him from the scaffold when he too was convicted on 16th August 1540 of treasonable conspiracy to assassinate the king. He was executed on the same day but his real crime may well have been his wealth, which the king appropriated.

The case of Janet Douglas, Countess of Glamis, has always excited pity and horror, and not simply because she was a young mother, and an uncommonly beautiful one at that, she had originally been charged with her Douglas brother for *'art and part assistance'* in 1528 during the first Douglas purge in the first year of James's personal rule and was granted remission. Later she was charged with having poisoned her first husband, John Lyon, Lord Glamis in 1532 but once again the prosecution case was dropped. Janet then married her second husband, Lord Lyon, a kinsman of her first husband, and resumed her title to the Glamis estates.

But James had not forgotten her from nine years ago for her simple offence of being a Douglas. On 17th July 1537, the 33-year-old Countess was charged again, and convicted this time, on two points of treason, conspiring to poison the king (as well as her husband), witchcraft and assisting her brothers. Immediately after being sentenced, her husband was imprisoned while she was taken out to Castle Hill in Edinburgh where the execution was carried out. She was chained to a stake, with barrels of tar packed around her, and burned to death. Sadly, her 16-year-old son was present and watched his mother burn. Next day, her husband, while trying to escape from the castle, plunged to his death onto the rocks below.

Convicting Janet on witchcraft was one thing, gaining evidence was another. Apparently to gain 'evidence' of poisoning her husband, James had the servants of Janet's family subjected to torture.

Historians agree that the charge of attempting to poison James was totally fictitious. Perhaps it should be noted that her forfeited estates brought the crown a total of £5,770 from 1538 until the end of James's reign in 1542.

As with so many of the Stewart monarchs, James had a powerful sexual appetite. He is known to have had at least seven mistresses: Lady Margaret Erskine (the wife of Douglas of Loch Leven), Elizabeth Beaton, Elizabeth Stewart, Elizabeth Shaw, Elizabeth Carmichael, Euphemia Elphinstone and Christina Barclay. By them, he had a number of illegitimate sons, at least eight, one of whom was James, the future Earl of Moray and future Regent of Scotland. His sons were appointed titular abbots of Kelso, Melrose, St Andrews, Coldingham and the Abbey of Holyrood House, which was nothing short of abuse of ecclesiastical appointments. The appointments were highly advantageous for James because the profits from these foundations went straight into his pockets.

For many years, his marital status was the object of discussion in the courts of Europe, despite Scotland being a minor player on the European stage. By this time, Henry in England had divorced Catherine of Aragon, who had subsequently died, and moved on to Anne Boleyn. Anne was beheaded in 1536 and been replaced by Jane Seymour, who had just delivered Henry his one and only son Edward in 1537 after two daughters, Mary to Catherine of Aragon and Elizabeth to Anne Boleyn. The birth was difficult and Jane died two weeks later from an infection. The euphoria that had accompanied his son's birth became sorrow but eighteen months later, he had recovered enough to marry Anne of Cleves.

Watching Henry, James must have realised that he needed to marry and have legitimate children, sooner rather than later.

By the Treaty of Rouen negotiated by the Duke of Albany in 1517, the 5-year-old James had been promised a French princess as a bride, but in the shifting alliances of the time, Francois I of France was reluctant to commit himself to such an anti-English stance. Henry had tried to woo the Scots away from France by offering the hand of his daughter, Mary Tudor but Scotland refused and began engaging in an intriguing round of proposals and counter-proposals over the years to put pressure on France. Various possibilities were publicly explored: a sister of Emperor Charles V, a daughter of King of Denmark, even a Medici ward of Pope Clement VII.

In 1536, as Anne Boleyn was heading to the gallows, a contract was arranged for a French bride, Marie de Bourbon. After seeing her rather unattractive portrait, James asked for a pension of 20,000 livres in addition to her dowry of a 100,000 livres. His conditions were accepted and James sailed to Dieppe with an escort of some 5,000 men in order to inspect Marie. When he saw her in the flesh, he broke off the match.

Next he turned to King Francois I of France with an offer for his daughter Madeleine de Valois. Being of delicate health, her father was reluctant to let her go but in the end he agreed and on January 1st 1537, James married Madeleine at Notre Dame and given the title 'Defender of the Faith' by the Pope. Madeleine fell ill in March but in May the couple sailed for Scotland. Within two months, Madeleine died in Holyrood Palace.

A French bride was still what James wanted and negotiations began for his marriage to another princess by the name of Marie de Guise, who had been adopted by King Francois I. Marie was the wife of the Duc de

Longueville when James first met her but the duke had died a few weeks before Madeleine's death and there was now no obstacle to her marriage with James. Henry had also been interested in marrying her after he lost the real love of his life, Jane Seymour. By now, Henry was a serial widower by reputation and his offer was refused while the marriage to James was arranged by proxy. In June 1538, Marie de Guise sailed to Scotland and Henry had begun looking for wife number four.

Marie de Guise was a remarkable woman. She was the sister of Francois Duc de Guise and of Charles, Cardinal of Lorraine, which made her a member of the most powerful noble house in France, perhaps all of Europe. She was highly intelligent and well-verse in the subtle intricacies of high politics, both domestic and international, and was about to play a tremendously important part in the governance of Scotland as Queen Regent after the birth of her daughter, Mary Queen of Scots.

Marie had brought with her another dowry of 150,000 livres and the money was of huge importance to James. Like so many of his ancestors, he was determined to improve the finances of the crown.

The background to the last years of James' reign was the growing wave of protests in many countries of Europe against the corrupt medieval order, especially against the power faults of the papacy and the churchmen. In Germany, Martin Luther, a monk who had married a former nun in flagrant breach of papal authority, had thrown down the gauntlet against papal supremacy by drawing up a list of 95 opinions on the sale of pardons for ordinary people.

In Scotland, the first of the 'heretic martyrs' had been burned in 1528 during the last year of James' minority, a young theologian by the name of Patrick Hamilton, a great-grandson of James II who preached openly of his principles when he returned to Scotland from Paris and Wittenberg, for 'teaching opinions of Luther and wicked heresies'. He was arrested and tried and on 29th February 1528, Patrick Hamilton was found guilty of heresy and burned in front of St Salvador's College in St Andrews. He was the first known Scotsman to die for his beliefs and ten other Protestant intellectuals were to go to the stake in the 1530's, although many others fled Scotland to continue their careers abroad.

After James' marriage to Marie de Guise, Henry VIII was even more concerned about the 'Auld Alliance' between Scotland and France. In 1541, as the crisis in the Church deepened, Henry's policy was more than ever aimed at trying to persuade his nephew James V to make the same break with Rome that he had made and James was invited to meet Henry at York to discuss their theological and religious differences. James did not formally accept the invitation but Henry seems to have assumed the he would attend, and expected to meet him during a royal progress to the north of England that summer. James probably saw no point in meeting his uncle at this stage since he was quite happy to preserve the status quo regarding the Scottish Church for as long as it was providing so much income for the crown. In any case, he had the support of both the King of France and the Pope. He didn't think he needed Henry's.

Henry waited in York until the end of September. When it became obvious that James was not coming, contrary to his usual outrage, he sent a letter to James in February 1542 forgiving him for his non-attendance. In the devious diplomacy of the time, Henry was even now planning to join the Holy roman Empire in a war against France, which he did in July 1542 when Francois I and the Emperor Charles V went to war.

With France otherwise engaged, Henry now felt able to deal with Scotland without fear of French intervention. Late in July, he put the north of England on a war footing and James responded in August by sending George Gordon, 4th Earl of Huntly, to Kelso as royal lieutenant to organise the defence of the Borders. After a flurry of raids and counter-raids, the English sent a force of three thousand men under Sir Robert Bower to harry the lands of the Merse. This force was scattered by a smaller force of two thousand men under Huntly at the Battle of Hadden Rig at the end of August, leaving hundreds of English prisoners in Scottish hands.

Before the news had even reached Henry, he had already commissioned the Duke of Norfolk to prepare to invade Scotland in October. On 22nd October, the English army left Berwick-upon-Tweed and proceeded to burn Kelso Abbey and Roxburgh Tower. The army had been at least 20,000 strong, enough to deter Huntly from trying to intervene with his small force, but Norfolk complained that he had been desperately short of supplies and could not sustain a longer incursion into Scotland.

As obstinate as ever, Henry officially declared war. He resurrected the English claim to superiority over Scotland and recommended that the full invasion should be launched in June 1543. James responded to the Norfolk incursion by ordering a general mobilisation in the belief that Norfolk was planning to attack Edinburgh.

James' strategy involved spreading a good deal of deliberate misinformation for the benefit of English spies. He feinted an assault to the south-east but at the same time he was planning an assault through the Merse in the west.

There was nothing wrong with the plan, only with the execution. James left Lauder and moved rapidly to Peebles to meet his 'western army' but the English had been alerted in the nick of time at Carlisle. James had promised his wife not to take part personally in any fighting and departed for Lochmaben while a large raiding party of Scots under the command of Lord Maxwell moved to the mouth of the Esk, leaving the main bulk of the army in reserve.

The geography of the Battle of Solway Moss which ensured is confusing in that the English reports contradict one another. There is no contemporary Scottish accounts of the battle and the scale of the fighting is in dispute as to whether it was a real battle or merely a brawl. Whatever the truth, the Scots quickly fled. What had been intended as a preliminary raid had ended in debacle.

James returned disconsolately to Edinburgh, his military strategy in tatters. Many of his nobles had been captured at Solway Moss and further raids into England were clearly out of the question. From Edinburgh he issued instructions for strengthening the Border defence to meet any English attempts to follow up their victory, then he went to Linlithgow where his queen was about to give birth.

James himself was terribly unwell by then, perhaps suffering from dysentery or cholera after drinking contaminated water while on campaign. He retired to his favourite palace of Falkland where he took to his bed on 6th December. He was only 30 years old, a strong, sturdy young man, but cholera in particular was a deadly disease. At Falkland he heard of the birth of his daughter, Mary, at Linlithgow on 8th December but the news brought him no pleasure for he must have been hoping for another son who would survive to be his heir. It was then that he said to have uttered his gloomy deathbed saying: *'The De'il gang wi' it. It will end as it began. It cam' wi' a lass and will gang wi' a lass.'*

On 14th December 1542, James died.

The baby was a weak, sickly child and you can believe Scotland were remembering with trepidation the sickly 6-year-old, Maid of Norway, who died in Orkney on her way from Denmark to accept the Scottish throne after her grandfather's death. Her death caused the Great Cause and the War of Independence when Robert the Bruce finally won over Edward I. But it came at a great cost and they would definitely not want to repeat that exercise. The *'lass'* James was referring to was Robert the Bruce's daughter, Marjory, from his first marriage. She married Walter Stewart, the 6th Steward of Scotland, and produced a son Robert who became King Robert II. But it was through Marjory, not a son, that the Stewart line had begun.

This time, it was Henry VIII who was lurking instead of Edward I and already, Henry could be held indirectly, if not directly, responsible for the death of two Scottish kings, James IV (the child's grandfather) and James V (her father). Both kings died as a result of unnecessary battles and Scotland would never forget that Henry was at the route of both deaths.

Historians may have unfairly treated James, portraying him almost as the anti-Christ. He did some dreadful things, but so have most monarchs. James may have not been particularly likeable (but which Stewart king has been?) and his reign ended in a humiliating failure although not as disastrous as Flodden was. Perhaps the real problem is that James V died such an untimely death. Had he lived longer, Scotland's later history would have been very different. James was a young and vigorous king in full control of his kingdom, facing an ailing Henry VIII approaching the end of his controversial and infamous reign. By then, Henry had just beheaded his fifth wife and was looking for his next bride. His search would end with a wealthy widow who was smart enough to outlive him. Had James lived, Marie de Guise might well have produced the son and heir who would have secured an adult Stewart succession free of the crises brought on by the accession of the infant Mary.

For me, the death of James V at Falkland Palace in 1542 was every bit as disastrous for Scotland as the death of Alexander III at Kinghorn in 1286. Another historical 'what-if'.

We all know the tiny child survived to become one of Scotland's most celebrated monarchs – the ill-fated Mary Queen of Scots.

MARY QUEEN OF SCOTS

Born 1542
Died 1587

Mary is one of the great celebrities of the British monarchy. Everyone knows the story of Mary's tumultuous life or some version of it. Born into a powerful royal dynasty that was already at the heart of the religious and political war between European nations intent on destroying each other, Mary's life was never destined to be easy. Born and raised to be the queen of not one but potentially three different nations, Mary fit the part of a great monarch in her looks, intelligence and wit. By the time she reached her wedding day, her future looked brighter than the rising sun.

But the tragic events of Mary's adulthood eclipsed those of her happy childhood. As Mary's support system disintegrated, she sought solace in the arms of disloyal men. She was betrayed time and time again. Unable to hold together her fatally unstable country, Mary failed to maintain her grip on the ever-tottering crown on her head and was finally removed from the Scottish throne by an armed rebellion.

To her champions, Mary was a victim of the Scottish lords, the French and English politicians who constantly plotted her demise. But to her critics, she was an ineffectual queen, ruled by her emotions and more concerned with her love affairs than repairing her fractured country. This vivacious, beautiful, thrice-married, thrice-widowed, woman was an infinitely unhappy queen whose storm-tossed life and horrendous end has held the world's imagination in thrall ever since. More has been written about Mary than any other monarch in Scotland, perhaps the world. Over the centuries, scholars have worked themselves into a frenzy of passion either for or against her. Her decisions and actions have been endlessly debated, her personality and motives endlessly dissected. The cast of characters is enormous, friends and foes, husbands and lovers, champions and traitors, and above all the people of Scotland.

Her story is complicated and lengthy because there was far more to Mary Queen of Scots than meets the eye.

She was born at Linlithgow on 8th December 1542, where her father had been born 30 years earlier, the 3rd child of James V and Mary of Guise. Mary and James had already lost two sons in infancy and as Mary was premature, her mother, and Scotland, feared they would lose her too. Just in case, she was baptised almost immediately.

Even at birth, Mary was a fighter. She not only survived but she took her father's throne at just six days old as Mary Queen of Scots and promptly became the source of discord in Scotland, England and even Europe. She was nursed for the first nine months of her life in Linlithgow and then moved to the greater security of Stirling Castle where she was solemnly crowned Queen of Scots on 9th September, the 30th anniversary of Flodden, whilst sitting on her mother's knee.

Mary's mother, Mary of Guise, was a powerful player in the House of Guise, a French noble family that was heavily involved in the politics of 16th century France.

As the child of Mary of Guise, Mary represented French interests but as the great-niece of the infamous Henry VIII, Mary also had strong ties to the English. At this stage, England was not yet Protestant but it was certainly heading that way. Meanwhile, France and Scotland was resolutely Catholic although some Scottish nobles were watching Henry carefully as he rejected the authority of the Pope and broke away from the Roman Catholic

Church. Henry's reformed Church of England was winning converts, even in Scotland, and many noblemen became rich beyond their dreams as he redistributed the spoils of the church amongst his allies.

Since Mary was a new born when she inherited the throne, a regent was needed, and since her mother could only remain her protector, (she not permitted to rule), the role of regent fell to the next in succession, James Hamilton, 2nd Earl of Arran and the great-grandson of James II.

Little is recorded in the early years of Mary's childhood but the machinations behind the scene were constant as a husband was being sourced for her. Knowing it was a win-win solution for him, Henry VIII proposed a future marriage between Mary and his own infant son Edward, not yet 6 years old. After the marriage, everything Mary owned would automatically become Edward's and the Tudors would be kings of Scotland and England combined. Six months later, Hamilton accepted Henry's offer and a treaty was drawn up to seal the deal. The Treaty stated that Mary should be taken to England where, at the age of ten, she and Edward would marry and Henry would have a hand in her upbringing.

Henry may have been happy with the treaty but Mary of Guise was definitely not. Pro-French factions led by Cardinal Beaton intervened and the treaty was finally rejected. At this stage, Hamilton stepped in and suggested his own son, after all he had Scottish royal blood running through his veins and he would make a better husband for Mary than the English Prince Edward.

Again the offer was refused and one month later, in September 1543, Mary of Guise felt her fragile daughter was strong enough to travel to Stirling Castle where Mary would be crowned Queen of Scots.

It was a brave thing to do for Mary of Guise to cross Henry VIII. By then, his temper and reputation was appalling and not too many people were brave enough to side-line him. Of course, he was furious and shortly after the coronation, he ordered the arrest of Scottish merchants heading for France, (an entirely illegal thing to do), causing an uproar in Scotland. Not finished yet, he then resorted to burning the border abbeys of Kelso, Jedburgh, Melrose and Dryburgh to the ground. Three years later, Cardinal Beaton would be murdered in St Andrew's Castle.

Even Henry's death one year later in 1547 didn't stop the onslaught.

The Duke of Somerset, acting as Lord Protector to young Edward, led an army north and defeated the Scots at the Battle of Pinkie Cleugh.

Desperate to protect their infant Queen, the Scots turned to the King Henry II of France for help. His wife, Catherine of Medici, sometimes called The Serpent Queen, had given him 9 children, 4 of which were boys, and their second son, Dauphin Francis, was put forward for the betrothal.

Once again, Hamilton agreed and with a French armed envoy, 5-year-old Mary boarded Henry II's own galley and headed to France to be raised in the French court. With her was her illegitimate half-brother Lord James Stewart, her mother's closest confidante Lady Fleming, Lords Erskine and Livingstone, her nurse Janet Sinclair and the 'four Mary's', her four best friends all named Mary. After the gruelling crossing, she was welcomed by her grandparents, Claude Duke of Guise and Antoinette of Bourbon, ready to spend the next eleven years of her life in readiness to enter the French Court as queen consort.

Vivacious and beautiful, Mary had a wonderful childhood with the best available education in languages, poetry, horsemanship, needlework and music. By sixteen, she was a cultured married woman with the world at her feet.

Despite Mary being quite tall for her age at 5 feet 11 inches and her husband quite short at 5 feet 3 inches, the two seemed happy enough. Francis' father, Henry II, led an unusual household. He lived in harmony with his wife Catherine de Medici and his mistress Diane de Poitiers, who even had a hand in the education and upbringing of Henry and Catherine's children.

Despite the complexities of the French king's domestic arrangements, Mary flourished and was much loved. With auburn hair and a fair complexion, Mary was a beautiful young woman who was said to be graceful, self-assured and intelligent. She became fluent in French, both written and spoken, in less than two years and in later years added Italian, Latin, Spanish and Greek to her list of languages. She played lute, wrote prose and poetry and her horsemanship and falconry was astounding.

Mary's childhood in the French court is the stuff made of fairy tales. But while Mary thrived in the French court, Scotland was becoming more unsettled, as was England. Between 1553 and 1558, Henry Tudor's eldest child, Mary Tudor, had become Queen of England and had aggressively set about restoring the Roman Catholic church, using methods that would later give her the name 'Bloody Mary'. In 1554, she married Price Philip of Spain who boasted that for every fort built by the French in Scotland, he would construct three more on the English side of the border. Once again, battle lines between England and Scotland were being drawn.

While he was alive, and because of the friction, Henry II of France had publicly proclaimed France and Scotland to be 'one country', a presumptive statement given Mary and Francis who were yet to be married. It raised the possibility that when they did marry, Scotland could become a French satellite land incorporated into France. Furthermore, Mary of Guise's regency in Scotland depended heavily on the protection of French troops stationed in Scotland and many viewed the French presence in Scotland as occupation.

A number of important events happened in 1558.

Firstly, in January, Mary of Guise's father, the Duke of Guise, led a French attack on the town of Calais, an English possession, and led a victorious procession through the town.

Secondly, in April, Mary Queen of Scots was married in an event as spectacular as you would expect. The wedding made Francis King Consort of Scotland and together the King and Queen were set to unite the crowns of France, Scotland and England as one, shaping a dynasty that would come to dominate the whole of Europe. However, before the wedding, Mary signed two important documents. The first stated that no matter what happened, Scotland would remain independent. The other document, signed in secret, stated that in the event of her death without an heir, the King of France and his successors would inherit Scotland and her claim to the English throne.

Then, in November 1558, Mary Tudor (remembered as Bloody Mary because of the number of religious executions she ordered) died childless of ovarian cancer in England.

According to Henry VIII's will, his only son Edward was his heir but after that, the throne would descend along the female line of Tudors. The young woman next in line was Mary Tudor and after her came Elizabeth Tudor. But Elizabeth had been declared illegitimate by an Act of Parliament since Henry had married her mother, Anne Boleyn, while his first wife, Catherine of Aragon, was still alive. Henry had repudiated his marriage to Anne when he tired of her and wished to marry again and had her executed in 1536.

For the Catholics in England, Scotland and France, Elizabeth Tudor was not the legitimate heir and if the English throne was to pass down the female line, then Margaret Tudor, Mary's grandmother, and her descendants were the legitimate heirs to the throne. It was only when Mary Tudor died without an heir that it became clear that there was both a Tudor and a Stuart claim to the throne. And Mary Queen of Scots was legitimate whereas Elizabeth was not.

With Mary Tudor dead, Mary Queen of Scots watched England with mounting interest waiting to hear news from England, summoning her. In those brutal and uncertain days, we can only assume she was waiting for the right moment to step forward and stake her claim. Then when Elizabeth took the throne of England, the eyes of Europe were also watching and waiting. Everyone knew that Mary Queen of Scots had a far better right to the throne than Elizabeth.

At this time in history, there were three women who held power in England, Scotland and France: Elizabeth in England, Mary in France and Mary of Guise, her mother, in Scotland. And with the force of France behind her, Mary stood a good chance of gaining the English throne.

Despite this, Elizabeth was crowned Queen of England in November 1558, a virtually bankrupt nation torn apart by religious discord, while in Paris the news was met with scorn. It seemed an illegitimate queen was better than a French one.

Elizabeth's life was troubled from the moment she was born. Despite the challenge of being Henry VIII's daughter, or perhaps *because* of it, she was a quiet and studious girl who could write English, speak Latin and Italian before progressing further on to French and Greek. By the time her formal education ended, she was the best-educated woman of her generation quietly living in the shadow of her father. When he died, everything suddenly and irrevocably changed.

Elizabeth was not only very aware of Mary's legitimate claim to the throne but also her capability to gather Catholic supporters in Scotland, England and Ireland. And if Mary had been smart, she would have used that incredible opportunity to her utmost advantage. But despite Mary's meticulous education, you can't teach someone how to cope with dangerous and complex situations. Trouble was never far away from Mary.

Mary fell ill early in 1559, but the exact cause of her illness remains a mystery. It seemed that Mary, in times of great stress, could succumb to breathlessness and fainting and it has been speculated that she was just one of a number of royals in her family line to suffer from porphyria, a rare blood disease. Perhaps it was porphyria, perhaps it was stress, because in June 1559, her father-in-law, Henry II of France, was taking part in a tournament and was struck down by a lance that slid under his helmet and into his face. Even the finest surgeons couldn't save Henry since the lance had struck his brain. He died of a stroke ten days later and Mary's husband Francis succeeded his father as King of France just days from her 17th birthday. On that day, she became Queen of France, Queen of Scotland and the rightful heir to England because more importantly, she was legitimate. It was a far cry from Elizabeth's circumstances where her father had declared his marriage to Elizabeth's mother, Anne Boleyn, as null and void, effectively making her illegitimate.

If Elizabeth's sister Mary Tudor had been considered a suspicious queen, Elizabeth surpassed her hands down. News was arriving daily in England that the French were plotting to assassinate her and Elizabeth began taking every precaution. Around her, she gathered Protestant supporters who would rather die than let any harm come her way and she hired bodyguards as food tasters where everything was fully examined and tasted before she would even lift it to her mouth.

Despite both being so closely related to Henry VII, the two cousins were nothing alike. Mary was unable to separate emotions from politics while Elizabeth had learnt from her bitter childhood to be in vigilant at all times. With her auburn hair, fiery temper and almost inexhaustible energy, there was never any doubt who Elizabeth's father was. Unfortunately, like her father, there were also fits of melancholy followed by buoyant cheerfulness and then sudden, convulsive rage.

Without a doubt, she was suspicious of everyone but her greatest concern was always Scotland. The danger from Scotland loomed even more threateningly as France declared their support for the French Queen and her French mother. As Elizabeth watched anxiously, it looked definite that French troops would land in Scotland at any time. If the French gained control of Scotland, their next move would certainly be to move south and attack her in England.

As always, a lack of money was the big issue for Elizabeth. With very little money in the treasury, it was a scant fleet hurriedly put together to try and blockade ports against French reinforcements.

And then disaster after disaster struck Mary.

The year 1560 turned out to be just as traumatic as 1558 and 1559 for Mary.

For over a week, her mother had been seriously ill in Scotland. Her mind had begun to wander and on some days, she could not speak at all. On the 8th June 1560, she made a will and three days later, she was dead. On that day, everything changed. At the news of her death, France instantly withdrew their troops from Scotland and Elizabeth was let off the hook.

In modern times, Hollywood has speculated that she died of poisoning because of the suddenness of her death, perhaps even on the order of Elizabeth herself. But at the time, in a paranoid political climate when many royal deaths were suspected to have been murders, none saw her death as 'foul play.' It was diagnosed as dropsy, a swelling from fluid accumulation in body tissues. It most commonly occurs in the feet and legs but as the body is primarily made up of water, excess fluid sometimes collects in the lungs and the heart tissues, which can cause a heart attack or the brain to swell.

In France, Mary was still in mourning when her husband began suffering from seizures and pains in his head, more specifically his ear. One month later, he was dead from an abscess on his brain caused by an ear infection and Mary became a widow at nineteen. He was succeeded by his 10-year-old brother, Charles, and things went from bad to worse for Mary.

Relations between Catherine de Medici and Mary had been strained for years. It was the 1st day as a widow when Catherine forced Mary to hand over all of her jewels as Queen of France, even creating an inventory of the items and their value. Mary was then sent into a period of solitary mourning that lasted for forty days while Catherine managed to craftily outwit other members of the family and began effectively ruling France as his Regent.

Mary wasn't stupid. She weighed up her options and decided the best course of action for her was to return to Scotland via England.

As the *legitimate* grandniece of Henry VIII, Mary Queen of Scots could be forgiven for thinking she had been robbed of the throne of England. Three months later, she could also be forgiven for thinking that France had turned its back on her as well. She could also be forgiven for thinking that

England had gone too far when they refused her request to dock in London on her way to Scotland from France.

Mary was furious at the insult. Putting aside the fact that she had a legitimate right to *contest* the English throne, and some would have stated that her claim was an even *better* one than Elizabeth's claim, her cousin should have at least awarded her a certain level of courtesy, given her plight and predicament. Inevitably, with the snub, Mary had no choice but to return to Scotland by another longer and more dangerous route. And England fervently prayed that danger stepped in quickly. Elizabeth didn't want her in England but she certainly had no want for her to return to Scotland either. The religious balance in Scotland was already delicate and a strongly Catholic monarch would probably start a civil war with the Protestants. If Mary won that civil war, she would probably turn her attention back to England again since she was regarded as the rightful queen in the eyes of many European leaders.

Before Mary left, dark storm clouds began to gather menacingly in the distance as she stood on the bow of the ship cursing Elizabeth profusely and praying that all the power of God would reap vengeance on her cousin. Later that night, it seemed that God had been listening to her prayers.

It was the summer of 1560 on the evening that Elizabeth had sent the letter to Mary refusing her permission to enter London. She had watched as Mary's ship left the harbour, growing smaller and smaller until it had become just a tiny black spot on the horizon. She would have been imagining it was Mary's red cloak that she saw fluttering wildly in the breeze. As she watched, storm clouds gathered menacingly in the distance.

As dusk fell, a vicious storm broke over London sending everyone scurrying through the flooding streets to escape the raging torrent of rain. As the temperature dropped dramatically, winds howled and trees were blown almost horizontally. Then at midnight, a lightning bolt struck the highest point of St Pauls Cathedral, sending it up in flames. An hour later, the steeple had been destroyed and the spire had fallen through the nave roof. The fire was hot enough to melt the cathedral bells, and lead that covered the wooden spire poured like lava through the burning roof. It was only at two in the morning that the fire was finally extinguished.

As Elizabeth stared in shock at the blackened ruin of St Pauls Cathedral, had she been wondering if she was being punished for refusing Mary to enter the harbour? Had she been too hasty in that refusal?

No doubt, it was an evening Elizabeth would never forget, especially with certain events not too far in the future.

From here on, England and Scotland's history is closely intertwined.

As in England, Scotland was torn between Catholics and Protestants and many different religious groups had established themselves throughout the countryside. With news that Mary was on her way home, Catholics were rejoicing that their ruler, who had declared herself a fervent Catholic, would soon be back in Scotland to take matters in hand. While Mary had been in France and after her mother's death, Scotland had been under the control of her illegitimate half-brother James Stewart, who was also the leader of the local Protestant group. Local sporadic fighting had broken out but things had settled down a little with news of Mary's imminent arrival.

Mary arrived in Leith and was astounded to find the country in so much disarray. Within weeks, she made her first mistake.

It's true her half-brother James Stewart said all the right things to Mary. He offered his undying support and he gave the appearance of steadfast loyalty. But words are just words and appearances can be deceptive. Unfortunately for Mary, she would find that out the hard way. So instead of dismissing James, she kept him on as her chief advisor. Not only that, she made him the 1st Earl of Moray. Sometimes your worst enemies come disguised as family members.

But if she'd looked to England, they were in a worse position.

In art galleries, we are shown pictures of Elizabethan countryside and what we see are ruggedly beautiful landscapes of sweeping meadows full of flowers and banks of lush green trees on hillsides. Most English people in those days saw England as anything but beautiful. For most people, it was a gloomy place worthy of murder around every corner, and you wouldn't hang around for too long. In the countryside, dotted around you would see cottages but they were far from idyllic. Families were poor and their houses were dark. Few people could afford the luxury of candles. Most houses were basic dwellings consisting of one room with a single fireplace. It was gloomy and smoky and windows were no more than a hole in the wall so little light entered the house. Their only possessions were a few pots, a ladle, some plates and if you were lucky, mats on the ground to sleep on. At night, the only sounds would have been the crackle of the fire, raindrops on the roof and the soft breathing of the children. And vermin were plentiful. And of course, with vermin came disease.

You would have been very aware of the diseases that could affect your everyday life. There were so many diseases lurking in the shadows: the flu, dysentery, small pox, the sweating sickness, typhoid and of course, the plague, although by the 16th century, the plague was not as prominent as it had been in the 14th century. In earlier days, half of the population of Europe was wiped out. By the 16th century, a 250,000 people would still die from this disease alone. If you had a swelling in your arm pits, if you were very thirsty, had a racing pulse, a headache or vomiting you knew you were in serious trouble. You also knew it was fleas that caused the disease so you made sure to air your bedding. But by then, it was way too late.

With the number of diseases so abundant, death was common in everyday life. Most children lost one parent by the time they had grown up and most parents lost half their children. In 1560 alone, there were 63 baptisms and 43 burials. Of course, added to everything else, sanitation was almost non-existent and it would be another 300 years before wealthy people could afford a flushing toilet. Until then, you had to make do with squatting over a running stream. With that came the stench and most times you could smell a village before you saw it.

For most people, options for work were very limited and your best bet was to go from farm to farm asking for work. You grew your own vegetables if you could and you made your own clothes. The question of whether to marry or not was based on the whether you could earn enough money to feed and support a family.

At the heart of everything, was their church. In those days of religious upheaval, attending church was compulsory every Sunday and if you didn't attend, you were fined £20. In England's chequered religious history, there were Protestants and Catholics but a new religion was raising its head with members calling themselves Puritans. Everyone believed in a God and if you said you were an Atheist, it was like saying you did not believe in trees and you could expect to be hated for it.

Where there is population there is crime and after dark, it was terrifying. In a place where so many had so little, it is hardly surprising. Many people carried a dagger and they kept their eyes open and their wits about them especially as ale was the only liquid available to drink due to a lack of clean fresh water. The combination of tempers and alcohol produced a dangerous and volatile situation and everyone could expect to be punished severely if they were caught breaking the laws.

Punishments varied and the level of cruelty won't come as a great surprise. The first was straightforward hanging on a gallows, the second was being hung, drawn and quartered. The third was to be burnt at a stake but the fourth was more severe and longer lasting. With this punishment, you were laid on the ground and a large rock was placed on your body. Blocks were added one by one until your body was crushed under the weight. It could take up to twelve hours to die.

It was an unbelievably painful, harsh time for most but it was a time of power and glory for a few others. Not everyone was at the bottom of the ladder. For the elite, it was a time of extravagance and wealth. In the same art galleries that depict a typical English countryside are portraits of noble men and women displaying these luxuries. When you look at these paintings what you see in their eyes is supreme confidence and a lifetime of privilege. But if you look a little closer and deeper, you may also see something else. Perhaps doubt and uncertainty? Perhaps fear? It was a dangerous time and it is worth remembering that those who possessed the most had the most to lose. Everyone liked to complain a little over a glass of wine or two, but you had to be very careful what you said and in whose company you said it.

Elizabethan England did not share our obsession with soap and water. In fact, they thought that using water could make you unwell through the pores of your skin. Looking at the rivers running with excrement, they had a good point. So the key to hygiene and keeping clean was not through water but through linen. Linen cloths were rubbed over the body and through their hair to soak up the sweat while shirts and undergarments were made of linen. So you kept yourself clean, not by washing, but by washing these linen clothes and by using perfumes to improve the smell of your clothes. While taking care of your body odours, you had to take care of your breath. There were no toothbrushes so you had to use a toothpick made of wood or bone or the quill of a feather. As to freshening your breath, you would have chewed cumin seeds or aniseed but most just rinsed their mouths out with white wine. Having done all your hygiene requirements, most gentry still believed that you should still take a bath once a month, whether you needed it or not.

Even after using these basic health care tips, you could also come across some illnesses like dysentery, typhus and scurvy. With dysentery you could die in as little as two weeks, as her father James V had, but with syphilis, you could live for twenty years, gradually and slowly going mad and at the end, dying from it.

While Mary settled in to life in Scotland in 1561, Elizabeth kept a low profile. Her movements during this time are somewhat scarce in history books until 1562 when it's known she contracted smallpox.

With no heir apparent apart from her cousin Mary Queen of Scots, England waited in abject horror to see if Elizabeth would pull through. To add to that fear, she made several unusual demands while she was delirious with fever, including requests to her advisers that Lord Robert Dudley be made Protector of the Realm. He was also to have a pension of £20,000 a year and an income was arranged for a servant of Dudley's, a man called John Tamworth. '*Which one was worse?*' the nobles were thinking. '*A Catholic barbarian queen from Scotland or a wolf in sheep's clothing scheming to snatch the throne for himself?*'

And then miraculously, Elizabeth showed signs of recovery and England let out an almost audible sigh of relief.

While Elizabeth was recuperating from her bout of smallpox, back in Scotland, Mary was having second thoughts of the wisdom of crossing Elizabeth years before. To make up for the breach, she invited Elizabeth to visit her in Scotland and of course, Elizabeth refused. A year later, arrangements were again made for the two queens to meet, this time fixed for York. Once more, Elizabeth's caution took over and she cancelled at the last minute. Then in 1563, Elizabeth made an extraordinary proposal.

When we consider her 'affection' for Robert Dudley, the proposal seems laughable in so many ways. Elizabeth's solution to the growing problem was that Robert Dudley should marry Mary and they should all live happily together as a family at the English court, so that she would not have to lose her favourite's company. Stunned, Mary asked Elizabeth if she was serious (a thought that crossed my mind as well). Elizabeth countered that she would only be prepared to acknowledge Mary as her heir on the condition that she do as she was requested and marry Robert.

To Mary's utter surprise, her Scottish advisors warmed to the prospect of having Robert as her consort and in September 1564, Elizabeth gave him the title of Earl of Leicester to make the offer even more tempting and acceptable.

Despite what Elizabeth or Mary's advisors thought, both Mary and Robert proved very unenthusiastic about her arrangement for a happy threesome and on 29th July 1565 Mary put paid to the suggestion and married her cousin Henry Stuart, Lord Darnley, instead.

Henry Stuart carried his own claim to the English throne through Margaret Tudor, Henry VIII's elder sister. After the death of Margaret's first husband James IV, she had married Archibald Douglas, Earl of Angus. From that marriage, there was one surviving daughter who in turn delivered a baby boy. Henry Stuart Lord Darnley. As a descendant of a daughter of James II of Scotland, Henry was in the front of the line for the throne of Scotland and a good chance for the English throne to boot, which is more than likely what he had in mind in the first place.

Mary had briefly met her cousin in February 1561 when she was still mourning her husband Francis. Darnley's parents, the Earl and Countess of Lennox, had sent him to France to ostensibly extend their condolences but in the back of their minds there was hope that a potential match could be arranged between their son and Mary. Nothing came of the visit but the seed had been planted. When the two met again in February of 1565, Mary fell in love with him.

And Darnley had plenty to offer. Three years younger than her, he was brought up conscious of his status and inheritance. He was well educated speaking Latin, Scottish Gaelic, English and French and he excelled in singing, lute playing and dancing. He was handsome, tall, strong, virile and athletic, a good horseman with a passion for hawking, hunting and dancing and he had a sound knowledge of weapons. Who could forgive Mary for falling head over heels in love and snapping him up?

If ever there was a whirlwind romance, this was it. On 22nd July, Darnley was made Duke of Albany in Holyrood Abbey and the banns of marriage were called. A proclamation was made in Edinburgh that government would be in the joint names of the King and Queen of Scots, giving Darnley equality and precedence over Mary and a silver coin was circulated in the names of Darnley and Mary. On the 29th, they made it official and married at Holyrood Palace without the papal dispensation for the marriage between first cousins.

Moray expressed his anger at the match by raising his Protestant supporters in rebellion. Mary rode valiantly with her troops, setting out from Edinburgh to confront Moray and his men and for the next month or two, both Mary and Moray roamed around Scotland with their troops, never actually coming to blows.

It wasn't just Moray who was angry. The marriage both infuriated Elizabeth and made her very nervous. It was, after all, the marriage between her two strongest claimants to the English throne and Darnley was the natural choice for many of Elizabeth's enemies because he was male, English born and a Catholic. But to do it without her permission, (he was after all an English subject), was unforgivable.

But Elizabeth need not have worried. With all of Darnley's accomplishments, he would have been a real catch except for one major flaw. He had a mean, violent streak in him, which was aggravated by his drinking problem.

It's no wonder this impulsive marriage was a disaster from the beginning. With literally a world of choices at Mary's feet, Mary had chosen to marry an arrogant man with a drinking problem who soon began making demands to be recognised as the co-sovereign of Scotland as well as having the right to keep the Scottish throne for himself ... if he outlived her.

Mary must have had an inkling of the significance of the suggestion and the ominous overtones because she adamantly and constantly refused his request. Apparently, she was smarter than she was given credit for. But her refusals put great strains on the already unsteady marriage and all too soon, he took a mistress in his first few months of marriage and Mary became disturbed by his taste for 'low company' and his frequenting of brothels, including male brothels in Edinburgh.

Then Mary realised she was pregnant.

With news of her pregnancy, Darnley decided the honeymoon was definitely over. It meant the child would be in front of him in the queue to the throne and more than likely, he would never become the king. And now for the magic words: *as long as the child was his and as long as the child lived.*

It's pretty safe to consider the possibility that the throne was all he ever wanted from the beginning. But with that option taken away from him, he had to come up with an alternative plan.

Months before, Mary had employed a secretary by the name of David Rizzio, who was himself a descendent of a noble Italian family. As her secretary, David was in close and regular contact with Mary, which must have sparked the idea into Darnley's head. What if he could convince everyone that Rizzio was really the father of Mary's child?

Over the ensuing months, the thought grew and festered in Darnley's head until it all came to a head when Mary was seven months pregnant.

The plan to murder Rizzo and potentially harm Mary was a complex one full of 'ifs' but Darnley decided to put it into action on 9th March 1566 anyway. Together with some of his supporters, Darnley was hoping that *if* Rizzio died, it would have such a traumatic impact on Mary and that it would result in a miscarriage and would ultimately damage her health permanently. *If* she became ill and *if* that illness resulted in her slow death before the baby was born, and *if* the baby died as well, then Scotland would be forced to hand the crown over to him as her husband. As I said, complex and iffy.

It would seem Mary had no idea of the ideas running through her husband's mind. On 9th March, as she and her secretary were bent over, intent on a document. Darnley, Lord Ruthven and her half-brother Earl of Moray burst into the room at around 8pm demanding that Rizzio leave immediately with them under arrest. There was very little she could do at seven months into her pregnancy but she valiantly stood her ground at gunpoint with Rizzio cowardly hiding behind her skirts as she tried to protect him. Demanding they leave her presence was all she could do and it was useless. The men had violence on their mind and a scuffle broke out.

The hysterical screams of both Mary and Rizzio echoed through the palace and into the dark streets of Edinburgh. Many of the locals were warming themselves in the taverns when they heard bloodcurdling screams coming from Holyrood Palace. It was enough to send most of them pouring out of taverns with makeshift weapons and running to the palace. With a gun held to her side, Mary was told to go to the window and dismiss them. In the uproar, Rizzio was stabbed an alleged 56 times then thrown down the main staircase after stripping him of his jewels before people were able to crash through the main door to help them.

Needless to say, the marriage was over. After the rather botched attempt on his wife's life, Darnley knew he'd have to suffer the consequences of the fiasco sooner or later. Before they could relieve him of his head, he fled.

In England, Elizabeth was horrified by the news filtering back from Scotland. When Mary delivered a baby boy two months later, naming him James in memory of her father, Elizabeth's horror turned to resignation. One year after that, when Elizabeth heard that Darnley had suffered a rather sudden, unfortunate death, resignation turned to suspicion. And then she heard the rest of the story.

We know that Mary was prone to making mistakes but this one was the worst one of all. The scandalous story was that Darnley had been recovering from a bout of smallpox (some said syphilis) when two explosions rocked the foundation of Kirk O'Field where he was staying. Later on, the explosions were attributed to two barrels of gunpowder placed in the small room under his sleeping quarters. Dressed only in his nightshirt, Darnley had fled from his bedchamber but was later found dead outside, murdered, not from the explosions as originally suspected, but apparently smothered since there were no visible signs of violence on his body. Suspicion quickly fell on a rather *close* friend of Mary, the Earl of Bothwell, whose shoes had been discovered at the scene of the crime.

Now you don't have to be a rocket scientist to join the dots together here.

The Earls of Bothwell were the hereditary Lord High Admirals of Scotland allowing them to claim any treasure found on wrecks foundering on the Scottish coast, a valuable source of revenue. They were also hereditary keepers of Liddesdale and, from their stronghold at Hermitage, they held sway over the eastern Border region on behalf of the Scottish Crown. Both roles caused them mistrust with the English. James was the son of Patrick Hepburn, 3rd Earl of Bothwell and Agnes Sinclair. His parents had divorced, after Patrick had ambitions to marry Mary of Guise after the death of her husband James V, although she turned him down. Yet he remained unfailingly loyal to her, as was his son, who definitely 'supported' her daughter, Mary Queen of Scots.

An unpopular and quarrelsome man, the Orkney born nobleman, Bothwell, seems to have appeared when he visited Mary at the French Court in the autumn of 1560. He supported Mary's mother, Mary of Guise, in Scotland and together with twenty-four followers, he took 6000 crowns of

English money destined to be used against Mary of Guise at an ambush near Haddington on Halloween 1559. After her death, he appears to be no more than a troublesome nobleman at court, although he was obviously smitten with Mary, until the Darnley murder when he showed his true colours.

Mary was in a state of despair. Still only 24 years old, she had lost her father-in-law, her mother and husband just a few years before. Now, over the course of eleven months, she had witnessed her best friend stabbed to death in front of her and her second husband murdered in cold blood.

Bothwell was brought to trial but was acquitted of any wrong doing on 12th April 1567 and rumours still crackled that he had been the murderer.

The acquittal left the way open for him to win Mary's hand in marriage. That is until eight bishops, nine earls, and seven Lords of Parliament put their signatures to what became known as the *'Ainslie Tavern Bond'*, declaring that Mary should marry a native-born subject and handed it confidently to Bothwell.

Four days later, while Mary was on the road from Stirling Castle to Edinburgh after visiting her son, Bothwell suddenly appeared with 800 men and assured her that danger awaited her in Edinburgh. She was to come with him to his castle at Dunbar, out of harm's way.

A strong man and a leader, Bothwell seemed to be someone with whom Mary could trust. It appears Mary agreed to accompany him and arrived at Dunbar at midnight where she was taken prisoner by Bothwell and allegedly raped. Bothwell's reasoning was that this would secure his marriage to her (although whether she was a willing accomplice or an unwilling victim remains a controversial issue.) Bothwell had already obtained a quickie divorce from his first wife twelve days beforehand and his intention was that the happy twosome would then marry.

Mary made another serious mistake. She married Bothwell at Holyrood House just four months after Darnley's murder and on 15th May, she created him Duke of Orkney and Marquess of Fife.

In England, Elizabeth was livid as the updates filtered back to her.

It wasn't just Elizabeth who was adding two and two together, the Scottish nobles were doing the same thing as well. As the suspicion suddenly hit them that Mary was probably involved in Darnley's murder, they knew a decision had to be made. And you can believe that her half-brother, the Earl of Moray, played a major part in making that momentous decision. Without too much delay, a council informed Mary that she would have to abdicate in favour of her 1-year-old son James. Coincidently, they said, her half-brother had helpfully and willingly stepped forward and nominated himself as Regent and the nobles had already accepted his generous offer. As a finishing touch, they informed Mary that after she abdicated, she was then to be imprisoned in Loch Leven Castle ready for the charge of murder to be heard in a court of law. There was nothing she could do, they informed her. It was a done deal.

By this time, Bothwell had seen the writing on the wall. Twenty-six Scottish peers had rebelled against Mary and Bothwell and raised a formidable army against them. They in turn raised one of their own but it soon dispersed leaving Mary and Bothwell completely vulnerable.

With one final embrace from Mary, Bothwell left her to face the music alone.

Mary had become a prisoner of the very people she had come to rule. On the streets of Edinburgh, shouts and insults were hurled at her from her people lining the streets. But despite the disgust her people showed her, the nobles knew that she still had supporters who could stage an uprising. The only solution was to transfer her to Loch Leven Castle on an island in the middle of the loch. The next day, Lord Moray, the half-brother she had loved and at one time trusted implicitly, threatened her into signing abdication papers, a betrayal she never recovered from. Still reeling from the desertion of her new husband and half-brother, Mary miscarried a set of twins. Unbeknownst to her, Bothwell had been captured without proper papers off the coast of Norway where he was taken prisoner and later died a terrible death, chained to a post in a prison cell and driven insane.

From somewhere deep in her soul, despite her immense grief, Mary must have been determined that her rights as queen should, and would, be restored. Inside a month, she had lost a husband and a set of twins: she was not about to lose her throne as well.

Loch Leven Castle was actually a grey stone house with small windows that barely kept out the cold winds that blew across the water. Outside was a narrow strip of scrubland and further still was the lake that took half an hour for a strong man to row to the mainland. When the weather turned foul, the strip submerged and the waves lashed the stones of the perimeter wall.

It was a hard prison from which escape and endurance seemed impossible. For someone like Mary who had been raised in a glittering court in France surrounded by priceless jewels and expensive clothes, attending banquets and plays, it was beyond hell to endure. The boredom would have driven her almost insane. During her time in the prison, she constantly declared that her abdication had been forced upon her under the threat of death and most of Scotland believed her. And she continually plotted her escape.

It took Mary almost a year to accomplish, but on 2nd May 1568, with the help of George Douglas, the handsome half-brother of Sir William Douglas, owner of Loch Leven, she escaped. Whether she granted George certain 'favours' more than mere kisses, (if you know what I mean), is unknown but I would assume that anything more would have been risky with her already besmirched reputation. But then again, she had made some terrible blunders up until then. In any case, Mary's supporters smuggled her out and whisked her away, hoping to reach the safety of Dumbarton Castle.

News of Mary's imprisonment had not been popular with the Scots in the first place so when word circulated that she had escaped, the news was widely welcomed. With an escort of fifty supporters led by Lord Hamilton, she rode in to Lanarkshire to join up with many more nobles who were willing to take up the fight with her and within a few days; she had managed to gather 6,000 men. With this sizeable army standing at the ready behind her, plus the assistance of eight earls, nine bishops, eighteen lords, twelve abbots and nearly 100 barons, the council was more than willing to pass a ruling that the Earl of Moray's actions had indeed been treasonable.

They say the road to death is a long march full of terrors and Mary had every intention of dodging that horrific end to her story. One of the ways to do that was to avoid battle at all cost. Her plan was to retire to Dumbarton Castle while expected reinforcements came from the north to help and with this added strength, she was certain she could take back the country by degrees from her half-brother.

With the full intention of temporarily bypassing Moray, Mary rode to Rutherglen Castle intending to pass on the north side of the Clyde estuary to avoid a direct confrontation with him. She had no wish to ride into a trap so until she had a full army at her disposal, she had to err on the side of caution.

Unlike Mary, Moray wasn't about to give up without a serious fight. His plan was to draw up his army close to the village several miles south of Glasgow, well within the city limits, and attack at the moment when Mary would least expect it. One of his commanders noted Mary's movements and he ordered his musketeers to stand ready behind each of the horsemen hiding among some cottages, hedges and gardens bordering a narrow lane through which Mary's army needed to pass. Moray would lead the rest of the army across a nearby bridge.

Moray's army had only just established themselves when Mary's army advanced through the village. The battle was on.

Mary's commander, Lord Argyll, had very little military skills so he hoped to simply push Moray aside by sheer force of numbers. As Lord Hamilton advanced slowly, Mary remained safe and secure at the rear. All was going to plan until Hamilton was met with fire from the musketeers and it was as if the world exploded in an almighty crash of metal. Many in the front were killed but Hamilton determinedly pushed on through the mayhem, finally reaching the top of a hill. What he saw frightened him. The enemy had totally blocked them off and they were advancing quickly.

What happened next has happened many times throughout history. Both armies collided in a forest of spears so thick, it is said that if anyone had thrown their discharged pistols at the enemy, the weapons would have come to rest on top of the shafts rather than falling to the ground. Forty-five minutes later, the Battle of Langside was over.

As the cries of screaming men and horses reached her, Mary watched in abject horror as over 300 of her men were slaughtered. Feathered shafts protruded from bodies, limbs had been hacked off and the smell of blood hung heavily in the air.

As dreadful as it was, if Moray had not called a halt to the fighting, it was certain the count would have been much higher. But if Mary had been in danger before, her capture at this crucial moment would certainly have been her final chapter. In a panic and with an escort, Mary fled across bleak windswept moorland, burning bridges behind her to slow pursuit, in an attempt to reach Dumbarton Castle. But then suddenly, she changed direction and turned south, heading towards a magnificent Gothic church by the name of Dundrennan Abbey on the south coast of Scotland. We can only assume she believed the Abbey seemed more reachable and safe. From there she could head for England and be out of harm's way.

After all the mistakes Mary had made, leaving Scotland was the worst. She would never see her homeland again.

In Mary's mind, the only choice she had was to throw herself on Elizabeth's mercy. And Elizabeth may have initially been tempted to do exactly that and take her cousin in. Especially when she remembered the night she'd refused Mary permission to dock in London on her way back to Scotland from France after the death of her French husband. That night, it was as if God had unleashed a powerful, vengeful storm following her refusal and the result had been that St Pauls Cathedral had been reduced to ashes, burnt to the ground and in ruins.

But with this horrific memory came doubt. The Mary of old had been dangerous enough but this new Mary was more dangerous and treacherous to Elizabeth than the one she'd sent that letter to years ago. This new Mary seemed out of control. Could she even be trusted?

If there was one thing we can be certain of is that Elizabeth would have remembered the past mangled generations of her dynasty. She would have remembered the stories of how her grandfather, Henry VII, had kissed the ground reverently as he invaded England before slaughtering Richard III and she would have remembered the stories of his tyranny. She certainly would have remembered that her father had excelled at disposing of anyone who stood in his way. Her own mother had been one of those disposable people. And I'm sure it would have been those same horrific memories that made Elizabeth hesitate and finally resist her government's advice. Beheading traitors was one thing, but beheading someone of royal blood, more to the point her own cousin, was something she could not bring herself to do. All you had to do was look at how the War of the Roses has turned out if you were in any sort of doubt. For a woman and a queen who had suffered first-hand at her family's brutality, there seemed only one option available to her. Rather than risk temporarily sheltering Mary and then returning her to Scotland at a later time with an English army, or even sending her back to France, Elizabeth imprisoned Mary in Carlisle Castle and then one month later, moved her a little further away from the Scottish border to Bolton Castle.

As it turned out, Elizabeth was wise not to trust Mary. As you would expect, Scottish supporters schemed and plotted against Elizabeth at every turn during the early months of Mary's imprisonment and in 1569, the threats became a reality.

In Elizabethan England, there was not only a religious division between the North and the South, nobles in the north felt threatened by Elizabeth's power. With the increase in threats on Elizabeth's life, the question of who would succeed to the throne of England was being asked more often. No one wanted another Catholic queen so it was becoming obvious to the government that Elizabeth needed to rid England of Mary before Catholics got to Elizabeth first. And their advice to her was she needed to do it quickly.

You can be sure Mary's supporters were thinking the exact same thing, only in their minds, Elizabeth was going to be the one disposed of.

It's not clear who first suggested the idea of a marriage between Mary and 30-year-old Thomas Howard, 4th Duke of Norfolk although his name had been floating around as a possible suitor for Mary for several years. Norfolk himself was actively discussing it by mid-October of 1568.

Norfolk was a second cousin to Elizabeth through her maternal grandmother, Elizabeth Howard, and he considered himself, as England's only duke at the time, as terribly undervalued in the English court. Self-worth had never been a problem in the Norfolk family and seems to have been a familial flaw. It led his father and great-grandfather to the executioner's block under Henry VIII and his grandfather had only been reprieved by the death of Henry himself. To add to his sense of incredible self-worth, after the deaths of his three previous wives, he had become the wealthiest landowner in the country as well as Earl Marshal of England and Elizabeth's Lieutenant in the North. As such, he had the means, the numbers, the family connection and he had the financial support of a Florentine banker by the name of Ridolfi behind him to make himself well and truly heard.

'The Ridolfi Plot', as it was called, was an intricate scheme in 1569 to murder Elizabeth, free Mary and marry her off to Norfolk then put Mary on the English throne. With the assistance from Catholic English peers in excess of 39,000 men, the plan was looking incredibly positive. With this impressive array of support, it seemed only logical that he could progress further and make a considerable attempt to depose Elizabeth.

It could have been a great success. Alongside the Duke of Norfolk and his family connections, they had Ridolfi's money and the support of the Bishop of Ross who was surreptitiously delivering letters to Mary of their progress while she was under house arrest in Bolton Castle. Then there were the armies of both Phillip of Spain and 10,000 loyal men standing behind a Duke from the Netherlands to back them up. They even had the go ahead and the nod of approval from Pope Pius V.

But common sense tells us that the plot was doomed to fail even if it hadn't been discovered prematurely. For one thing, 10,000 roaring Spanish and Dutch soldiers waving swords and guns would have been more than a little difficult to hide. For another, they would still have been absurdly inadequate to overthrow Elizabeth's newly formed army. Thirdly, the vagueness of the invasion point was terribly confusing. What let them down at this point was administration.

The plan they'd hatched was to land at either Harwich or Portsmouth, not a bad location by any means for an invading army. But by not telling Ridolfi *exactly* where Harwich was in the first place, they made a colossal blunder because the banker had no idea where to go. Another stumbling block for Norfolk as a future king was that a lot of nobles considered him a rather dubious contender anyway. Most regarded him as a bad leader, and heaven forbid, he wasn't even a Catholic. All this, plus the fact that both he and Mary had been married three times before this new proposed marriage, seems to have made the attempt a little too farfetched for anyone to conceive.

Elizabeth's extensive spy network didn't have to work too hard to uncover this plot. Ridolfi's talkative nature was always going to be a problem and rather stupidly, he trumpeted his plan all over Europe, more particularly to Cosimo I de Medici, Grand Duke of Tuscany, who sent a private message back to Elizabeth. Ridolfi's messenger was then arrested at Dover with his pockets full of compromising letters and money and he soon spilled every bean in his possession.

From being the most powerful nobleman in England, Norfolk became damaged goods overnight. Elizabeth ordered him to be arrested and sent to the Tower of London on her 37th birthday on 7th September but he left court, evidently hurt that his cousin could believe the terrible rumours of his implication in the plot. She reissued the order later that month and he removed himself further away to his palace in Kenninghall, outside

Norwich, claiming illness. His distress seemed understandable, caught between public shame at becoming a person who could eliminate the queen and the private horror waiting for him while imprisoned in the Tower.

Three days later, Elizabeth wrote again demanding his return '...*without any manner of excuse*'. By the 28th, all semblance of patience was gone. Norfolk was placed under house arrest on October 3rd and he was in the Tower by the 11th. By January the next year he was tried and convicted of three counts of high treason and beheaded six months after that.

Mary watched in stunned silence as Norfolk and hundreds of rebels were executed for treason. As the death toll rose, Elizabeth's government again pushed hard for Elizabeth to sign Mary's death warrant as well. Still she refused to shed royal blood, stating that Mary would continue to remain in her prison.

That year marked the time when most recognised the fact that Elizabeth would probably never marry or have children. Her outright refusal had finally been accepted by Parliament who had repeatedly asked her to make a decision and they'd repeatedly been refused. The House of Commons had even threatened to withhold funds from her if she did not marry. Still she held her ground and refused. And as ever, the question was, '*who will be her heir?*'

What is clear is that Elizabeth's advisors regarded Mary as a serious threat and an enemy of England. Elizabeth was nine years older than Mary and as the years went by, men feared Elizabeth may die before Mary. The memory of Mary Tudor's reign and attempt to bring England back to Catholicism was still fresh in the minds of these men. If a Catholic rebellion was to put Mary on the throne of England and Scotland, they knew they would be the first to the gallows.

In England, Francis Drake had returned from a trip that had taken him around the world and he'd brought back Peruvian gold and spices as well as captured Spanish treasures. As a reward, Elizabeth had knighted him and given him his own personal coat of arms. With his experience, there was never a doubt that he would be the one to lead the expedition to attack the Spanish. Drake left Plymouth in command of 1800 soldiers and 21 ships, freeing up Elizabeth's time so she could concentrate on Scotland.

With Drake on his way to fight the Spanish, Elizabeth needed as much support as she could get. And what she had was a rabbit in her hat, well ... in her prison. Mary Queen of Scots. By then, Mary had been imprisoned for nineteen years and during the whole time, her son James had continued to petition Elizabeth for the safe release of his mother so she could return to Scotland.

Mary's confinement was long and dreary and Mary spent much time in needlework and fussing over her many pets. Over the years Mary's health worsened and as she approached her forties, she is said to have looked like a much older woman. Clinging to the hope that her son would gain power and force her release, but ever more secluded from the outside world, Mary turned to her religion for solace.

Where once upon a time, Elizabeth would have scoffed at the idea of sending Mary home, considering how Mary and her supporters were continually plotting to murder her.

But things had changed in those nineteen years and she began to see the value of the notion. What if she too could kill two birds with one stone? What if she gave Scotland back their precious queen, with a little quid pro quo, of course? Slowly, a plan began to formulate in her mind. What she could do would be to send James an ultimatum. On the threat of losing his 'heir apparent' status to the English throne, she would demand that James sign a treaty with England by which he pledged to protect her, and vice versa. They would both come to each other's aid in the event of any attack. Only *then* would she consider releasing his mother.

The unspoken words to James were 'Spanish attack' aimed at shutting out the Spanish and of course, with his mother's freedom hanging in the balance, James willingly signed. His mother's release was everything he had been hoping for and if her release meant pledging his support to protect England from Spain in the process, then so be it.

Being the only son of Mary Queen of Scots and the ruler of Scotland since he was 13 months old seems incredible enough on its own, but James' early childhood years were lonely ones, full of murder and intrigue, and they undoubtedly had a profound effect on him.

He had heard the story of his father's death presumably planned by his mother and executed by her lover who then fled when his complicity was discovered. He knew of his mother's desperate attempt to escape only to be arrested and imprisoned in Loch Leven Castle after abdicating in his favour and he knew she'd been forced to leave him in the care of her half-brother,

James Stewart, Earl of Moray, while she had fled to England in the dead of night to escape the consequences.

To him, these stories were wild, romantic tales told by men sitting around a fireplace with a tankard of ale in their hands while the bitter cold winds blew snow in from the north. He was unaware that those same men were determined that the wild stories they told held just the right amount of danger to ensure James would remain submissive and pliant. They were meant to show James what would happen if he didn't comply. What they actually did was fill James' heart with a desperate longing for the shadowy figure of his mother. She was a figure he had no hope of ever remembering since she left Scotland when he was so young, never to be seen again. Despite this, or possibly because of this, those old men failed. James desperately wanted her to come back to him at any cost. He *longed* for it. It was a yearning however that was never fulfilled.

Scotland was ripe for a change when his mother had fled to England and there seemed no end to the ruthlessness that men were prepared to go to. As a consequence, James had seen 4 of his regents die horribly one after the other. When he was 4 years old, the Earl of Moray had been assassinated and James' care had been transferred to his paternal grandfather Matthew Stewart, 4th Earl of Lennox. Two years after that, his grandfather was shot dead in a skirmish with Mary's supporters and was replaced by the Earl of Mar who in turn was poisoned at a banquet given by James Douglas, Earl of Morton two years after that. Morton lasted for ten years until James' second cousin, the then current Earl of Lennox, established himself as James' dominant male 'favourite' and convinced James to have Douglas executed for the overdue complicity in his father's murder fifteen years before. For a sensitive young man not even out of his teens, James had been surrounded by death and intrigue for most of his life.

By then, the juicy carrot of the English throne had been dangled in front of him and James wanted it more than anything else, even as much as his mother's return. He was already James VI of Scotland but he wanted England as well. After all, it was his due as the great-great-grandson of Henry VII. But that same carrot was also being dangled in front of another member of the Stuart clan: his cousin Lady Arbella Stuart.

For some time, from around 1592, Arbella was being considered as one of the serious candidates to succeed Elizabeth I. Arbella's father, Charles

Stuart, 1st Earl of Lennox, and James father, Henry Stuart Lord Darnley, had been brothers and both brothers were great-grandchildren of Margaret Tudor – James through Margaret's first marriage to James IV and Arbella through Margaret's second marriage to Archibald Douglas. This made them both great-great-grandchildren of Henry VII and both with equal rights to the English throne. Everything depended, of course, on Elizabeth's choice of heir and it could have gone either way.

At 17 years of age, Arbella had many childbearing years ahead of her while at 26 years of age, James was displaying little interest in women and the government was beginning to show signs of uneasiness as male favourites came and went at a steady pace. Things weren't looking very rosy for James at this stage.

Then Arbella made a big mistake. Word reached Elizabeth that Arbella was making plans to marry Edward Seymour, 1st Earl of Hertford, the son of Edward Seymour, Duke of Somerset, eldest brother of Jane Seymour and Elizabeth was far from pleased with her choice.

It wasn't the fact that the Seymours were a powerful family who had rightful claims to the English throne. And it wasn't the fact that while Edward's father had been regent for her young brother, Edward VI, people were suspicious at the speed with which he accumulated his wealth and power. Both were bad enough, but it was more Edward Seymour's predisposition for clandestine marriages that made Elizabeth hesitate.

Edward's first marriage had taken place in December 1560, without Elizabeth's permission, to a potential claimant to Elizabeth's throne, Lady Catherine Grey, (the sister of Lady Jane Grey, the Nine Day Queen). It had been kept hidden until Catherine was so visibly pregnant in August the next year that the secret could no longer be kept quiet. She had confided in Robert Dudley of her predicament and there had been no doubt that Robert was going to tell Elizabeth. When the truth came out, both were sent to the Tower, where their first son was born. It was only after Catherine died of consumption eight years later that Edward had been released from the Tower.

His stay in the Tower apparently hadn't taught Edward a single thing. In 1582, he married a gentlewoman of the Privy Chamber by the name of Frances Howard and that marriage was kept a secret as well for almost a decade. The truth only came out when he had tried to have it set aside so he could establish a relationship with Arbella.

Of course, Arbella denied any intention of marrying Edward without Elizabeth's consent but the damage had already been done. Elizabeth's opinion of Arbella hit a disastrous low and Edward was once more sent to the Tower, only to be released when Frances died in 1598.

During all of this, James was feeling pretty buoyant.

But James' big problem was that he needed an heir just as urgently as Elizabeth did. To achieve this, James needed a wife and the search was on to find him one. Denmark became the prime choice since it was a growing and affluent country and James had very little money in his Scottish bank. Scottish ambassadors initially focussed on King Frederick's elder daughter, but they were informed she was out of the race because she was already betrothed. Their attention then shifted to King Frederick's younger daughter, Anne, at James' suggestion, although she had only just turned 14. Despite her youth and within months of the initial negotiations, everything was quickly finalised and James married Anne by proxy at Kronborg Castle in Denmark. Within weeks, she set sail for Scotland to meet her new husband for the first time. Who said romance was dead?

Despite being spellbound with Anne at first, James' enchantment quickly evaporated and whispers resumed of his fondness for male company. As for Anne, she had been very underwhelmed by her new husband and her eyes had been caught wandering on many occasions.

As with most queens, Anne had been very aware of her role and producing heirs to the throne was her main duty in life. Finally, and to everyone's relief, she gave birth to her first child four years later, a boy they named Henry and over the coming years, two further children would arrive.

At the same time, Europe had been restless with religious turmoil. Men talked and they wrote and they printed thousands of copies of their own writings and beliefs. In this culture, the discordant Puritans thrived. Elizabeth soon realised that not only did she have to face the Roman Catholics but she also had to face the Puritans led by the exiles of Mary's reign. England seemed divided between those who thought things had gone too far and those who wanted to go a step further. Silence had become impossible.

It was a time when John Calvin and his writings were inspiring French

Protestants and his supporters were being called Huguenots. This group was growing stronger in strength throughout the world and France, as a Catholic nation on the whole, was feeling very threatened.

It all came to a head after an important wedding on the 18th August 1572. Many leading Huguenots had remained in Paris after the wedding to discuss some grievances with the king but what happened four days later stunned Europe. Admiral Coligny, a leading Huguenot, was walking back to his rooms from The Louvre when a shot rang out from a nearby house and wounded him in the arm. A smoking gun was discovered in the window of an upstairs window, but the culprit had made his escape from the rear of the building and on to a waiting horse. In a state of shock, Coligny was carried to his lodgings at the Hôtel de Béthisy, where a surgeon removed a bullet from his elbow and amputated a damaged finger with a pair of scissors. Considering all the possibilities, the damage could have been far worse, but the bloodbath that followed was soon beyond the control of any leader.

The St. Bartholomew's Day Massacre began two days later, after Catherine de Medici's son, King Charles IX, ordered, *"Kill them. Kill them all! Don't leave a single one alive."* The thinking was clear. Catherine and her advisers were expecting a Huguenot uprising to avenge the attack on Coligny but instead of waiting for it to happen, they chose to strike first and wipe out the Huguenot leaders while they were still in Paris. It was the beginning of a wave of Catholic mob violence that continued unabated for weeks.

The slaughter began in Paris but soon spread outwards to the French countryside. Estimates of the number of dead across France range from 5,000 to 30,000 but for Paris alone, the only hard figure was the payment by the crown to workmen to collect and bury 1,100 bodies washed up on the banks of the Seine downstream of the city ... in the first week alone.

The horror of the massacre and the hostility it aroused still created a great deal of controversy throughout Europe. And everyone was pointing a finger at Catherine de Medici as the instigator.

It was at this time when everything began to unravel. No sooner had James signed the agreement than a new plot surfaced aimed to kill Elizabeth. Letters from Mary were discovered by Elizabeth's spymaster Sir Francis Walsingham suggesting another attempted assassination and the threat from Scotland could not be denied anymore.

The chief instigator had been Anthony Babington, a young man recruited by John Ballard, a Jesuit priest who had wanted to rescue Mary and place her on the English throne. At Ballard's instruction, Babington had sent a coded letter to Mary, who added his name to the complicated plot, and Mary had responded back in code ordering the would-be rescuers to assassinate Elizabeth. When Mary signed the letter, she had been in a dark mood thinking her son James had betrayed her since she had been dependent on the Spanish to help rescue her. She even stated in the letter that she was in favour of a Spanish invasion of England.

Mary couldn't have picked a worse time to write the letter. John Ballard was arrested on 4th August and under torture confessed. Then he'd implicated Babington. Within days, the names of other conspirators were added to the list and all were rounded up and taken prisoner.

For Mary, the 11th August 1586 dawned like any other day except for some subtle differences and if she'd been watching closely, she would have been aware that a change was taking place. Up until that day, Mary had always been treated like a royal prisoner with every luxury at her disposal. In Bolton, she had been living very nicely in the South-West tower with a full retinue of fifty-one knights, servants and ladies-in-waiting. Her household included cooks, grooms, a hairdresser, an embroiderer, an apothecary, physician and a surgeon. Elizabeth had even sent tapestries, rugs and furniture from nearby Barnard Castle and she had herself loaned some pewter vessels to Mary as well as a copper kettle. But much to Mary's annoyance, she had been moved one year before to Chartley Manor owned by Robert Dudley's stepson, Robert Devereaux, 2nd Earl of Essex, because the house had a deep moat, which helped with security. She was still allowed relative freedom of her prison, along with her servants, and every day she was allowed to go out riding while her servants left the house to do her laundry. On this particular day however, her servants were refused permission to leave the manor.

At the time, Mary hadn't seen this as a threat. It had surprised her, but she nevertheless continued with her plans to go out riding with her doctor and several others. But as she came to the crest of a hill, she was startled by a group of armed soldiers waiting for her in the shade of a leafy outcrop. It was only then she learnt that instead of riding back to the manor, she was to be taken to Tixall where she would wait to stand trial for treason.

For weeks it was unclear whether Elizabeth would be able to bring herself to sign Mary's death warrant or whether she would simply keep her incarcerated until one of them died. Elizabeth's own mother, Anne Boleyn, had suffered the ultimate indignity of being beheaded in front of a baying crowd at her father's command. Could she inflict the same horror on Mary?

If Mary thought she had a hope of defending herself, she was wrong. Even though the assassination order had not come from James, Mary's supporters had instigated it and it was the final straw for Elizabeth. Knowing she could not wait any longer, she was forced to make a fateful decision regarding Mary. Parliament was still pushing for her execution and at last, a stoic Elizabeth signed the death warrant. It was all just a formality anyway.

Within twenty-four hours, Elizabeth regretted it but by then, it was too late to stop the ball from rolling.

While Mary waited for word of her fate, her supporters were given no such luxury. On 20th September, seven Catholic men were bound to hurdles in the Tower of London and dragged on their final slow journey through the streets to a hastily erected scaffold in the open field at the upper end of Holborn to what is now known as Lincoln's Inn Fields. Most of the condemned were well-connected and wealthy men, wearing fine silks for their last day on earth. Just a week before they were tried at Westminster and found guilty of treason and only six weeks before that, they were free men enjoying the good life. Authorities had searched the homes of known conspirators who had been seen having furtive conversations and the list was a long one.

The crowd, numbered in the thousands, gathered at the scaffold and authorities had to fence off the site to stop people blocking the view. The gallows were even raised so that no one could miss seeing justice being done. Seven more executions would follow the next day.

It was customary for a traitor's death to be by hanging but on that day, it was be different. One after another, the men were left to swing briefly by the neck until half-dead and then cut down, still alive and conscious. Then they were made to watch as an executioner hacked off their genitals with their own knives before digging out their intestines. If they were still alive after all of that, they knew their heart would be next. As their insides were cast into a burning brazier, each man's body was then dismembered and the severed head set high above the gallows.

The first man to die was Ballard, arguably the ringleader, and the second was Babington. He stood unflinchingly beside the scaffold and watched Ballard die, waiting coolly for his turn, not even removing his hat as others turned away in apprehensive horror.

The outcry from their executions was so intense that Elizabeth changed the order for the second group to be allowed simply to hang until 'quite dead' before disembowelling and quartering.

Weeks later, Mary was sent to be tried at Fotheringhay Castle in Northamptonshire by forty-six lords, bishops and earls. There would be no legal counsel, no permission to review the evidence and there would be no witnesses called. Portions of the letter were simply read and Mary was convicted of treason against the country of England.

Mary is said to have been in good spirits, perhaps disbelieving that her ordeal would end in actual execution. Then on 4th February 1587, three of Elizabeth's earls arrived at Mary's apartments at Fotheringhay Castle and informed her that she was to be executed.

It was on the 7th February that Mary began to hear faint banging in the distance and she would have been aware that a scaffold was being erected. It wasn't until after dinner that evening that she was notified of her forthcoming execution at 8am the following morning. She was not allowed to see a priest, despite one being in the building, and she was not given permission for him to hear her confessions or to receive the Last Sacrament. She could however receive the consolation of *their* minister. She quickly distributed her belongings to her household and wrote her last will as well as a letter to the King Henry III of France, her former brother-in-law, who she had known since he was born.

At just past 8am the next day, the Sheriff arrived for Mary and they made their way down the great oak staircase of Fotheringhay Castle. At the foot of the stairs, the Earl of Kent refused to allow Mary's servants to proceed any further but after heated words with Mary, six of her attendants were granted permission. Just not a priest.

From around the countryside, the gentry gathered to witness her death. Mary appeared in black satin and walked down the quiet hall to the cloth-covered scaffold draped in black. In the hush, she slowly disrobed revealing a blood red bodice and a petticoat of crimson velvet, the colour of martyrdom in the Catholic Church. She was then blindfolded by one of her servants and ordered to kneel in deathly silence. Throughout the hall, awed spectators watched and held their breath, expecting Elizabeth's soldiers to rush in and halt the execution at any moment. After years of refusing to kill her cousin, no one really expected Elizabeth to go ahead with it. Surely this was just a terrifying warning to the Scottish queen to stop her rebellious threats and plots. Wasn't it?

It took two strokes to kill Mary. The first blow missed her neck and struck the back of her head, at which point Mary's lips moved (her servants reported they heard her whisper *"Sweet Jesus"*). The spectators in the Great Hall gasped and screamed. The second blow severed the neck, except for a small bit of sinew that the embarrassed executioner split by using the axe as a saw. The executioner then held the head up and at that moment, the auburn tresses in his hand came apart and the head fell to the ground, revealing Mary's head of very short, grey hair. She had tried to disguise the greying of her hair by wearing the wig that had matched her auburn hair before her years of imprisonment. She was 24 years old when first imprisoned and she was 44 at the time of her execution.

In a final gruesome twist, Mary's favourite dog, who had been hiding in the folds of her dress throughout, emerged and lay in the thick pool of blood at her severed neck and refused to move. The execution was never forgotten by any soul who witnessed it and has gone down in history as one of the most shocking and macabre displays in the history of British monarchy.

As Mary died, Elizabeth sat in her room and cried.

To the very end, Mary stood by her hereditary right to the English throne, wishing only to be recognised as Elizabeth's successor, and in a way she succeeded.

Queen Elizabeth died on the 24th March 1603 and famously refused to the very end to name her successor. Elizabeth's wishes were unknown or disregarded and James was proclaimed King of England and Ireland on the back of a proclamation that declared his right to the crown by 'lineal succession and undoubted right'. Mary is not mentioned but the meaning of the proclamation is clear: Mary was always the rightful successor to the throne in the eyes of the law.

Mary was an enigmatic queen. Beautiful, vivacious and courageous. She was loved by all who knew her but was a victim of circumstance time and time again, betrayed by almost every influential person in her life. Mary's fairy tale upbringing and early adulthood in France came to a tragic end when her father-in-law, husband and mother all died within a few years of each other. From then on, Mary swapped the sunny, carefree days of life in France with the grey skies and murderous politics in Scotland. She made a number of poor choices, particularly when it came to husbands, forced down the wrong path and embroiled her in a series of unfortunate events that ultimately led her straight into Elizabeth's jealous hands.

But many would consider that Mary won after all because every subsequent ruler of Great Britain to this day is descended from Mary Queen of Scots and not Elizabeth, the *'Virgin Queen'*.

Some could forgive James for rejecting his mother during her incarceration. He did very little to free her and when he did attempt to arrange for her release, it was too little and too late.

In 1603, James' prayers were answered when Elizabeth died in the early hours of 24th March and he was informed that he would indeed be the next King of England as James I. A month later, eager to start their new life in England, full of wealth and promise, James, Anne, and their three children left Edinburgh for London. With a fervent promise to parliament that he would return every three years, James set off with his family on their high adventure.

His promise to return to Scotland was never fulfilled. After hearing the endless stories of English wealth, told around his inadequate fireplace on cold wintery nights, he had no want to return. He was even heard to say it was like *'swapping a stony couch for a deep feather bed'*. Compared to Scotland, England offered incredible prosperity and he was going to take every advantage of it. That fortune was now his and he had no intention of being parted from it, or the benefits of having it, for any length of time whatsoever.

Once he became King of England, James set about atoning for his behaviour and commissioned the building of 2 magnificent monumental tombs at Henry VII's chapel at Westminster Abbey, one for Elizabeth and one for his mother, Mary.

END OF THE STUART DYNASTY

*W*hether by bad health or bad luck, the Stuart dynasty came to an end on the death of James' great-granddaughter, Anne. There would still be Stuart blood pulsing through the veins of the coming generations: George I's great grandfather was James VI / I after all. But it was the Stuart dynasty that had withered on the vine and failed to continue after Queen Anne's death.

No one can agree why Anne's health had been bad for so long. Sure she was overweight, which everyone knew caused difficulty during births. But lots of overweight women gave birth children. Hughes syndrome, an autoimmune disease affecting the blood, has been suggested, even porphyria, which can potentially cause recurrent miscarriages and is also associated with other complications such as premature birth and stillbirth. And don't forget that James I more than likely suffered from porphyria.

Historically, the poor health of a monarch may have had political importance, but it is the inability to produce a suitable heir that has been the usual cause for the end of a dynasty, as well as bad luck, I suppose.

The Stuart dynasty began with Robert II in 1371 and although we grow up with children's stories that give us a picture of kings, queens and fairy tale princesses in medieval Scotland, the reality was far from being a fairy tale. Their lives were constantly at risk from enemies within their kingdom and they had to keep watchful eyes out for ambitious nobles.

Many died 'mysteriously' and many died simply trying to protect themselves and their family, as with James I of Scotland in 1437 and Charles I of England in 1649. Through the centuries the Stuarts had endured. They survived wars, crusades, bouts of the plague, smallpox, a great fire, murder and ill health. And they'd survived years of captivity, as we know with Mary Queen of Scots.

But when looking back over the last four generations of Stuart Kings of England, each one seems to have been precarious. After Elizabeth I's death, James VI of Scotland became James I of England in 1603 when he was 36 years old. His weak legs remain unexplained, as do episodes of jaundice, but a shrunken kidney containing stones at his post mortem explains the evidence of blood and tiny stones in his urine. From 1616 he was disabled from arthritis, and began showing signs of dementia six years before he died. The possibility that his thyroid glands were not functioning properly has been a recent speculation.

Henry also seems to be an unfortunate name to be called if you were a Stuart. Firstly, the family name came originally from Henry Stuart Lord Darnley who lost his life after his wife Mary Queen of Scots took a lover and had him assassinated. James I of England's first son Henry lost his life to typhoid and James' son, Charles I, had a son, Henry who died of smallpox – both at 18 years of age. If only Prince Henry had survived his bout of smallpox, there would have been a Protestant Stuart who would have been fit, well and acceptable to Parliament and the dynasty could very well still be with us today. The same would have happened if just one of Anne's seventeen children had survived to adulthood. Perhaps it was fate, not just ill health, that severed the line from future generations, given that the decapitation of Charles I was not truly a surgical procedure.

The story of James' children does not make for easy reading. First there was Henry, Prince of Wales who was intellectually remarkable but died of typhoid in 1612 at 18 years of age. Four of James' children died before they reached the age of two and Charles II's wife, Catherine of Braganza, failed to produce a child despite the many illegitimate children he was able to father out of wedlock. It would be James' daughter Elizabeth who would marry the Protestant Prince, Frederick of Hanover and of her two children, one would die of pleurisy while the only surviving daughter, Sophia, would live to give birth to the future King George I of England.

With each generation, it wasn't just producing an heir that was a problem. It was keeping the heirs alive as well. James lost five children, as did his sons Charles I and James II.

The jury is still out on James II. Was he an egotistical bigot and a tyrant who rode roughshod over the will of the vast majority of his subjects? Was he simply naïve? Was he perhaps just plain stupid? Perhaps he was only doing what he thought was best and he was actually an intelligent, clear-thinking strategically motivated monarch? After all, English taxes had remained low during James II's reign, at only about 4% of the national income. This would suggest that he had no intention of modelling England after France whose taxes were at least twice as high.

Things seemed like they couldn't get any worse for England when James II's first wife died and he married an Italian bride, a *Catholic* Italian bride, from Modena in the hope of fathering a male heir. But things *did* get worse because she gave birth to a healthy baby boy two years later and England knew their nightmare was only just beginning. Where James II's only two possible successors were his two Protestant daughters, Mary and Anne from his first marriage, this new birth opened up the possibility of a permanent Catholic dynasty. When Catholic after Catholic stepped into prominent positions of power, even James II's most faithful supporter, his dead wife's brother Laurence Hyde, Earl of Rochester, turned against him.

Parliamentary ministers sent heated letters to James and he sent equally heated ones back to them. Backwards and forwards the letters continued until James finally put his foot down and declared that the Protestant religion was false and he would not promise to support them in any way. To prove his point, he went on a rampage of more promotions, replacing Protestant office-holders at court with his own Catholic favourites. By May 1686, he was in full swing and had begun to dismiss judges in the Common law courts who disagreed with him as well.

It was the final straw or parliament. They wanted James out and the most likely candidate was James' eldest daughter Mary, married to William of Orange. In their minds, Parliament could see James aligning himself with Louis XIV in France in a 'holy league' to destroy Protestantism and as the idea took root, it grew at an amazing rate. While James revelled in the birth of his son, the heir to his throne, seven nobles, later known as the 'Immortal Seven', were on their way to Holland to invite William to invade. Which he did with relish. He had no qualms about ousting his father-in-law off the throne.

William of Orange was jubilant when he and Mary arrived in London. They rode through the streets, waving happily and were greeted with cheers by people who had come out and lined the streets to see them. William was about to fulfil his promise to be a Protestant monarch and to defend the country against Catholicism and in doing so, he would secure the throne for himself and his family.

But in William's mind, there were still the Scots to deal with for their complicity in an uprising in Derry in Ireland led by his father-in-law in an attempt to take back the throne.

James wanted the throne back at any cost and the best way he saw to do that was to take control of Ireland before moving on to England. But standing in his way were the Protestants in Ulster, in particular Derry. He knew if he did not have control of Derry, he would never have control of Ireland and therefore England.

In Ireland itself, tension was mounting. James' friend, Richard Talbot, holding the position of Viceroy in Ireland, knew that the Protestants in Ulster could not be trusted to support the Jacobites, a Latinised name given to James supporters. From the Protestant side of it, they saw Talbot as the one responsible for disrupting their power base. As for Talbot, he was determined that they would remain under Jacobite rule, whether they liked it or not.

Central to this disturbance was Derry, a strategic city full of supporters loyal to Scotland. Desperate to avoid trouble at all costs with the Scots, Talbot arranged for the military garrison to be replaced by a regiment of Scottish highlanders and clansmen, known as Redshanks. As Catholics, their loyalty to James was unquestionable.

Arguments raged throughout the city at the decision. The Protestants thought that once the Redshanks were in, they would never leave, even though the Anglican bishop urged them to be allowed to enter the city. They were, after all, James' soldiers and he was still their king. But the Presbyterian bishop thought otherwise. He stated that the gates to Derry should be locked immediately and they shouldn't waste any time dithering about it if they valued their lives. If they delayed, all would certainly be lost.

It was a critical moment. Eight or nine young men, acting on the impulse of the moment, ran to Ferry-Quay gate, drew their swords and raised the drawbridge. They seized the keys and locked the gate against the Redshanks when they were only 60 yards from the spot. They literally slammed the gate shut in their faces. Three or four others joined in and with no time to lose, the other gates were secured as well.

It was a major step to take and one that left no allowances for going back. They had taken matters into their own hands and had started a rebellion that was inviting the king's anger. Soon after, when the garrison at Enniskillen heard what had happened, they followed suit by shutting their gates against the Scots as well, knowing full well that their show of solidarity could bring the whole of the English army down on them.

In Dublin, Talbot was furious by the turn of events but in France James was simply stunned. It was all going terribly wrong. Ireland was a Catholic nation, just as he was a Catholic. This wasn't how it was supposed to be.

Knowing that word was probably on its way to William, and with time running out, the siege in Derry forced James to put his plan into action sooner than he had hoped.

It was not a complicated plan. All James hoped for was for the support of Catholics in Ireland. He also hoped that if he could hold out, he could use Ireland as a launch pad to take back Scotland and England. Then he would march on to London and seize his throne. And there was no time to waste. William and Mary were about to be crowned king and queen of England. But if worst came to worst and they actually pulled it off, James was determined that it would be the shortest reign in history, daughter or no daughter. But the fly in the ointment was the Ulster Protestants.

On the 12th March, James landed in Kinsale, along with several French generals and 6,000 of their men, ready to start his fight-back. Together, they would join another 5,000 loyal Catholics under Commander Richard Hamilton who was already on his way north to subdue Derry's rebels. What James didn't realise was that there were just as many Protestants in Ireland who supported William and they were already taking up arms and preparing to attack James and his supporters.

James advanced north, taking town after town, until he finally reached

Ulster. By April, he was at the gates of Derry, hoping that his tremendous show of strength would force them to surrender. James had thought that the mere sight of his soldiers would shock and awe Derry into submission.

It never occurred to him that this might never happen.

What James didn't know was his commander, Richard Hamilton, had already spoken to the leaders in Derry and he had guaranteed that Jacobites would not approach the city.

It was inevitable that there would be confusion on James' part. Part of that confusion was that he had no idea that there had been any sort agreement made. When the guards saw James and his army standing outside the gates demanding entry, there was no doubt in their minds that it as an act of duplicity. Derry had been offered an agreement, and they had accepted, and yet here was the king himself breaking that very agreement.

Before James knew it, the guards on duty were firing at him and his troops. He had ridden straight into a storm of anger as the city prepared themselves to fight against him to the death.

Outside the walls, James was in no mood to hang around for the fight. Talbot had already sent word that 4,000 Dutch troops had arrived in Belfast to help William, which meant James was needed in Dublin. Leaving the French generals in charge until the additional 6,000 troops promised by Louis in France arrived to help, he left to make plans with Talbot. He gave the generals clear orders. Take Derry at any cost. He left before the smell of smoke reached his nostrils and women's screams filled the air.

You would think that 17,000 men would be invincible but from the very beginning, the lack of armament and the lack of discipline were evident. Cannonballs crashed into the rooves of houses and smashed into their walls but it was the Williamites who made the important strikes and in the chaos, two of James' French generals were killed.

But as bad as it was on the outside, inside the walls of Derry was worse. They were suffering from malnutrition and starvation, forced to eat rats, horseflesh and even their own dogs. It was a slow death for some in the bitter cold and due to the unavailability of fresh water; the streets ran with faeces and urine. Soon, disease was rampant.

It was an epic power struggle to decide, not only who would control England and Ireland, but also the balance of power in Europe and it shaped the course of our history to the present day. It was a remarkable 105 days where the people of Derry defied James and refused to surrender the city to his Catholic army. The words 'No surrender' are as meaningful today as they were when they were first shouted three centuries ago.

On 26th July, starving and rife with disease, the remaining citizens of Derry were just about to give in and begin negotiations when reinforcements from London arrived. At the 11th hour, Derry was saved.

What *they* hadn't known was that six weeks earlier, on 14th June, William had arrived in Ulster, pale and asthmatic, but ready for a fight. Although his face was lined with constant pain and fighting ill health, he had marched south at the same time that James was marching north from Dublin. As Derry was struggling to survive, the two armies had met on 1st July at the River Boyne, thirty miles north of Dublin on the outskirts of Drogheda.

No year in Irish history is better known than 1690 and no Irish battle is more famous than William III's victory over James II at the River Boyne.

It would be the last time in history that a king would fight on a battlefield.

On one side, there was James who had fought with his brother Charles in Europe and although he was prone to panicking under pressure and making rash decisions, that was 1658 and a lot had changed in 30 years. Still, he was a man in his late fifties and his best years as a military leader were behind him.

On the other side, there was 40-year-old William, a fragile man but a battle-hardened commander known for his reckless courage in countless campaigns who was yet to win a major battle. But William had one advantage over James. William had 36,000 strong, composed troops gathered from all over Europe and all of them were better trained and better equipped than James' 23,500 troops.

On the night before the battle, soldiers on both sides prepared themselves nervously for the day ahead. On the march down, both armies had taken whatever metal and lead they could find, mostly from churches along the way, and they were sitting by their campfires, melting it all down to make bullets for their muskets. After the lead had melted, they prepared cartridges with rolls of paper in which they poured gunpowder and then dropped the bullets on top. In battle, the soldiers would bite the top off the cartridges to release the bullet, literally biting the bullet.

As his men worked, William walked around his soldiers with his arm in a sling after a near miss earlier on in the day. He believed that his presence would encourage his men and he'd even bought with him a portable house so he could sleep among his men.

On the other side of the river, it was a different story. James sat alone in his tent, never showing his face.

The fight started in the early hours of dawn as the sky became a watercolour of pinks, reds and oranges but after four hours of fighting, neither side could say they were ahead. By noon, William decided he had to do something and the only possible option was for his army of Dutch and English cavalry to go down to the riverside and cross over to the south side, meeting the Jacobites head on. But in making that decision, he had chosen the most difficult place to cross where the banks were deep and muddy and for a frail king, getting across the river was going to be more than a little bit difficult.

Sure enough, his horse got stuck in the mud halfway across and as he tried to move his horse forward, he had an asthma attack. One of his men saw that he was in trouble and waded back across the river and threw William over his shoulder, carrying him to safety on the south bank. Behind him, 2,000 cavalrymen were still struggling to cross the river and face the Jacobites along the mile and a half stretch of mud.

By early afternoon, William's vast number of men were beginning to make progress. With the Jacobites heavily outnumbered and worn down by the relentless attacks, their only chance for survival was to make a stand on high ground. Ahead of them, they saw a church on top of a hill and they desperately ran towards it with the Williamites hot on their heels. But by doing that, they'd actually allowed themselves to be surrounded on three sides and by late afternoon, it was all over. They simply couldn't hold out any longer.

Throughout the battle, William fought bravely alongside his men. James however was nowhere to be seen. Instead, James had remained behind in a ravine where he could see the battle raging on the hill three miles away. When it was obvious that his wearying army could not possibly win, James sped down the road to Dublin ahead of his men.

He was unaware that his men had seen him running and they already knew he was miles ahead, having deserted them in a cowardly attempt to get himself to safety. Two days after his victory, William triumphantly marched into Dublin as James was making a speedy retreat back to Louis in France. His cowardly behaviour would earn James the title *Seamus an Chaca* or 'James the Shit'.

William was jubilant when he returned to London. He rode through the streets, waving happily and was greeted with cheers by people who had come out and lined the streets to see him. Even Parliament praised him. He had fulfilled his promise as a Protestant monarch to defend the country against Catholicism and in doing so, he had secured the throne for himself and his family.

But as successful as he was, he hadn't finished yet. Not by a long shot. There were still the Scots to deal with for their complicity in the Jacobite uprising in Ireland and there were many Highland clans who were still loyal to James, and as such, a possible threat to William, despite James' recent defeat at The Battle of Boyne and his spineless behaviour of running back to Europe with his tail between his legs. Many of them had sworn allegiance to James and William wasn't about to forget about it. What he wanted was for the clans to pledge allegiance to *him*, and he didn't think it would be too hard considering the Derry debacle either. With that out of the way, he could continue his own war with Louis.

Knowing William's history for patience, it's not surprising he took his time in thinking long and hard about what to do. It took him a year to come up with a plan but by August 1691, he was ready to put the plan into action. He would offer the Highland clans a pardon for their part in the Jacobite rising, but only if they took an oath before a magistrate and agreed to pledge allegiance to him instead of James before New Year's day. That date was 4 months away and it would give them plenty of time to take affirmative action. It was also a symbolic date for William representing the beginning of a new reign and the start of new era.

Of all the clans in Scotland, the clan Donald was a huge force in the Highland system and the MacDonalds of Glencoe were only a small segment. Glencoe had a rugged beauty and it had been their home since the early 14th century when they had supported Robert the Bruce. It was one of the most magnificent areas of natural wilderness in all of Britain with Loch Leven to the north and the vast empty spaces of Rannoch Moor to the south. Skirted on both sides by huge imposing mountains was the Glencoe pass.

Alasdair MacLain was not a man who could hide in a crowd. The head of the MacDonald clan was a huge man with flowing white hair, beard and a well-respected leader and who was very much old school. His clan were constantly involved in trouble with both the law and with neighbouring clans for consistently raiding, pillaging and cattle rustling. Unfortunately, they also had a fervent dislike for the nearby Campbell clan. And the feeling was entirely mutual.

William's order came through with promises of money and land for the clans who signed the oath but by the time it was circulated publicly, the terms had changed and were much more threatening. The clans would sign the agreement or be punished with the utmost extremity of the law.

One of the problems for the clans was that many of them were already bound by an oath to James now back in France. James had promised to return to Britain to reclaim his throne and the Highlanders were not-so-patiently waiting for him to fulfil that promise. James' delay put them in a difficult spot. While they *wanted* to wait for his return, and had promised to stand by him and fight with him and beside him when he *did* return, they had William's dire threat hanging over their heads if they didn't sign allegiance to him. If James didn't come back soon, their families' safety would be at risk. That meant signing the allegiance to William, like it or not. According to Williams's instructions, their lives depended on it.

They sent urgent word to James of their predicament, outlining the importance and speediness of his reply and informing him that the deadline was January 1st.

Weeks turned into months and still James dithered with a reply, convinced that he was close to returning. It wasn't until December 12th that it became apparent this wasn't going to happen before the deadline so reluctantly James sent orders back to Scotland releasing the clans from their oath. The problem was that due to his prolonged delay, his messenger only arrived back in the Highlands during dreadful winter conditions and with only three days before the deadline.

Cruel winter winds swept through Glencoe on December 31st as MacLain arrived at Fort William ready to sign the oath, fearful for his clan's safety. When he arrived, Colonel Hill told him that the oath had to be taken before a sheriff, which involved another 60-mile trek further on to Inverary. And Inverary was the hometown of his enemies, the Campbells.

Colonel Hill knew about the friction between the Campbells and the MacDonalds, which is why he gave MacLain a letter of protection and a letter for the sheriff, Sir Colin Campbell, requesting that he receive MacLain's late oath since he had come to him within the allotted time. Hill assured MacLain that no action would be taken against him but he urged MacLain to make haste to Inverary in any case.

MacLain may have met the deadline had Campbell soldiers, commanded by Captain Drummond serving with the Earl of Argyll's regiment, not captured him along the way. They detained him for a full day and then finally sent him on to Inverary where he was held for several more days due to the absence of the sheriff, who was visiting his family across the waters of Loch Fyne. When Sir Colin returned, MacLain pleaded with him to accept the late oath. He gave him the letter from Colonel Hill and explained the reasons why he had been delayed. Reluctantly, the sheriff accepted the late oath.

But other forces were already in play as MacLain headed back to Glencoe, sure that his signed oath was on its way to London.

In Edinburgh, the Secretary of State, John Dalrymple and John Campbell, 1st Earl of Breadalbane and Holland, had other things in mind. John Campbell, a senior member of the Campbell clan, saw an opportunity for revenge for the decades of raids on Campbell lands and the tradition of sheep and cattle rustling by the MacDonalds. As such, he had a strong dislike for the MacDonalds and he'd already decided to decline the late-delivered oath. Together with his cousin, Archibald Campbell, 10th Earl of Argyll, they found a willing accomplice in John Dalrymple who had been disappointed in the fact that the clan leaders were taking the oath of allegiance at all. He was rather hoping they would have declined. Together, the three men sent an order to London for William to sign, stating that MacLain and his den of thieves had not signed within the allotted time and they should be punished severely.

I suppose we should give William some credit for not knowing the full circumstances surrounding the late oath. He had given a specific order and his commanders in Scotland had informed him that that order had not been carried out. They'd just omitted a small, rather important, part of the story but William didn't know. As a result, he had to show that he meant what he said. If you make a threat, you had to carry through with it.

He signed the order and sent it to Sir Thomas Livingstone, commander of the forces in Scotland. With the order, he gave explicit instructions to John Dalrymple: the MacDonalds were to be slaughtered. From there, the order was sent to a Major Duncanson who then sent three of his commanders, two from the Campbell-dominated Argyll regiment and lastly, Colonel Hill from Fort William, with an infamous letter.

"You are hereby ordered to fall upon the rebells, the McDonalds of Glenco, and put all to the sword under seventy. you are to have a special care that the old Fox and his sones doe upon no account escape your hands, you are to secure all the avenues that no man escape. This you are to putt in execution att fyve of the clock precisely; and by that time, or very shortly after it, I'll strive to be att you with a stronger party: if I doe not come to you att fyve, you are not to tarry for me, but to fall on. This is by the Kings special command, for the good and safety of the Country, that these miscreants be cut off root and branch. See that this be putt in execution without feud or favour, else you may expect to be dealt with as one not true to King nor Government, nor a man fit to carry Commissione in the Kings service. Expecting you will not faill in the full-filling hereof, as you love your selfe, I subscribe these with my hand att Balicholis Feb: 12, 1692. For their Majesties service. (signed) R. Duncanson"

Unaware of what was happening in Edinburgh and London, the MacDonald clan were billeting 120 English soldiers hospitably in Glencoe. The soldiers were under the command of a Captain Robert Campbell of Glenlyon but most of the regiment was recruited from the Argyll estates and only a minority bore the Campbell name.

Captain Campbell was actually related by marriage to MacLain and so it was natural that he should be given special treatment and billeted in the old chief's house. Each morning for the past two weeks, Captain Campbell had visited the home of MacLain's youngest son, Alexander, who was married to Campbell's niece. This niece had a brother by the name of Rob Roy McGregor.

During the day on 12th February, the sky was a seething cauldron of clouds and a light dusting of snow had fallen, making all the paths cold and slippery. The feeble afternoon sun had only persisted occasionally through the thick dark clouds and in the winter light, there seemed to be no colours except grey, white and black. Captain Drummond arrived in Glencoe and due to his role in detaining MacLain and ensuring that he was late giving his oath, he would not have been welcomed at all. What they didn't know was he was bringing a letter from Major Duncanson bearing fateful instructions to give to Captain Campbell.

In his heart, Drummond must have known what he was about to do was wrong. He'd eaten their food and accepted their hospitality. He even spent the evening playing cards with them before retiring, wishing them a good night and accepting an invitation to dine with MacLain the following day. Still, he continued with his instructions.

By evening, a blizzard howled through Glencoe and snow blanketed the rugged landscape as the MacDonald clan slept restlessly. As they slept, the soldiers were preparing to carry out their instructions to systematically kill everyone they could.

In the early hours of February 13th, MacLain had woken from his fitful sleep to the sound of muffled cries. Before he could rise from his bed, he was killed along with thirty-eight others. Forty women and children managed to flee the massacre but they would soon be dead of exposure after their homes were set alight and burnt to the ground. A few survivors had managed to escape into the hills finding makeshift shelters but they would lose their lives as well in the relentless blizzard. Among the death was MacLain's elderly wife who died on the mountainside just outside of the town.

The survivors told stories of how a few of Captain Campbell's soldiers had alerted the families and given them time to rug up and escape. Two lieutenants had even broken their swords rather than carry out the orders. In addition to the soldiers who were actually in Glencoe that night, two other detachments, each with 400 men, were to have converged on the possible escape routes. But both were late in taking up their positions, and it was suggested that the lateness of the two other companies was not purely because of the snowstorm, but a ploy *not* to be involved in the atrocity. What they *did* know was that Colonel Hill from Fort William had brought the orders for the massacre.

An inquiry was held under the category *'murder under trust'* but nothing would ever come of it. The King himself had signed the orders and he could not be held responsible. The conclusion of the enquiry was that William was to be exonerated and the blame placed firmly upon Secretary Dalrymple's shoulders. Not long after the enquiry, Dalrymple resigned his position but no other action was taken.

William did not wait for the verdict from the enquiry. Europe was waiting for him to deal with France and he left immediately. As good as his reign was, this would forever mar it and would go down in history as the Glencoe Massacre.

While William was away, Mary sat on the throne. She had tremendous difficulty dealing with the curses from her angry father who constantly sent her seething letters berating her for her role in the invasion. She had broken one of the Ten Commandments that stated she should respect her parents and she lived in fear of never being forgiven by God. It was a difficult situation for her and it put her under constant psychological stress as her husband and her father jockeyed for her loyalty.

Perhaps because of William's physical frailties and Mary's mental fragility, Mary was unable to produce a child. When she died William took the throne and when he died, James' youngest daughter, Anne took the throne.

Anne's gynaecological record is horrific. In 16 years, she had seventeen pregnancies: twelve were either miscarried or stillborn, having died weeks before in her womb. Then in 1687, her two surviving girls contracted smallpox and died within six days of each other. There was nothing more heart-breaking than seeing Anne and her husband mourning together over a tiny empty cot. Sometimes they would weep uncontrollably together. Other times they would just sit in silence, staring at nothing. It was unimaginably awful.

While Anne suffered miscarriage after miscarriage, Parliament searched desperately through the Stuart family tree looking for a suitable candidate to step in after Anne. But with fifty of Anne's Catholic relatives standing in a long queue to claim the throne, they needed to be quick. One by one they went through the list, crossing names off as they went, even the names of those who had a legitimate claim to the throne were discarded in their frantic attempt to find a Protestant heir.

And then, like a light shining down from heaven, they saw a solution. There *was* a relative. Sophia Electress of Hanover was the granddaughter of James I through his daughter Elizabeth who had married Frederick of Hanover and as such, she had Stuart blood running through her veins. And she was a Protestant. In their desperate attempt to find a Protestant heir, Parliament overlooked Anne's fifty other relatives, many who had a much better claim to the throne than Sophia, on the grounds that they were Catholic. That, they stated, would have been absolutely unacceptable. In something bordering on panic, they quickly passed an Act of Settlement stating that if Anne died without issue, Sophia would inherit the crown.

Although considerably older than Anne, Sophia of Hanover enjoyed much better health. But at 83 years old, Sophia knew her demise could come at any time. She constantly sent letters to Anne begging to be allowed to visit, but angrily, and rather rudely, Anne constantly refused. It was only after receiving yet another angry letter from Anne refusing her permission to enter the country that Sophia began feeling ill. Two days later she was walking in the gardens of Herrenhausen when she ran to shelter from a sudden downpour of rain. It was there, alone in the garden, that she collapsed and died.

One month later, at only 49 years of age, Anne suffered a stroke and died as well. After twelve months in bed, obesity, gout and seventeen pregnancies had finally taken its toll on her body and it finally caught up with her.

It would be a new era for England and they were to find that their new king, Sophie's son George of Hanover, was a short, quiet German who could barely speak a word of English. But at least he was a Protestant and if you disregarded the Catholic Stuarts in France, the Hanoverians were all England had left.

Never again would there be a Stuart on the throne of England, although heaven knows both James' only son to his Italian bride, James Francis Edward Stuart (the Pretender) and James Francis Edward's son Bonnie Prince Charles (the Young Pretender) tried unsuccessfully to remedy that.

THE TARTAN KINGS WHO NEVER RULED

It didn't take long for George's first big crisis to arrive. It was barely four weeks after his coronation in October 1714 when an uprising of the Jacobites in Scotland took off.

James II died in 1701 and the Jacobite leadership fell to his 13-year-old son, James Francis Edward Stuart, 'The Pretender' as he was called. But when George I died, James Francis wasn't a little boy anymore. He was 20 years old and eager to fight and take his kingdom back.

John Erskine, 6th Earl of Mar, had already mustered highland chiefs in September and declared James Francis Edward Stuart to be their rightful king. But now they were determined to physically remove George's son from the throne if they had to and replace him with James as James III of England. With his army of about 12,000 men, Mar proceeded to take Perth. Some Tories had even joined the rebellion.

But things didn't go quite according to Mar's plan. There were still men who did not support the Jacobites and many of them were Campbells, in particular John Campbell 2nd Duke of Argyll, based in Stirling. This man was the son of Archibald Campbell: the very man who had been King William's chief Scottish advisor and who had been present when orders went through for the massacre of the MacDonalds at Glencoe. While Mar had been leading his army south, spies were informing John Campbell about

Mar's actions and in an attempt to halt his progress, he moved his army of around 4,000 men to Sheriffmuir on 10th November 1715. Three days later, on a remote elevated plateau of heathland lying between Stirling and Auchterarder on the northern fringe of the Ochil Hills, their armies finally met head on.

Argyll knew he was seriously outnumbered but he surprisingly managed to halt the Jacobite advance. By evening, both armies were seriously reduced, (the Jacobites had lost 800 while the government had lost 600) and not wanting to risk any more of his men, Mar allowed Campbell to withdraw.

Considering the size of Mar's army, it seems astonishing that the Jacobites failed and that both sides claimed it as their victory. An historian by the name of Neil Oliver has gone so far as to say that if Mar had not led his army like the leader of a parade instead of a campaign, the army could have easily bypassed Argyll and linked up with the English Jacobites and Catholics in the north of England. Also, if Mar had decided to continue fighting instead of allowing Argyll to leave, history may be very different from what it is today.

It wasn't until 23rd December that James Francis Edward Stuart set sail for Scotland as gales raged across the Channel. As he looked up at the vast sky full of wheeling gulls, his legs were splayed to ride the surging deck as the boat crashed over the waves against the hull. Wind stung his face, turning his face scarlet, but he didn't care. He was heading back to Scotland to claim his throne. What he didn't realise was his cause was already largely lost. There was too little money and too few arms.

When he finally set foot on Scottish soil at Peterhead, he was disheartened and disappointed at the little show of support that was left for him. As for the Scots, when they first saw James standing before them, they were more than a little disappointed themselves. This James Stuart was the son of James II who had captured and executed Monmouth after a bloody battle. His uncle Charles II had declared wars and defied Parliament time and time again almost until the day he died. His grandfather Charles I had been brutally beheaded for steadfastly standing up for his beliefs. The quiet, timid man standing before them, who seemed almost uncomfortable with crowds, was not the leader *they* had imaged he would be. As he stood shyly before them, whispers of the 'warming pan' incident were muttered, arousing doubts of whether he truly was a Stuart after all as the past rumours had insultingly suggested.

The 'warming pan' incident they were referring to was actually James Francis' birth. James II seems to have been more like his philandering brother Charles II than we thought when it came to women. During his Italian wife's pregnancies and childbirth horrors, he still felt the need for female 'companionship' and had continued an affair with a woman by the name of Catherine Sedley, Countess of Dorchester. Three years after the death of her last child, Mary became irritated by James' continued affair with Catherine and moved into new apartments of her own in Whitehall in February 1687.

Then towards the end of 1687, Mary visited the spa city of Bath, not yet the popular resort it would become later in the Georgian period, but a place that was said to have had 'healing waters'. When she returned shortly before Christmas, the jubilant couple announced happily that while she was on her retreat, Mary had discovered that she was pregnant.

To say feelings were mixed is an understatement. English Catholics were ecstatic but the English Protestants were seriously doubtful. Bath's PR people had credited the therapeutic spa for restoring her fertility but the Protestants were sceptical and openly suspicious that it was Bath's reputation for licentious behaviour that should be credited instead. Rumours spread that the baby was not James' child at all.

After the baby was born, an even wilder rumour took hold. James' enemies claimed that a male baby had been smuggled into the Queen's chamber in a warming pan to replace her own stillborn child. Witnesses to the birth were called but these witnesses were even doubted since they were themselves not of royal birth and hence not to be trusted. Everyone knew that money spoke volumes. It was mainly due to James' mismanagement, but the rumours had substance since he had excluded many from the birth whose testimony would have counted as valid and most of the witnesses were either Catholics or foreigners. When James' daughter Mary was alive, she had been convinced that it was just a plot to trick her out of her inheritance by replacing her and William with the boy from her father's second marriage. A male child was needed and indeed, a male child had been produced.

It wasn't just the cool reception from the Scotsmen that bothered James.

He was unprepared for the bleakness of a Scottish winter as well. Howling icy winds blew constantly with persistent, bleak snowstorms unlike anything he had ever endured during a French winter and he soon fell ill with a fever that eventually worsened. By the time he recovered, the rebellion had all but fizzled out. He met with Mar at Perth but he could not find the means, or the words, to rouse the disheartened army. By 4th February, he had already decided to return dejectedly to France.

As James stood on the shores of Montrose, a coastal town in Angus 61 kms north of Dundee, ready to board his ship, the thought must have crossed his mind that it wasn't quite the glorious return he had imagined it would be. He would have taken one last look around and remembered the swashbuckling stories his father had told him. The Danes had plundered Montrose in 980 and razed it to the ground, but they'd endured. William the Lion, King of the Scots in 1165, had built the Red Castle nearby where Edward I had visited with 30,000 of his men. Edward had stayed at the castle for three nights, humiliating John Balliol the whole time. The following year, William Wallace destroyed the garrison, slaying every soldier in sight. As James stood on board the ship his last night on English soil, he would have seen his own final chapter as something vastly different. It marked a failure that he had never imagined or foreseen. He knew his departure would be seen as abandonment and he fully understood the ill-feeling and disillusionment it would create. The shame it caused him was almost more than he could bear. He was returning to France disgraced and defeated.

His decision to return to France was one he would regret for the rest of his life. He arrived in Avignon to find that during his absence Louis XIV had died and he was not welcome in France anymore. Pope Clement XI eventually offered him a residence in Rome at the Palazzo Muti, which he gratefully accepted, plus a life annuity of 8,000 Roman scudi, (large silver coins), and four years later, on 3rd September 1719, he married Maria Clementina Sobieska, the granddaughter of King John III Sobieski of Poland.

Maria brought with her a dowry of 25,000,000 francs and the fabled Sobieski rubies, an heirloom of scarcely calculable value. As a wedding present the Pope have the couple the Palazzo Muti in Rome – a relatively small palace situated at one end of the Piazza Dei Santi Apostoli. It was here, one year later, in 1720, their first son was born and named Charles Edward

Louis John Casimir Sylvester Xavier Maria Stuart. Later he would be called Bonnie Prince Charles. Five years later, another son called Henry Benedict Stuart would be born, destined to become a cardinal.

The rocky marriage lasted barely ten years. Maria was impetuous and wayward and soon developed a hearty dislike for her husband. After the birth of her second son, she retreated to a convent for eighteen months, deeply depressed, and fasted so stringently that she became anorexic and died at the age of 33.

In Britain, after the failed Jacobite uprising in 1715, it was a very different story for George. He was jubilant at the news that James had left the country. It was his first victory and with it, after a few executions and land forfeitures along the way, the Whigs finally gained the upper hand over the Tories.

Britain didn't quite love their new shy German king but they were in love with the idea of steadiness. That, above all, was what they craved after the constant upheavals caused by the Stuarts. But by the end of his thirteen year reign in 1727, through the constant bickering between he and his sons and associated family members, England was beginning to wonder if perhaps the Stuarts were better after all.

Things were just not going the way George had planned. His heart had always been in Hanover and he missed the clean, fresh smell of pine in the air wafting down from the lush mountains and he missed the small hamlets and towns nestled at the base of them. But most of all, he missed the people. They had never laughed at his crude manners or called him a 'turnip king' or snickered at his strange accent. He missed the people who had loved him so much before he had departed to start his new promising life in England. With his character in tatters in England, he returned many times over the years to the homeland that he never really wanted to leave in the first place.

It was the perfect place for George to die and it would be on one of his trips home that he was to have a stroke and die.

With his death, anti-German feeling subsided a little, just in time for his feisty son George Augustus to begin his own reign as George II.

It was a warm summer's day in June 1727 when the Chief Minister, Robert Walpole, arrived unannounced at the country residence of the Prince and Princess of Wales. He was out of breath and in a panic. He had come to tell him that the man he had been locking horns with in a 'do or die' struggle for most of his life - his father King George I - was dead.

Prince George received the news with barely a frown. His seething anger at the pain and suffering his father had caused him was still so intense, it didn't cease at the news of father's death. To him, his father was an obstinate, self-indulgent, miserly tyrant and George decided not to even travel to Germany for the funeral, using the excuse that he was needed more in England than at the gravesite of the man he loathed.

What they soon found was George loved a fight just as much as his father had. If he wasn't fighting with Robert Walpole, he was fighting with his son Frederick. When he wasn't fighting with someone in England, he would go back to Hanover and fight to protect his borders against the Austrians. People were getting thoroughly sick and tired of it all. So when problems began with the Spanish, they knew George would be completely delighted.

If it was at all possible for things to worsen any further, it was when Charles of Austria died at the end of October 1742. Overnight England became embroiled in another succession issue with Charles' daughter Maria Theresa fighting to become the only female, and last ruler, of the House of Hapsburg. With war threatening the borders of his beloved Hanover, George and his youngest son, William Duke of Cumberland, left for Germany to protect their boundaries. It would be the beginning of a long military career for 21-year-old William.

Instead of fighting the Austrians, George should have been spending more time watching the Stuarts in Italy. Bonnie Prince Charlie had grown up now and both he and his father, James Francis Stuart, were making preparations to take back what they saw as rightfully theirs. James had already made his son his regent and invested him with the title Charles III and by 1745 money had been raised with the help of France. Charles was basically an Italian who was challenging the Germans with the help of the French for the British throne.

When Bonnie Prince Charlie set sail for Scotland, hoping for a warm welcome from the Highland clans once he'd landed, he must have been feeling more than a little nervous. With only two ships, it was always going to be difficult and he was going to need every bit of his charisma and leadership skills considering he only had seven companions with him as well.

Scotland can be bitterly cold in autumn but there is nowhere much colder than the small isolated island of Eriskay, north west of Scotland. If Charles had missed it, his next stop would have been Iceland. Today, ferries take 40 mins to cross the causeway to Barra, another equally isolated spot on the mainland, but for Charles, it would have taken him many days to make the crossing in the constant drenching rain.

When Charles landed on the cockle shore, the sky was a steel grey and the winds were howling. But despite the weather, he was able to sail for the mainland a hundred kilometres away and drop anchor by the northern shore of Loch nan Uamh at the mouth of the Borrodale Burn in Arisaig.

His initial welcome was discouraging. He had not brought any money to speak of and none of the promised French support. The powerful Skye chieftains, Norman MacLeod of MacLeod and Alexander MacDonald of Sleat, flatly refused to join him and he was strongly advised to go home. But for him, there was no turning back so soon like his father had done in 1715. He sent his ship back to France and announced that he would raise his standard at Glenfinnan on 19th August.

The 12th August was a long day for Charles. When he arrived at Glenfinnan in the middle of the morning, there was no one there apart from two shepherds who wished him God-speed in Gaelic. He retired to a nearby hut to await events and see how many clansmen would respond to his call to arms.

Early in the afternoon, a contingent of 150 MacDonalds under MacDonald of Morar arrived along with James Mor MacGregor, son of the celebrated Rob Roy MacGregor, who brought the welcome news that the MacGregors were on their way. At four o'clock, the sound of pipes heralded the coming of the 800 Cameron men, followed by Alexander MacDonnell of Keppoch with another 300 MacDonalds.

These Jacobites were in love with the past. They seemed to have forgotten about his father's failed attempt years before and were still intent on bringing the Stuarts back home along with their divine right to rule. With support from the Highland clans, both Catholic and Protestant, the Royal Standard of white, blue and red silk was unfurled by the aged Duke of Atholl. Charles gave a short speech which no one understood but they cheered themselves hoarse and hurled their bonnets joyfully into the air in the setting sun.

The force was large enough to march on to Edinburgh and by early November, Edinburgh surrendered to him.

The anxiety in the English court was palpable as news arrived that Charles had set up court at Holyrood Palace and had issued a public declaration. He stated that the Germans were engaging Britain in a personal, irrelevant foreign war that was a pointless drain on English money and that war was disrupting English trade. It wasn't George who was suffering, it was the English people and they'd had enough.

England was certainly listening. Everything Bonnie Prince Charlie was saying was true. England *was* being run by barbaric foreigners who had no idea or care about the English people. Their king *was* spending too much time in Hanover. A satirical note had even been pinned to St James Palace decrying his absence. *'Lost or strayed out of the house'* the note quipped and it had been read by thousands of people before George had it ripped down from the gates. They were certainly in full agreeance with Charles who then added, *'who wanted to be ruled by a foreigner anyway?'*, perhaps conveniently forgetting he himself was a foreigner.

It was a clever way to run down the Germans to the British public and you can see how this touched a raw nerve. Even the new Prime Minister, William Pitt, had stated that they needed more self-confidence as a nation and that the Georgians were treating the country like a province of Hanover not the formidable country that it was. *That* statement certainly did not win him any favours with George.

As Charles marched south at the head of approximately 10,000 men, tension mounted even more in the English court. George was busting for a fight as usual and he was ready to leap onto his horse and lead the charge. Ever the diplomat, Pitt tactfully reminded George of his advancing age and eventually convinced him to leave the fight to his youngest and favourite son, William Duke of Cumberland, since his eldest son, Frederick, had stated he would have nothing to do with it all.

There was no love lost between the two brothers. Frederick was well aware that his younger brother was in his father's good books and even without the added aggravation, they were like chalk and cheese. Frederick was busy trying to impress on the English that he was a much more gentle person than his overweight, obnoxious younger brother who had a penchant for picking fights and starting wars like their argumentative father.

It was probably the final straw for George. He had been thinking recently about his will and this fresh declaration only served to annoy him even more. He already regarded Frederick as the 'black sheep' of the family, and even his mother once famously described him as *the greatest ass and the greatest liar ... and the greatest beast in the whole world'*, adding *'and I heartily wish he were out of it.'* Frederick had just pushed George that one bit further to making a final decision. He came up with the idea to reshuffle the line of succession after his death by giving Frederick the role of Elector of Hanover while putting the crown of England firmly and squarely on the head of his favourite son William instead.

While the two brothers bickered savagely with each other, as well as with their father, Charles was taking full advantage of the volatile situation and had been on the move again. He had taken Carlisle and Manchester comfortably and continued further on to Derby. But as he travelled further south, he found a totally unexpected and worrying lack of support for the Jacobites in England.

Bonnie Prince Charles was thirty years too late in his attempt to take back his throne. Though no one could say they particularly *liked* the Hanoverians, George and his family were firmly established in England by then and no one seemed interested in yet another monumental change. Sure, the English disliked the Germans. They were boorish and cold and could barely speak the language. And they fought callously and endlessly with each other. But England had not been happy with the arrogance of the Stuarts either.

Perhaps England was spot-on in their observation because arrogance seems to have been Charles' biggest downfall. Because of the lack of English support, Charles was given advice, good advice, from his colonels to return to Scotland to rethink their plans. Charles on the other hand didn't want to return. By returning to Scotland, it would look like he was retreating and that was not his intention. It was so far from the actual truth it was laughable. He wanted England to know that he wasn't afraid of a battle. That's what he'd come for and that's what was going to happen.

As adamant as he was, his council wouldn't budge either. They'd heard that the English army was gathering force and as much as Charles tried to convince them that France was launching an invasion as well, no one wanted to listen.

In the end, Charles had no other choice but to reluctantly take the advice of his colonels and begin the long march back north. They withdrew on 6th December 1745, Black Friday it's been called, marching north through freezing snowstorms, taking whatever food and money they needed from the already cash-strapped towns. It was when they reached Glasgow that Charles' army made their fateful and worst mistake. They threatened to ransack the city if they weren't housed and fed. They even demanded all the boots and shoes of the townspeople of Dumfries since they'd worn their own out on the long trek.

It wasn't the way it should have been done and because of it, he lost even more valuable support from men who would have joined him willingly otherwise.

As Charles marched, George recalled William from Austria to act as his Commander at the head of the army to deal with the rebellion up north. By January, William had arrived in Scotland, taken control of the English army and made his first decision. They would wait out the cruel winter in Aberdeen until reinforcements from Prince Frederick of Hesse joined his rejuvenated army.

What he didn't know was the Jacobites had mustered a considerable force in Perth under Lord John Drummond and his original eight hundred men had been reinforced by thousands of clansmen encouraged by the news of Charles's unopposed march into England. By now, his army numbered four thousand men and on 2nd January, 1746, the Jacobites moved off in the direction of Stirling to link up with Lord John Drummond and mount an assault on Stirling Castle. On 5th January, a drummer was sent to Stirling to demand the surrender of the town which by now was almost completely surrounded by Jacobites. Stirling, however, stood firm and Charles accordingly ordered the castle to be besieged, entrusting the task to a French artillery 'expert' of Scottish descent, by the name of Monsieur Mirabel de Gordon.

Monsieur Mirabel, who never seemed to be sober, ordered the digging of trenches for the Jacobite cannons. Unfortunately, he chose a hillside site with only fifteen inches of soil on top of solid rock. Not just that, the site was lower than the level of the castle's own guns and well within their range.

Meanwhile, there was simmering dissension among the Jacobite commanders rising to the surface who resented Charles's decision not to hold councils and his increase in drinking. Since Derby, he had been drinking very heavily late into the night and getting up very late in the morning when the army was already on the move. He seemed to have lost all his gaiety and charm and his decisions were becoming wilful, ill-considered and erratic.

The Battle of Falkirk Muir on 17th January 1746 was fought in a blinding storm where six thousand men confronted and defeated the best regular force the Hanoverian government was able to put up. There were more than 12,000 combatants on the field and the battle itself was a confused, scrambling affair fought in a storm of wind and driving rain. It was so confused that neither side was sure who had won.

The Jacobite regiments were almost a the top of the Hill Falkirk before the English commander, General Hawley, saw them. His artillery was bogged down in mire at the foot of the hill and his infantry were scrambling.

The weather worsened during the day and by then it was blowing a gale into the face of the dragoons as they scrambled up the steep slope. As it grew dark, the storm raged even more fiercely. No one knew where the enemy was or even where most of their own men were. General Murray gathered his troops as best he could and pushed into Falkirk to seek shelter for the night and before he knew it, news arrived that the Hanoverian troops were in full retreat along the road to Linlithgow.

Despite losing many faithful nobles, the Jacobites had won a spectacular victory but no one even realised it yet. Charles was urged to follow in pursuit and capture Edinburgh before it could be reorganised but for some reason he seemed incapable of making a rational decision. After a day of dithering in Falkirk, he left Lord Murray and the clan regiments and moved back to Bannockburn with the rest of the army. He settled himself in Bannockburn house with the daughter of a Jacobite, Clementina Walkinshaw, after developing a cold and stayed put while Monsieur Mirabel continued the siege of Stirling Castle. Ten days later, he held a letter from Lord Murray in his hands urging an immediate withdrawal to the Highlands.

By then, Charles wasn't listening to anyone. He'd already decided to face Cumberland face to face to 'decide the fate of Scotland'.

He waited until a rainy day in April 1745, one day after his 25th birthday, to pack up and move his well-rested army towards Culloden Moor, north east of Inverness. It would be the last battle on British soil and it would be catastrophic.

Charles was ready for a fight but he should have listened to Commander Lord Murray when he was told not to stop on the bleak, heather-clad, marshy ground of Drumossie Moor, three miles south of Culloden.

Charles' original plan was to carry out a surprise night attack on the government's sleeping camp. The plan was to set out at dusk and march to Nairn, 16 miles north of Inverness, and as Murray attacked Cumberland's rear, Charles would bring up the second line. Unfortunately, there were countless delays and they only started out at 8pm, leaving Murray to lead the slow-going, tired army across the countryside in the dark.

The terrain was bad enough but it wasn't the only problem Murray was facing. His men were from Highland clans and they were basically wild, untrained ruffians fighting with pitchforks, scythes and axes. Only one-fifth of them had a sword. Even the colonels from the MacDonald clan considered their men to be uncontrollable.

By the time the leading troop reached Culraick, it was one hour before dawn and Murray decided there was not enough time to mount a surprise attack. He sent another commander to inform Charles of the change of plan, but he missed Charles in the dark.

It ended up a disorganised shambles. In the darkness, while Murray led one-third of the Jacobite forces back to camp, the other two-thirds continued towards their original objective, unaware of the change in plan. Not long after the exhausted Jacobite forces made it back to Culloden, reports came in of the advancing government troops. By then, many of the Jacobite soldiers were starving and freezing, while others were asleep in ditches. Meanwhile, William's army struck camp at about 5am after breakfasting on bread and cheese and tots of brandy and were well on their way to Culloden, their bayonets fixed and ready.

Before the Jacobites knew it, the pipes and drums were resounding on the cold dawn of Wednesday 16th April, and everyone was in a state of confusion. Only 1,000 answered the call to arms and officers were forced to gallop in all directions trying to round up stragglers. By 10am, only 5,000 exhausted and disoriented Highlanders massed on the ground which had been elected for the battle.

By 11am, both armies were within sight of each other with open moorland. Between them was 500 metres of level moorland lying soggily between them. Commander Murray claimed Charles had chosen a death trap but by then there was nothing he could do about it.

As the government forces steadily trudged across the moor in the driving rain, sleet blew into the faces of the already exhausted Jacobite army, hindering their progress even more.

The Jacobites just didn't stand a chance. Within an hour, any who had not been shot were being butchered and run through with redcoat bayonets and any survivors left standing were simply dropping their weapons and running. Cameron of Lochiel, whose ankles had been shattered by a cannonball, was carried from the field on the shoulders of a faithful clansman while Lord Murray managed to round up as many as he could and withdraw. He was the last to leave the field. Charles, shocked at the amount of dead bodies and in tears, was escorted from the field on horseback by his Irish officers. The sight of the fleeing prince was too much for the young commander Lord Elcho. As Charles fled from the bloody field, Elcho yelled, *"Run, you damned cowardly Italian!"*

It was the day the Jacobite cause bled to death on the marshes of Scotland and a day they would remember losing 1500 - 2000 loyal men. In striking contrast, William is reported to have lost only 50 Englishmen with 259 wounded, although a high proportion of those wounded would most likely have died of their wounds later on.

It was a relatively short battle but the significance cannot be underestimated. The story of Culloden represents the last stand of an ancient royal dynasty that could trace its ancestry back to the Dark Ages and quite simply, it was the end of an era for Scotland.

The morning after the Battle of Culloden, written orders were sent out by William *'to give no quarter'* and his men followed his orders to the word. Settlements were burnt to the ground and around 20,000 cattle, sheep and goats were confiscated from already impoverished local farms and sold at Fort Augustus where the soldiers split the profits. Some Jacobites had headed south in an attempt to escape abroad while most went north to Inverness. These were the ones William was waiting for.

William had been thinking long and hard about what to do. The orders given to his men were being carried out to the letter but the question in his mind was *'where will they run when they had nowhere else to go?'* Then, like a bolt of lightning, he knew. Most would head north to the biggest city they knew in an attempt to hide before eventually escaping to France. They'd head to Inverness.

William had thought of everything and it turned out he was absolutely correct. In no time, as more and more weary Jacobites flooded into the city, the refugees were captured and the gaols were filled. Later, they would be loaded onto prison ships and taken south to England to stand trial for high treason.

Of the total of 3,471 Jacobite prisoners, 120 men were hung, drawn and quartered, four died by beheading because they were peers, and one third of the prisoners from the British Army were executed as well for deserting. Amongst the remaining prisoners, lots were drawn and only one out of twenty were alive to actually stand trial. With the journey taking upwards of eight months, not too many of these remainders were alive at the end of their journey anyway. Although most of those who stood trial were sentenced to death, almost all prisoners had their sentences commuted to transportation to the British colonies for life. Whole clans such as the Camerons and almost all the tribes of the MacDonalds, except some of those in the Isles, were transported although the Campbells were spared. Most had fought on the Hanoverian side.

In all, 936 men were transported, 222 were banished and another 382 obtained their freedom by being exchanged for prisoners of war in France. The high ranking 'rebel lords' were lucky enough to be simply executed on Tower Hill in London.

Following Culloden, William was rewarded with an extra £25,000 per annum for his war effort. To the Whigs, William was nothing less than the conquering hero who had saved Britain. To the Tories, well supported by Frederick who openly encouraged them, William had earned the title of *'The Butcher'*. It was at this time that Frederick met Flora and eventually obtained her release during his constant unsuccessful campaigning against his father and brother.

For some, Charles' flight has become a romantic legend with songs and poems written to tell the sad story. They tell of his escape, hiding in the moors of Scotland and criss-crossing the country for more than five months to evade capture while government troops scoured the country for him. He had no intention of staying in Scotland: he was on his way back to France.

Many highlanders who saw him were told it was every man for himself. A few helped him, but none of them betrayed him for the £30,000 reward that had been offered, although heaven knows, they could have used the cash. The songs tell how 24-year-old Flora MacDonald, the stepdaughter of minor gentry in Armadale on the Isle of Skye, helped Charles escape in a small boat dressed as a milkmaid in a blue-sprigged calico gown with a quilted petticoat, over to the Isle of Skye in the hope of fleeing back to France. They also tell of a heart-wrenching longing for Charles to return to them one day. In their perhaps misguided loyalty, they had worshipped him and sacrificed their lives for his cause and they were so sure he would remember that fact and return.

He never did. On the 19th September, 1746 Charles set sail for France from Arisaig, the place where he had landed in Scotland almost fourteen months earlier.

For her effort in saving Charles, Flora was captured and sent to the Tower to await trial for treason for six months. She was already hailed as a heroine and Frederick rather wisely decided not to make a martyr of her.

There was no happy ending for Bonnie Prince Charles. He spiralled after his failure and although money was given to him from Pope Clement XI that helped him live in splendour and helped fund future attempts, future *failed* attempts, to restore the Stuarts to the British throne, Charles never emotionally recovered from his unequivocal defeat. He met briefly with his father James Francis Edward Stuart but things were never the same. They were estranged and never met again after the defeat, even when James died in 1766.

Charles went from affair to affair, drinking heavily all the way, until he slipped back into France then London incognito where he met up with Clementina Walkinshaw again.

The relationship was disastrous from the beginning. It lasted 9 tempestuous years until she finally left Charles, who was using his title Duke of Albany as a disguise by then, taking their 7-year-old daughter, Charlotte, with her.

For the next 12 years, Clementina and Charlotte lived in various French convents, supported by the pension granted to her by her father-in-law. Despite circulating descriptions of them both, Charles never found them and he never forgave Clementina.

Charles's health deteriorated in later life, and he was reported to have suffered from asthma, high blood pressure, swollen legs and ulcers. In 1774, while in Florence, he suffered constantly from his illnesses, which required him to be carried by his servants to and from his carriage.

In 1776, Charles moved to Florence where years later, he sent for his daughter. By then she was married with three small children of her own but she left them to be brought up by Clementina while she went to Florence to nurse her father in 1784. By then, she had been legitimised by Charles and created Duchess of Albany. Four years later, Charles was dead.

During the years Charlotte lived and cared for Charles, she knew she wasn't well wither. It would seem the Stuart curse had trickled down to her. One year after her father's death, Charlotte would die of liver cancer at the age of 36 leaving Clementina to continue looking after her three grandchildren.

I've written that the Stuart dynasty was dead but when saying that, there is one thing that we should consider. We know that Charles II left no legitimate children, yet we also know of a dozen illegitimate children by his ten mistresses. The present Dukes of Buccleuch, Richmond, Grafton and St Albans descend from Charles in a direct male line and Diana, Princess of Wales, was descended from two of Charles's illegitimate sons: the Duke of Grafton and the Duke of Richmond. Also, through Charles II and his mistress Louise de Kerouaille, their son Charles Lennox Duke of Richmond would become the ancestor of Camilla, Duchess of Cornwall and Sarah, Duchess of York. Lady Diana's son, Prince William, first in line to the present British throne, is likely to be the first monarch descended directly from Charles II. Stuart blood will once more run through the veins of future kings and queens of England.

Something also to consider is the link that goes back to the early Vikings through Sweyn Forkbeard. With a touch of irony, Sweyn's descendants, through his daughter Estrid, continue to rule Denmark to this very day and one of his descendants, in another period of history when fierce battles would rage and countless people died, Margaret of Denmark married James III of Scotland. In another strange twist of fate, after James VI of Scotland inherited the English throne and become James 1 of England in 1603, Sweyn's ancestry was once again introduced into the English royal bloodline and Stuart / Danish blood became rulers of England.

Also noteworthy is that Prince George, Princess Charlotte and Prince Louis are the 14th great-grandchildren of Mary Queen of Scots. Although the dynasty eludes the Stuarts after 1701, the bloodline extends forward to the present day, and back again through Mary Stuart's paternal grandmother, Mary Tudor, to Owen Tudor's bloodline, and through her Stuart ancestors as far back as Robert The Bruce. Further still, his blood travels back through France and Russia and on to Brusse Sigurdsson, a Norwegian Viking who settled in the Orkneys and Ireland.

Bruce blood springs from countless generations of ethnic women in Wales, Ireland and Scotland and with it, over the centuries, strength, courage and determination has grown as well to become the essence of Scottish generations.

For better or worse, the story of Scotland and England is long, tumultuous and endlessly inter-connected and history has possibly never seen such an intense relationship between two countries. To the Scots, the English have been enemies, friends, allies, rivals, family and oppressors.

For now... they are one.

www.ingramcontent.com/pod-product-compliance
Lightning Source LLC
Chambersburg PA
CBHW072149070526
44585CB00015B/1052